W9-CMS-693

COLLECTED
AND NEW
POEMS

1924-1963

MARK VAN DOREN

 HILL AND WANG · NEW YORK

COLLECTED AND NEW POEMS
1924-1963

By Mark Van Doren

ACKNOWLEDGMENTS

The section of this book entitled "from NEW POEMS (1948)" includes all of the poems from the corresponding section of *Selected Poems* by Mark Van Doren. Copyright 1954 by Mark Van Doren. Reprinted by permission of Holt, Rinehart and Winston, Inc.

CONTENTS

from
NOW THE SKY AND OTHER POEMS (1928)

from
A WINTER DIARY AND OTHER POEMS (1935)

from
THE LAST LOOK and Other Poems (1937)

AMERICA'S MYTHOLOGY (1939)

THE SEVEN SLEEPERS AND OTHER POEMS (1944)

from
NEW POEMS (1948)

SPRING BIRTH AND OTHER POEMS (1953)

MORNING WORSHIP AND OTHER POEMS (1960)

LATE POEMS (1963)

xix

COLLECTED AND NEW POEMS
1924-1963

from

SPRING THUNDER

AND OTHER POEMS (1924)

Spring Thunder

Listen. The wind is still,
And far away in the night—
See! The uplands fill
With a running light.

Open the doors. It is warm;
And where the sky was clear—
Look! The head of a storm
That marches here!

Come under the trembling hedge—
Fast, although you fumble.
There! Did you hear the edge
Of winter crumble?

Travelling Storm

The sky above us here is open again.
The sun comes hotter, and the shingles steam.
The trees are done with dripping, and the hens
Bustle among bright pools to pick and drink.

But east and south are black with the speeding storm.
That thunder, low and far, remembering nothing,
Gathers a new world under it and growls,
Worries, strikes, and is gone. Children at windows
Cry at the rain, it pours so heavily down,
Drifting across the yard till the sheds are grey.
A county farther on, the wind is all:
A swift dark wind that turns the maples pale,
Ruffles the hay, and spreads the swallows' wings.
Horses, suddenly restless, are unhitched,
And men, with glances upward, hurry in;
Their overalls blow full and cool; they shout;
Soon they will lie in barns and laugh at the lightning.
Another county yet, and the sky is still;
The air is fainting; women sit with fans
And wonder when a rain will come that way.

Former Barn Lot

Once there was a fence here,
    And the grass came and tried,
Leaning from the pasture,
    To get inside.

But colt feet trampled it,
    Turning it brown;
Until the farmer moved
    And the fence fell down.

Then any bird saw,
    Under the wire,
Grass nibbling inward
    Like green fire.

Pigeon

This bird is used to sitting on bright ledges
And looking into darkness. Through the square
High window in the barn the mow is black
To one here by the fence. But there he sits
And treads the sun-warm sill, turning his breast
Toward all the musty corners deep within.
They flash no colors on him, though the sky
Is playing bronze and green upon his back.
Gravely he disappears, and spiders now
Must hurry from the rafter where his beak
Searches the seed. The afternoon is slow
Till he returns, complacent on the ledge,
And spreads a breast of copper. But the sun
Is nothing to a pigeon. On the ground
A grain of corn is yellower than gold.
He circles down and takes it, leisurely.

River Snow

The flakes are a little thinner where I look,
For I can see a circle of grey shore,
And greyer water, motionless beyond.
But the other shore is gone, and right and left
Earth and sky desert me. Still I stand
And look at the dark circle that is there,
As if I were a man blinded with whiteness,
And one grey spot remained. The flakes descend,
Softly, without a sound that I can tell;
When out of the further white a gull appears,
Crosses the hollow place, and goes again.
There was no flap of wing; no feather fell.
But now I hear him crying, far away,
And think he may be wanting to return.
The flakes descend. And shall I see the bird?
Not one path is open through the snow.

3

Immortal

The last thin acre of stalks that stood
    Was never the end of the wheat.
Always something fled to the wood,
    As if the field had feet.

In front of the sickle something rose:
    Mouse, or weasel, or hare;
We struck and struck, but our worst blows
    Dangled in the air.

Nothing could touch the little soul
    Of the grain. It ran to cover,
And nobody knew in what warm hole
    It slept till the winter was over,

And early seeds lay cold in the ground.
    Then, but nobody saw,
It burrowed back with a sun-white sound,
    And awoke the thaw.

History

I crossed the swinging bridge, and there
    The little town I came to see
Was ashes. In the April air
    Ruined rafters poked at me.

I ran, imploring why and when,
    But though I searched on every side
The little town was bare of men;
    The very voice of it had died.

Only past a pile of stone
    Was any sound. I crept, afraid.
There upon the grass alone
    Nell, the shepherd bitch, was laid

4

And seven puppies pulled at her
   That never saw the little town,
Or the angry wagoner
   Who whipped his horses up and down.

Barricade

Come to the other hole, and fit your tin,
And start your spike;
And if you hear the rat within,
Strike!

Rats can gnaw, but suddenly a nail
Can eat an inch.
Let him see our teeth, and quail,
And flinch.

Now he scampers—pound more loudly yet
To kill my fear.
The feet are what I must forget.
Hear?

Midwife Cat

Beyond the fence she hesitates,
   And drops a paw, and tries the dust.
It is a clearing, but she waits
   No longer minute than she must.

Though a dozen foes may dart
   From out the grass, she crouches by;
Then runs to where the silos start
   To heave their shadows far and high.

Here she folds herself and sleeps;
   But in a moment she has put

The dream aside; and now she creeps
   Across the open, foot by foot,

Till at the threshold of a shed
   She smells the water and the corn
Where a sow is on her bed
   And little pigs are being born.

Silently she leaps, and walks
   All night upon a narrow rafter;
Whence at intervals she talks
   Wise to them she watches after.

Driver Lost

Roads are flowing everywhere
   In the night, beneath the moon.
But one of them the homing mare
   Is certain of; and soon

The barn will be in plainest sight,
   Grey beyond the grove.
To her the misty way is bright,
   As if another drove.

She points an ear at every turn
   Before a hoof arrives.
What hand is here from which to learn?
   Who is it sits and drives?

Crow

A hundred autumns he has wheeled
Above this solitary field.
Here he circled after corn

Before the oldest man was born.
When the oldest man is dead
He will be unsurfeited.
See him crouch upon a limb
With his banquet under him.
Hear the echo of his caw
Give the skirting forest law.
Down he drops, and struts among
The rows of supper, tassel-hung.
Not a grain is left behind
That his polished beak can find.
He is full; he rises slow
To watch the evening come and go.
From the barren branch, his rest,
All is open to the west;
And the light along his wing
Is a sleek and oily thing.
Past an island floats the gaze
Of this ancientest of days.
Green and orange and purple dye
Is reflected in his eye.
There is an elm tree in the wood
Where his dwelling place has stood
All the hundred of his years.
There he sails and disappears.

To a Child with Eyes

Footprints now on bread or cake
Merely are what a mouse can make.
You cannot open any door
And find a brownie on the floor,
Or on the window where he went,
A fork, a spoon, a finger-dent.
Farmers climbing from the mow
Surprise no imp beneath a cow,

Milking madly. Breakfast bells
Are never tinkled from dry wells.
The commonwealth is gone that shut
Its felons in a hazelnut.
Forests are no longer full
Of fairy women who can pull
A leaf around them, and can dance
Upon the very breath of plants.
River rocks are bare of men
Who wring their beards and dive again.
Is there nothing left to see?
There is the squirrel. There is the bee.
There is the chipmunk on the wall,
And the first yellow every fall.
There is the hummingbird, the crow.
There is the lantern on the snow.
There is the new-appearing corn.
There is the colt a minute born.
Run and see, and say how many.
There are more if there is any.

Afternoon Alone

She leaves the kitten at her cream
And runs to watch. But all the glass
Is covered over with a steam
That hides the people who would pass.

Sad awhile, she draws a thumb
Across the pane and through the slit
Sees a purple face has come
To stare at her. Afraid of it,

All her hand she takes to wipe
The streak away; but now the tramp
Stands entirely with his pipe,
And his clothes are foul and damp.

8

So she flies and shuts the door
And is by the stove again,
Where the kitten lets her pour
Milk enough for nine or ten.

Noblesse

The stubble is an upstart thing,
    A summer's growth, that as we walk
Turns—the envious underling—
    And stabs us with its stalk.

Weeds, arriving everywhere,
    Are insolent as soon as come.
They shout upon the morning air
    Until the flowers are dumb.

But in this corner, past the gate,
    Safe from where the horses turned,
I used to lie till it was late;
    And here it was I learned

How blue-grass is the gentlest born
    Of all the gentle things that stand,
Holding, without a spear or thorn,
    Hereditary land.

Fall

Winter and Spring and Summer are this or that:
A white old man, a girl, a drowsing tree.
The Fall is a covered bridge that crosses the river
Down from my father's house. The foam and the rocks
Grow suddenly to a grey there, as the sky
Returns one day to roof the valley in.
The bridge's darkened mouth, so cool all summer,

Gathers descending leaves; already warm there,
The shadows settle to sleep, and a yellow cart,
Flickering through the leaf-shower down the highway,
Comes on with noiseless wheels and disappears.

Fallen Barn

The sun came white upon these shingles once,
And a few rotted edges let it in.
But the hay held it, as it held the rain
That dripped on other days and slowly dried.
No sky ever could pierce to where the stalls
Gathered familiar gloom. Their corners filled
Each year with heavier cobwebs, and the dust
Mingled with many odors never dead.
But yesterday the farmer hitched four teams
In turn to all the uprights; and they fell.
The sun has followed through, and soon the rain
Will soak the oldest timbers into sod.
Here in the weeds a manger plank was thrown.
You see it, bitten thin. The horse is gone
That found it every evening with his nose
And smoothed it, long ago. Nothing remains
Of what it was that made these beams a barn.

Water Wheel to Mend

There have been times I thought these paddles moved
To music, not to water. Should that hush,
And cataracts descend here with no song,
The axle would not answer with its groan;
The great spokes that swung in solemn circle
Would ponderously wait upon new tunes.
But water still is noisy in the sluice,
And the splashed wheel is motionless. The stream
Foams out below with even a louder voice,

Calling upon the mighty arms to go.
They cannot go; the axle, old and deaf,
Is unaware this Spring of water sounding.

Mountain House: December

Anyone on the road below
    Can see it now; the boughs are bare
That hung about it months ago,
    Beautiful, and thick as hair.

It is a white and silent face
    That some will talk of, driving by.
None will turn to reach a place
    So cold and high.

No summer walkers up that way,
    Arriving half in shadow, stand
And wait upon the sign to stay
    From a slow hand.

The house's hands are folded in,
    For warmth; but all the warmth is fled:
It climbed the stairs, and stricken thin
    Died one evening on your bed.

Waterfall Sound

In the middle of the wood it starts,
Then over the wall and the meadow
And into our ears all day. But it departs,
Sometimes, like a shadow.

There is an instant when it grows
Too weak to climb a solid fence,
And creeps to find a crack. But the wind blows,
Scattering it hence

In whimpering fragments like the leaves
That every autumn drives before.
Then rain again in the hills, and the brook receives
It home with a roar.

Alteration

I did not ask to have the shed
    Pulled down, although it leaned so sickly.
But, now the proper word is said,
    Let it come quickly.

Bring rope and pulley, axe and bar,
    And while you hammer I will pry.
Shingles can be sent as far
    As feathers fly.

Naked beams can tumble faster
    Than cobwebs in a sudden gust;
Floors can stand on end; and plaster
    Soon is dust.

I did not think this valley view
    Deserved that any roof should fall.
But, now the word is said by you,
    I want it all.

Premonition

It was September, and the weeds were mowed
For the last time along the narrow road.
Sunlight speckled down, as leaves would fall,
Shortly, upon the gravel; and by the wall
Chipmunks quietly ran that soon would sound
More loudly on the green and yellow ground.

A woodchuck crossed beyond me as I went,
So slowly that he seemed indifferent;
As if he slept already out of sight,
Deep in a burrow, with the meadows white.
I soberly advanced, and all the way
Was proof that nothing now could ever stay
Of the soft summer. Even when I stood
At last upon the border of the wood,
And the bright Hollow lay a mile below,
The light dazzled, and I thought of snow.

Grass

Poppies are burning; daisies dip their faces;
The gentle ageratum at my side
Offers a pale blue cheek to the afternoon.
Something has brought the swallows whence they hid;
They tumble up and dizzy the warm day,
Speeding against the calm or dropping straight:
Dropping to cut and float. Along the walk
A black hose runs, and ends in a tall spray;
Catbirds hop to the bath, and flirt and shine.
I look, but do not see these things; or care
When a brown, erring rabbit bounces in,
Fears the immaculate garden, and is gone.
Further across the way there quietly feed
A few round sheep in a shade. And out of sight
Momently there is a pattering among branches,
And ripened apples thud upon the ground.
I look and look, but do not see these things.
My mind is lost in the river of bright green
That, smoothly out from between those highest elms,
Issues under the sun. It does not pause,
But dreaming spreads and flows. So I am taken
Beyond all flutter of birds, all cry of flowers,
All nibble and leap and fall, to lie in grass.

Wind in the Grass

Are you so weary? Come to the window;
Lean, and look at this.
Something swift runs under the grass
With a little hiss.

Now you see it rippling off,
Reckless, under the fence.
Are you so tired? Unfasten your mind,
And follow it hence.

Afterward

The stalls were empty in the shed;
   Nothing grazed beyond the gate.
But there was straw to make a bed,
   And the four bridles dangled straight.

We heard the water running cold,
   As she had left it, round the crocks.
Linen lay for us to fold,
   And there was pepper in the box.

The very trap that he had set
   To catch a mole that loved the lawn
Hung above the passage yet;
   Another mole was boring on.

The wounded deer still fled the dog
   Within the gold and walnut frame;
The Fishermen Among the Fog,
   And The Young Mother, were the same.

We laughed to see a boot behind
   The stove; but then you wept
At your happening to find
   Spectacles where she had slept.

Identity

He knew a place on the mountain where he went
A certain kind of morning, clear and warm.
The sky was open there, and not a cloud
Came over; not a buzzard filled the blue.
The cattle never climbed so high, and the dog—
He left her in the shed. All day he walked
Without an eye upon him he could feel;
Or sat among the stones, himself a stone,
Watching an empty heaven till his mind
Passed out of him and poured the silence full.
His legs were his no longer, and a hand,
Resting upon a knee, was miles away.
All afternoon he sat, and when he moved
It was as if a stone settled a little
To firmer and longer sleep. Only the wind,
At evening, made him wake and stumble off
To stand upon a bluff over the farm.
The kitchen chimney then, and supper waiting,
Uttered his name aloud and brought him down.

Gardener

Under the window, on a dusty ledge,
He peers among the spider webs for seed.
He wonders, groping, if the spiders spun
Beneath that window after all. Perhaps
His eyes are spiders, and new veils are dropped
Each winter and summer morning in the brain.
He sees but silken-dimly, though the ends
Of his white fingers feel more things than are:
More delicate webs, and sundry bags of seed.
That flicker at the window is a wren.
She taps the pane with a neat tail, and scolds.
He knows her there, and hears her—far away,
As if an insect sang in a tree. Whereat

15

The shelf he fumbles on is distant, too,
And his bent arm is longer than an arm.
Something between his fingers brings him back:
An envelope that rustles, and he reads:
"The coreopsis." He does not delay.
Down from the rafter where they always hang
He shoulders rake and hoe, and shuffles out.

The sun is warm and thick upon the path,
But he goes lightly, under a broad straw
None knows the age of. They are watching him
From upper windows as his slippered feet
Avoid the aster and nasturtium beds
Where he is not to meddle. His preserve
Is further, and no stranger touches it.
Yesterday he was planting larkspur there.
He works the ground and hoes the larkspur out,
Pressing the coreopsis gently in.
With an old hose he plays a quavering stream,
Then shuffles back with the tools and goes to supper.

Over his bowl of milk, wherein he breaks
Five brittle crackers, drifts the question: "Uncle,
What have you planted for the summer coming?"

"Why—hollyhocks," he murmurs; and they smile.

Big Mare

The grass is deep in the field, and her four legs
Sink out of sight. She plunges lazily on
To a fresh circle, whence she lifts her head
And looks across the fences to the barn.
No voice from there, no swing of any door.
She lowers her nose to the ground; but suddenly shifts,
Looks up again; and stares into the quiet.
Yesterday, and as long as she remembers,

16

At this good hour there sounded a shrill cry—
"Here Chunk! Here Chunk! Here Chunk!"—and two thin arms
Were waved from a dark opening in the wall.
Now nothing; so she feeds until the sun
Comes cooler over the meadow, and starts home.
Her feet trample on clover, and her breast
Moves with superfluous might against the weeds.
She ploughs across the creek and through the gap;
Is halfway up the hillside; still no shout;
No corn upon an aged, trembling hand.
She hesitates, as if the barn were gone;
Had never been just here; and gazes long
At the half-opened door; then stumbles through.
Some stranger has thrown nubbins in the box;
Her salt is there; the timothy is down.
She munches, while no words are in her nostrils;
No feet in boots too big for them clump by.
The weak old man who never failed has failed.
Yet foolish whisperings, not of the hay, are heard;
Spidery pads of fingers now caress her,
Swiftly over a shoulder, down a flank,
Smoothing, smoothing her mane till evening is night.
Does a plain mare remember? And how long?
Tomorrow will come a slap and a careless whistle.
Tomorrow will come a boy. Is she to forget?

Spirit

A straight old woman, tall and very pale,
Moving from room to room of a musty house
No voice is ever heard in, stops, stone-white,
Her weakness come upon her. She can steer
To the kitchen only; yet it is enough.
Into a painted chair she drops, by the stove,
Reaches and lights the gas, then crumples down.
All black behind that white. Upon the plate
A kettle has been ready for the flame,

17

And water in it nearly to the brim.
Now, while she barely breathes, bubbles arise:
A few, then more, then many breaking fast
Until the water's face nowhere is still,
And the whole of it leaps as if to follow the steam.
Unseen the vessel shakes, untended hums;
A column pours to the ceiling, spreads, and fades;
And the woman never stirs. But now she reaches
Two thin hands to the rail of the stove, and stands
Like one of older time who worshipped fire.
The water boils for her. Water is strong.
While there is any water, it will work.
Suddenly she has smiled across the commotion.
She hears her blood again, and quietly goes
Upon the ancient round from room to room.

Javelins

I heard a hum grow loud in the winter woods,
So went to see. In the very furthest part
A clearing, lately cut, circled a sawmill,
A little shack that buzzed until it shook,
And breathed rankly of elm. I walked around;
The other side was open, whence I watched
The fat back of the sawman as he fed.
Both of his feet were hidden in the dust;
His legs were bundled tight, and his short arms
Heaved in a woolen coat that once was loose.
He stood, serving the poles, and never shifted.
I stepped to him; he turned a solemn face,
Red as the heap of elm, and only nodded.
I had to shout to make him hear at all:
"What are they going to do with these? Do you know?"
I thought his lips said "Javelins." That was wrong:
Javelins! So I screamed at him again.
This time he stopped the saw till he could tell me—
Gently, although he growled a little—"Javelins."

18

He started again. I waved a hand and went.
All of the way the woods were close and cold;
But as I walked they seemed to open themselves,
Spreading before me green and smooth. It was Spring.
The sky was soft, and white young men in the distance,
Posturing, flung their spears, and trotted after
To measure and fling again. I heard no sound,
But the air was swift with the darting. Then the road.
I passed a team. The field once more was forest.
A few rods on and the hum had quieted too.

Three Friends

You on the bed beside me hold
One arm straight up till it is cold,
Then let it fall, the softest part
Lying for warmth against my heart.
My fingers with your fingers' ends
Play in and out; a foot defends
Deep regions from another foot.
You turn and find my eyes. I put
A curious palm where it is seized
By a quick hand; but you are pleased.
There is a third one in the room.
See—in the sun, where the figures bloom
Blood-red on the rug—somebody kneels?
Time smiles at us, and rests his heels.
Outside a hundred horses graze.
He will drive on; but now he stays.
Soon I must follow hence, and slip
Into my place beneath the whip.
He smiles upon us. Come, forget!
He has not thought of rising yet.

Marriage

No wandering any more where the feet stumble
Upon a sudden rise, or sink in damp
Marsh grasses. No uncertain following on
With nothing there to follow: a sure bird,
A fence, a farmhouse. No adventuring now
Where motion that is yet not motion dies.
Circles have lost their magic, and the voice
Comes back upon itself. The road is firm.
It runs, and the dust is not too deep, and the end
Never can heave in sight, though one is there.
It runs in a straight silence, till a word
Turns it; then a sentence, and evening falls
At an expected inn, whose barest room
Cannot be lonely with the walls forgotten.
Laughter is morning, and the road resumes;
Adventurous, it never will return.

Reverie After War: 1866

I am the only man today
At the mill.
The rain will keep the rest away,
And leave me sitting on the sill
Alone:
Nothing around but my old pipe,
A bushel of bright corn crunching into meal,
Water below,
And the mountain.
The roof will drip
And the stones will grind;
I'll think and sit
Till the stones turn empty.
They don't mind.

Last winter once, in the Wilderness,
In the noise and the smoke and the stink and the wet,

All of us swore, if we got home,
To forget.
It's pleasanter now
To remember.

It's pleasant to have the leaves run rain
And you be under a board roof,
Dry.
It's pleasant to smell a hopper of grain
Cracking your food
And piling it by.
It's pleasant, the curl of the smoke
Of only tobacco.
It's pleasant to tighten the trigger finger
Warm on the stem of your pipe
And nothing go off.
It's pleasant, here at the mill,
With only your time to kill.

Down along the back paths the war isn't done.
Houses aren't built again; there isn't any smoke
Except where the long-haired men are having fun
Burning up barns: a good guerrilla joke.

I could have joined a band, and had a skinny mare,
Ridden down a woodroad, held up a stranger,
Killed him for a dollar bill, or maybe for a dare;
I could have gone and been a Cumberland Ranger.

I could have joined, but I'm tired of watching men,
Guessing where they'll go, and whether they'll turn,
Crawling under cover, and crawling out again,
Setting fire to something, just to see it burn.

Scouts are not around now, bullets don't crack;
Nothing happens suddenly to make you move faster;
I can cross the mountain now and never look back;
I can go home; I can be my own master.

I've got a house now, a little patch of corn,
A plough, and a shed, and a one-eyed mule;
As ignorant and as poor as I was when I was born;
But I'm my own pauper, and I'm my own fool.

from

7 P.M. AND OTHER POEMS

(1926)

I ৵

7 P.M.

Slow twilight bird,
Suspended, as you sail, along the nearer edge
Of nightfall and the beechwood, are you heard
In places past my ears? Are you a wedge,

Slow tapered wing,
Driving into the outer walls of time?
Eternity is not so strange a thing,
At evening, when the towers that were to climb,

Slow searching beak,
Lie level with your progress in the soft
Dark-feathered dusk, and there are known to speak
Gentle, wild voices from the dark aloft.

Memories

A child ran alone,
And nothing followed that he felt.
He never heard the sky moan
For old men. He never knelt

To call the hounds—that behind him ran alone
And searching smelt.

He did not hear their cries,
For there was curving earth between.
But he is taller now, and wise
Enough to listen as they lean
Upon the wind—that can turn and bring their cries
So clear and keen.

He still can look away
And do the business of his prime.
He has not foreseen the day
When he will sit and they will climb
And lick his face—that will never frown away
The tongues of time.

Good Night

This moonlight lies
Like a lovely death
On the darkening eyes,
On the yielded breath

Of the earth, that turns
So quietly now;
Letting its burns
Be soothed somehow

In the widening bloom,
In the tender blight.
It has entered our room.
We sleep tonight.

Apple Limbs

Lay them as neatly
Away as the wind
   Lays the soft grasses
   Through which it passes.

They waited all summer,
Just as they fell:
   On gnarl and prong;
   And the time was long.

But yesterday's hatchet
Straightened their knees.
   Now nothing will cumber
   Them in their slumber.

Apple-Hell

Apples, bright on the leafless bough,
In the high noon sun, with the sky above you,
Time will turn. For the white sky falls
And long, red shadows soon will shove you

Eastward, downward, into the room
Where the moon hangs low like a smoking lamp;
Walls lean in; and the studded ceiling
Shines no more; and the bins grow damp.

Apples, yellow on the naked limb,
Although you burn till the air be gold,
Time is tarnish. Skies are falling,
Noon is dead, and the day grows old.

Night-Lilac

Lilac alone,
Standing so quiet, so dim, outside
Till the door-light died
On cricket and stone,

Do you sleep at last?
Or beyond this night that has taken my yard
Do you stare more hard,
In a night more vast,

At the great white things
That move the outermost world: the whale,
The stallion, the pale
High planet with rings,

The raven, the bull,
And the midnight mountain that never is black?
Lilac, come back!
My lawn is too full

Of the dark; and the fine
Impalpable shadows will never be still.
Return as you will,
Dim lilac, and shine.

Remembered Farm

There was a line of frosty light
Along each roof and down the road.
All the rest was perfect night;
Not a field or window showed.

In my cool thought no morning came
To sweep the hills, no moon arose

To flood the meadows with its flame
As far as all this valley flows.

Now I am come, the fields are fair.
Yet not the greenest flesh atones
For when the skeleton was bare
And lightning ran along the bones.

After Dry Weather

If the people under that portico
Are happy, and point at the pattering drops;
If barehead boys are parading below
Musical eaves of tall house-tops;

If you lean out of the window here,
Contented so with the pavement's shine,
And laugh as the covers of cabs appear
With passengers in them dressed to dine;

If all of the stones that we can see
Are licking their lips, that waited so long,
A meadow I know to the north of me
By a hundred miles has caught the song.

I am certain the clover has lifted its head
For dark, intemperate draughts of rain.
Once even I thought I had heard the tread
Of a plunging horse with a sodden mane.

One Fall

Time grew so thin
That it could hang
Between these hills,
Where nothing sang

27

Save the silence.
All those weeks
Are now as one;
And it speaks—

Sharply now—
Of a suspended
Year that died
Before it ended;

Leaving only
A blue shell,
That turned to brown,
And never fell.

Winter Fields

Once they were black
And again they were green.
But the sun dropped,
And the wind grew lean,

And the crows dived
So fiercely down
That the grass blanched
In meadow and town;

And barns and fences
And rows of trees
Died to a brown
As brown as these.

Whatever can live
With the sun so low?
That wagoner there
But appears to go.

28

Soon you will look
And the wheels will stand:
Frozen asleep:
Locked in with the land.

Land Tide

The moon is in flood;
All things are going:
Grass uprooted
And fences flowing

Over the roads
And the meadows east
To the black immovable
Woods at least.

But the pump, there,
Knows how to resist.
The moon comes on;
It never will twist

And topple and go
As the current is laid;
With its rock root,
And pillar of shade.

Eighth Day

Water goes all ways; ships go one,
And now we can see what was never there before:
The low grey line where the ocean will be done;
Though yet there is nothing, no green shore;

Nothing but a faint thing that might have been fog,
No painted houses, and no small sheep

29

Scattered down broken cliffs, underneath a dog
Who growls at the water; but he will never leap.

Water goes all ways; fields keep fast.
Let me lean and look, then, if only at a cloud.
Ninety miles in lies the meadow where I last
Walked beneath a bird, and it was bright, and it was loud.

The Tuning-Fork

One dead tree
With arms upswung,
Silver cold,
Is the forest's tongue.

In the middle of the morning,
When the crows cry,
This oldest oak—
None saw it die—

Shrills with its far
Thin finger ends;
Till the body listens
And a scream descends

And the alleys open,
Making room
For another death
In a dateless gloom.

II ߢ

Beastless Farm

The paths again are solid green
That used to whiten in a drouth,

30

Whirling dust into the clean
 Heifer's nose and horse's mouth.

Stanchion-leathers crack and fall;
 Water runs, and is not heard.
No sudden thunder from a stall
 Stops a mouse, or starts a bird.

Fences might as well come down;
 Lanes are only ghosts of lanes:
Staring hither with a frown
 At smoke of rumps, at mist of manes.

Tree-Dwellers

Ants file past
To the end of the last
Thin twig, and finding
An ultimate, vast
Green meadow, graze;
While back in the maze
Of the body are winding
Worms in the dark,
That never this bark
Shall open to show
One small bird binding
Straws in a row,
And treading them, so.

Inference

Who made the evening made the fear
Of horse and bird and snake and deer,
Of all that do not learn they live
Till light itself, grown fugitive,
Goes breathing by; but turns about,

31

And the black pouncer puts it out.
Then bird and horse and deer and snake
Go posting home, before they break
The line that leads them; and their eyes
Hold all the day that slowly dies.

Crow Madness

There is no mandrake here to cry
As fingers rip it from the ground;
But any morning I can lie
And listen to the other sound

Of darkness tearing clear across
And fragments falling with a shriek
On lonely meadows, where they toss
And rise again with angry beak

That plucks at day and offers war
Against the green, against the blue;
Till night, returning, reaches for
All things that lost her as she flew.

Relief from Spring

Pastures trickle and shine in this new sun;
Hill roads gurgle; and hocks of shaggy horses
Drip with the melting mud. The winter is over,
And all of the world you know is water again.
But have no fear for the grass. It will not drown.
Yesterday noon I waded the upper meadow
And saw, in the farthest field, a lonely crow.
Where crows will walk it has to be dryer soon.
Crows have taken the very top of the world.
They caw, and the wind is warmer, and there is a rustle
Already of weeds to please their horny feet.
Listen now. The grasses are listening too.

Turkey-Buzzards

Silently, every hour, a pair would rise
And float, without an effort, clear of the trees:
Float in a perfect curve, then tilt and drop;
Or tilt again and spiral toward the sun.
They might have been a dream the timber dreamed;
But could have been a conscious thought, that cut
The warm blue world in segments. For the sky,
Unmeasured, was too much that afternoon.
It lay too heavy on us. Happy trees,
If they could so divide it, wing and wing!

Deduction

So smooth a field,
With the hummocks mown;
Moss peeled
From trunk and stone;

A stunted blade
Withdrawing under
A wall, afraid
Of the herd's thunder:

Only sheep
Could have kept it so,
With nibble and leap,
And lambs in tow.

Dispossessed

No hand had come there since the room was closed
To all but what could live with sifting chaff,
And dust, and pale grey webs. Mine at the latch
Startled the silence; and the wind I brought

33

Whirled powdery dust against the darkened panes.
No other sound; and so I went to work,
Making a room to put a table in
And sit where none could see me all day long.
No sound. I pulled a length of lining-board
Loose from the timbers, and a spider ran.
Another, and a wasp was at his hole,
Lifting an angry wing. I said of them:
They saw me, but with eyes no man can feel;
I still shall be alone; and laughed and pulled—
And did not laugh again; or go again.
For all I know the dust is quieter now
Than ever it was; with only the bright-black eyes
Of motionless mice on a beam to say if it is.

Contemptuous

Lying along the window sill,
With a low fire to feed his purrs,
He sees a misty meadow fill
With fly-light, that only blurs

And disappears the more he turns;
But comes again and dances down
The rainy slope to where it burns
The tops of trees. He seems to frown

And gaze away at rug and chair,
And settle further from the glass.
Not for him the dripping air,
Not for him the weeping grass.

Too Early Spring

The wind is mighty in the maple tops,
And the long grass is double.
The house leans that way too; but it stops,
Like a bubble,

Swaying softly. And there you walk
With the morning under your skirt.
When blossoms blow from a tender stalk,
Do they hurt?

Does it hurt, now, as you reach the gap,
And part of you whips the wire?
Go back in and straighten your lap
By the fire.

The Crime

Your cruellest deed, my dear,
Was not to threaten to be gone:
Running to graze your love and my lean fear
On a strange lawn.

But as you looked away
I looked at you; and heard the sound
Of whining in my head, as if I lay
On the green ground

And, fawning, licked your foot,
And waited there for any word.
It was that you were Circe, and had put
Me with the herd.

Confession in Part

Though I had strength
To stand alone,
I come at length
And half atone

For my old pride,
That would not keep
You by my side;
And would not weep.

With you away
I did not fall;
But on a day—
None heard me call—

I leaned and felt
The rock give in
Where you had knelt,
And sand had been.

By-Laws

Never be offended
At what your love forgets to do.
Something then is ended
Between your love and you.

Seek no healing salve
That lets a wounded lover live.
Dodge the poisoned arrow. Have
Nothing to forgive.

Outwardly be hard,
To save the tenderness within.
So impregnable a guard
Is love's thick skin.

Circumferences

Swallows' wings
In the day are swift,
And the hawk's drop,
And the lark's lift,

And mice's feet
That run to cover,
And the sidewise look
Of a jealous lover.

Light is racing
Round the seas;
And thought can distance
All of these.

But faster yet—
And what beyond?—
Is the curving edge
Of a quiet pond,

Or any arc
As soon as drawn,
That seems to sleep,
And plunges on.

Bitten

If ever age
Remembers youth,
Is it something sharp—
Time's tooth—

Or does it arrive
With sudden might,
Like all of the West
On a windy night;

37

Out of nothing,
Into the heart,
That leaps and follows
And roars apart;

Till the wind dies,
And the world is still,
And teeth begin
To drill, drill?

Segments

The first triumphant man was he that drew
His mind across a task and made it two;
And next, to be the creature nearest heaven,
Parcelled the endless mornings into seven.
Night yet unknown, nor fastened with a name,
Tomorrow and tomorrow flowed the same.
On-curving time, with terror in the folds,
Lies powerless in a hand that only holds
The clean-dividing knife, and nipping fast,
Labels the falling pieces to the last.
There are no lines in nature, false or true,
Till number cuts a door and pulls it to.

Employment

Who made the world was not so wise
As one that, opening his eyes
Ten thousand mornings, must again
Start making things that die with men.
Who made the world must think upon
Something never to be gone,
And his hands that never close
Are pale and dry, and his toes
Never leave their print in sand

Going to another land.
Who made the world cannot come home
Over grass or over foam
And shut his mind and so forget
All that will be coming yet.

IV ❧

Paradox

His eyes are so
Because they gleam
With an unbreakable
Soft dream.

They are stone
And they are cold
Because the world
Cannot grow old

Whereat so fiercely
Now they stare.
There was a vision
Fastened there

Before they opened
On our light,
That cannot ever
Dim to night

For one so sure
Of gilded things:
Mountains dancing
Round in rings,

Talking trees,
And never-tame

Lightning setting
Flowers aflame.

Only those
Have gentle eyes
For whom the hills
Had ceased to rise

Before they looked;
And now are laid
In rows that granite
Death has made.

Who would embrace
No sweeter breast:
Only he
Has any rest.

The Bird-Watcher

He is not lifted by their flight
Across the circle of his sight;
He is cold, and he is slow
Beside the least of them that go
And never heed the silent face.
But there is something that can race
With any wing, and no one see.
A piece of him is flying free
Beyond the further forest now;
And all the beating hearts allow
A path among them to be cut
By these wings that cannot shut;
By this beak that cannot learn
Of any season to return.

Survival

He is not yet
Too solid clay
Wherein no rivers
Cut their way.

Is he cold
And is he firm?
There is something
Like a worm

That can awake
And drill a path
Whereinto trickle
Drops of wrath

That quickly gather
In a flood.
Then all is fire
That was mud

As the edges
Break and go
Wherever now
His angers flow.

The Guide

Now to the right,
Between these bars.
This field by night
Is a field of stars.

Here I can sit
And here I can see
These boulders lit
For more than me:

41

For the stars on the other
Side of the sky.
Brother and brother,
Eye to eye,

They sing so long
That I have slept;
And stopped the song;
And the stones have wept.

The Picture

The only thing she kept
Was not a pretty thing at all.
She brought it down one evening from the wall
And put it in a bureau, where, except
On certain cooler evenings in the fall,
It lay and slept.

She would unwrap it, slow,
And touch the formidable frame;
Whispering that her father was to blame
For nothing: for the shepherd, or the snow,
The cottage, or the children, or the tame
Incredible crow.

Cornish Villages

They are nothing but sifted
Sand in the folds
Of round hills lifted,
I think, from molds,

So smoothly they rise,
And so grittily sound

The names—Pengrise,
   Trelithick, Germound—

Of the flint-grey places
   Beneath and between.
Hear the wind on their faces,
   Keeping them keen.

Cornish Castle

Pengerswick then was the title of it.
Here was the lord of the hideous wit
Who laughed to her death a farmer's daughter,
And drew night-foundering crews to slaughter
Down by the sands, that used to lie
But a fathom deep when the tide was high.
He knew too much; the ocean came
And covered him all except for his name
And the top of the tower with the narrow slit—
Pengerswick's Eye was the title of it—
Whence he would order his evil done,
Under the moon and behind the sun.
The gulls have forgotten to pick at it now—
That deepening eye in the granite brow—
But hear them cry from the parapet:
"Pengerswick's garden is wet! is wet!
And weeds grow there that are not of the land!
Salt! Salt! Sand! Sand!"

First Night Alone

He locked the window
   And lighted a candle,
Setting it where it would show him the edge
   Of the door, and the handle.

43

Then to the barn
    At an even pace;
Though once in the driveway cobwebs dangled
    And blanched his face.

The garden again.
    He looked to his light.
No other thing in the world was so firm
    As that tapering white.

Now on the path
    Once more his eyes
Turned to the quiet warm curtains—boy,
    That wasn't so wise.

Between the two fringes
    A circle of hair!—
Parted, as if a dead finger of chalk
    Had descended there.

The top of a head!
    Who bends to the flame?—
Drinks it, and vanishes, leaving the walker
    All night to his shame:

Afraid to go forward,
    Afraid to go back,
Afraid of his window, that once was so empty;
    And now so black.

The Encounter

Between the two hedges
    As high as a horse—
Stone, with their edges
    Broken to gorse—

44

I walked in a shade
    That was purple and brown;
And darkly I said
    As I went down and down:

"Nothing can meet me
    In this deep lane;
Though the sun will beat me,
    Ascending again."

But, talking, I rounded
    A gentle green curve;
And something had bounded,
    Before I could swerve,

Swiftly beyond
    And out of my sight,
Tipping each frond
    Of the bracken with white,

That might have been fear
    And that might have been foam;
For the ocean was near,
    And the wind was from home.

September Highway

"Why do you go so fast tonight,
In the endless dark, in the blowing rain?"
"One of these maples spat three bright
Red leaves in front of us, and the stain

"Is deepening there, though no one sees:
Blood on the roadway trickling down.
Summer is wounded high in the trees,
And red is black, and green is brown.

"Yesterday noon our lawn was bare.
So I would climb and find it still.
I am trying to beat the wind up there
That wants it lonely at the kill."

Burial

Nobody wanted this infant born.
　　Nobody wished it dead.
They wrapped it tight as an ear of corn
　　In a box of cedar and lead.

Nobody by had lighted a candle;
　　No one offered to moan.
The priest and I each lifted a handle.
　　The father followed alone.

Three in a Ford, that had been waiting
　　Most of the wintry day.
Boys on the river still were skating;
　　The wood and the road were gay:

Brown quick birds and scarlet-berried
　　Twigs, and snow begun.
The priest in the back seat sat and carried
　　What never saw our sun.

A blanketed horse was at the gate,
　　And someone's tracks led in.
We entered, and we ascended straight
　　To where the graves were thin,

And where, on a hill, the digger bent
　　In wind and thickening white.
Snow covered the box that two of us leant
　　To lower out of the light.

Then priestly words to cover the snow;
    The four of us stood bare.
Then clods to keep those words below.
    Now there is nothing there.

Ambush

At evening in the strange unlighted town
I sought the streets for comfort, turning down
Each covered dusky walk. There was a tree
Whereunder children swung and stared at me.
Some houses slept, with doors and windows locked.
I passed a shallow porch where people rocked;
They whispered. I went on, and met a man
Who trimmed the border where his grass began.
Across a garden, fragrant now and cool,
Three happy puppies played about a pool,
Until a boy behind them pushed them in.
The night was sweet as none had ever been.
I turned another way, to go and sleep,
When suddenly a cottage seemed to creep
Close to the walk and wait for me. I looked;
The porch was empty, and the screen was hooked;
But, dim within, two ancient women sat,
Motionless, their feet upon a mat.
I could not see an eye; but there were four
That fixed me as I hastened by the door.
Soon I was out of hearing; and I knew
There went no word between them as they grew
Expectant of the next foot that would fall.
I tried forgetting, but my thoughts were all
Of darkness, and a path before a den,
And silent, silent spiders watching men.

V 🙌

The Sage in the Sierra

EMERSON: 1871

Because I stand and smile, and am dumb,
They reckon it was vain to come.
Because I let my Journal lie
The thoughts are dead? The stream is dry
Wherewith my fountain ran
When I was man?
Why does the world that calls me sage
Pity the silence of my age?
Only sentences, only song,
Showed I was strong?
Has no one heard that it is weak
Forever to sing, forever to speak?
I learned it from a Concord brook
Ages ago, that could not talk.
I see it now, wherever I look,
Wherever I walk.
Merely to wait, merely to be,
Is the Sierra's destiny.
Merely to stand, merely to shine.
So is it mine.

The world lies round me as it lay
In the bright morning of my day.
There is no change from what I saw
When I looked skyward for my law.
The sun paints meadows, and the hills
Happily lift their daffodils.
Mountains are tall and valleys deep,
And forests in the distance sleep.
Midnight still unrolls a heaven
Wherein the Pleiades are seven.
The volume has not lost a leaf,

Nor the proud vessel any sail.
Felicity to come is brief;
It is not frail.

What though the index to the book be gone?
Each page is new again to ponder on.
In the green days my mind was a thick wood,
Wherein perplexing branches, as I stood,
Teemed with quick birds that my yet quicker thought
Darted to fasten, and in trembling caught.
My mind is still a grove, but I advance
With steady pace, in serene ignorance
Of what deep bird springs from what hidden bough.
I weave no net of words for capture now.
There came a storm! Now, all such seasons done,
I stand, an ancient smiler, in the sun.
Shadows of passing clouds that cool my head
Provoke no sign from me, and think me dead.
I am content with this eternal place;
Who will may look for sorrow in my face.

The sentences that once I spoke
To this pure fire were smoke.
The correspondences I sung
But proved me young.
I strove to learn and teach the rest
What sang the spheres, what thoughts were best.
But seeing is forgetting speech;
The lesson learned, I cannot teach.
Come thus far forward, I have lost
Remembrance of the care and cost.
Stationed among the stars, I lack
One syllable to whisper back.

Men for themselves will find the good;
I may no longer be their guide.
Here where I would
Let me abide.

I ৡ

We Come Too Late

June now, like any June,
Brings up its fountains of bright flowers;
Crows rise, and beetles fall;
Wind runs in the lengthening grass;
Squirrels labor; tall tree tops
Dip all day, and a long day, there.
And so I walk where once I walked.
The grass is mine as once it was.
Evening, morning, night, and noon:
There is no change in what they are.
I watch a hawk against the white
Of an upland cloud; I enter woods;
Yesterday there I looked again
For print of deer, and—turning thus—
Beheld a fox.
June is now like any June.
But I am changed from what I was.
I see, and pass. I do not stand
Deep in the grass and lose the day.
There is no longer any ground
That flows before me down the hill.
The hours are broken that in chime

51

Preceded me and laughed at time.
Still I rise, and still I go;
But there is something that I know.
I cannot walk the older way.
There is something I would say.

Arc of the sky,
Northward or westward, east or south,
There never has come any wisdom
Out of your mouth.

Waterfall sound,
And the rattle of air in the aspen above,
Language of endless grass,
And the woodbine's love

Wrapping the young
Sweet tree: no one of you ever will tell
The things in the world that are ill
And the things that are well.

The mole and the worm
Have a way, and the rain has a way, in the ground;
Birds see over the orchard,
And storms go round;

Clouds are driven,
And on to the mouse the field-hawk drops.
But here where the lesson begins
The lesson stops.

There was a boy who with the setting sun
Stepped westward from his father's house, and choosing
One of the five worn stones within a field,
Sat there and looked away. The sheep were resting,

Grey on the nibbled grass, and all the sky
Ran down in red to where his gaze was sent.
A few small birds were disobedient still,
Circling high and black to the East and South;
And noises, far behind on the townward road,
Disturbed the looker too. But soon he lost them,
Losing himself the while; and evening came
On delicate feet that only the blood could hear.
He sat, and the same pulse, his mind believed,
Went through the wrist before him and the long,
Low, undulating veins of the warm West.
He watched the clouds that sailed into the sun,
Watching until no bones of the world remained.
The body of all the universe, he said,
Dreamed now in his own thought, that could dissolve
Perfectly with the horizon. What he knew
Always had thus been known; and what he saw
The stars, coming so pale, saw long ago.
Yet there was more if pages could be turned.
The book was big that he had opened now.
Steadily he would labor while he lived
To arrive at the hidden end. And, so resolving,
Back with a burning face and home to bed.

Sickness of heart
And the crumbling away
Of former bright edges of courage;
Dearth, and decay;

Strength of a hand
That the seasons drain
Till it withers and hangs; and the husk
Of a harvested brain;

Death, and your sisters
Weakness and hate:

There never has risen a star
Explaining your state.

Nor you, the living,
The brave one, the lover,
There never has come any sky
To be none but your cover.

Boy, in the tree
Or kicking the white
Dust of the road, you are neither
The day nor the night.

Friended you come,
Friended you go;
But never the tops of those hills
Are conducting you so.

The hours of your doubt,
And your ecstasies after;
Calm, and forgetting, and sudden
Long moments of laughter;

Desperate days,
And help come soon:
Nothing discourses of these
In the yellow of noon.

Peace, peace?
The old man said,
There are two kinds of mortal peace,
And not another that I know.

There was the time
Before your birth,
And there will be a time as long
Commencing neatly with your death.

54

Each is deep
And each is wide,
And each is empty; which is cause,
From what I know, to call it peace.

Fill a world,
And trembling comes.
But the trembling goes; and in between
There is a space of quiet waiting.

These are peace:
Before a storm,
And after all the wind is dead;
Before the pebble breaks the pond,

And when the ultimate
Circle ceases;
When no enemy has come
And when the last of you is slain;

An open heart
To all assault,
And one, bruised, that bleeds and waits
Until the healing shall be over.

Not to know,
Or to have known
And to remember: these, he said,
Are all that be; and peace is either.

Many a dawning day and many a night,
Sitting, he looked about him for the light
That should be more than feathers from the sun:
Plumes that chance had plucked. Was no least one,
Hither so casually coming, sent to say
What feet should go in what deliberate way?
These beams that fell, was not a one concerned

With edging a perilous path until it turned?
He asked the question softly of the grass.
If that could hear, his sentences would pass
By wind and branch and cloud until they came
To where all spoken answers were the same:
All simple, and all sure. Or he would mark
The times of moonless nights, and ply the dark
With such entreaties as another sun,
Smaller and far away, could have begun
To ponder long ago when moons were not.
There was a moon, and planets in a plot
Came after one another, white and red.
All there, but separate now; and each was dead.
By nothing was he heeded, near or far;
No tuft of grasses, whispering to a star,
Took any message off or brought him back,
By twisted ways, along a glinting track,
The wisdom that he wanted. Nerveless now,
A world without direction, and a brow
Whereon no sign was branded stared at him
Through broken light that would be always dim:
All strange, with no circumference to hold
A universe of fragments growing cold.

When he no longer
Strove to know,
Straightway he knew.
The currents flow

Of stream and sky,
Of root and stem,
More smoothly since
He suffers them.

There is no saying,
He has said,

If there be laws
For heart and head;

Or if there be,
Another giver
Regulated
Grass and river

Long before.
We come too late
To hear the gods
Communicate.

Thus he says:
And that he finds
Comfort in
Those separate minds,

Unknowing now,
And caring little
If the greater
Frame be brittle

That encloses,
Mild and wide,
Mice and mountains
Side by side,

White and black,
And autumn red
That never misses
What is dead,

He smiling says.
Matter only
In the world
Is never lonely.

June is now like any June,
But hearing him I will not say
What seems to signify the moon,
What are the languages of day.

The earth is lovely as before;
I shall not ever cease to walk
Where it may lead. But nevermore
Shall I pretend that it can talk.

What is spoken I will speak;
What is done now I will do.
The bird had nothing in its beak
That cut my vision then and flew

Across the field, into the wood;
There was no word along the way.
So I pursue; but if I could
I would not say what it will say.

End of Travel

Here in a circle of maples I can sit
Half of a day in the sun, and before and after
Figure the speed of shadows; eastward, westward,
Going or coming, all of the shade is one.
Night, the centerless circle, widening, leaves
Me and the bounded brightness, whence I watch
Birds, coming and going—westward, eastward—
Clouds, and the smallest of all my circles, the sun.
Beyond this rounded silence there is nothing.
Roads go to the tops of hills and over,
Over to Canaan and over to all of the Cornwalls:
Eastward, westward, on to the two grey oceans.
For me they end on the hills.
                                And now there rises
Thunder of cars that pass below on the pike.

They pass, are gone; and still the Hollow is sounding.
Round and round it runs, the prisoned thunder,
Higher and higher yet in the curving trees.
I listen and follow, and laugh as the feet grow tired,
Falter, and stumble, and enter the death of hills.
Beyond there is crying of trains that people have taken,
Pointing them straight to the west. I do not listen.
Rim of the world, that cry is yours to devour.
Here am I nourished enough; remembering only
Men long gone who, never considering circles,
Straightened their eyes and pointed their steps to the West.

Through a cool
And speckled wood,
Where unseen
An Indian stood

And asked the meaning
Of their eyes,
They followed hot
Upon the cries

Of men ahead,
Whose going warmed
Paths no feet
Had ever formed;

Until there ran
A stiffened road
To where the first
River flowed.

Silver it came,
Lazily, widely, down from the North;
And one on a raft put forth
And gave it a name.

Word blew back,
Flushing the faces of men in file;
And, trotting the ultimate mile
Of the shadowy track,

Ten of them shouted,
Bringing the ferry again to the shore.
They crossed; and again there were more.
And some of them doubted;

Two of them turned,
Talking together of East and home.
But there was the river in foam,
And both of them burned

New now with desire;
Looking across where the water was walled
Once more with a wood, that called
Their feet to the fire

Laid far in the West:
Waiting for these who would touch it to flame.
So on, and ever the same,
And never a rest.

So over the biggest of rivers
And on to the plains,
Under a sun whose shadows
Were yellowing stains

On the green of the grass, and the white
Of the desert beyond.
At evening it reddened the world,
And the goers were fond

Of saying that this was the fire,
That this was the end;

Only a hundred mountains
Now to ascend,

Only a hundred valleys
And there it would wait:
Faggot and leaf and log
On an altar of fate.

The feet and the eyes drew on
Till the ocean was there.
Then silence. The hills were asleep,
And the beaches were bare,

And the sun going down in the sea
Went utterly out.
And the travellers looked at each other
And turned about.

Here in the circle of maples where I am standing
Only the bodies come back of these long gone.
Thinly they walk in the shade, and thinly endeavor,
Turning, to keep to the West. But they have lost it;
And so all afternoon I will see them circling—
Birds with a wounded wing—and never at rest.
The thoughts of a traveller never can curve and return.
Only the body comes back of one long gone
Straightly and far away. And bodies discover
Death in the hills, and death in a circle of sound.

End of Singing

This wind today
From the invisible West
Is the wind that carried the singing away,
Away from an Indian breast.

He sang to the four
Dark ends of the sky,
And they can remember, though song no more
Goes there in a quartered cry.

Snow tomorrow
Will blossom and fall,
Unknowing if it is the flower of our sorrow;
Nobody now will call

To the four dark ends
Of the covering grey,
To the wind, this wind, that catches and bends
The stem of no song away.

Now the corn
Stands alone
That was born
Of a green moan

From one beneath,
Who gave it milk
Within a sheath
Of yellow silk;

And the wind
Its father came,
Leather-skinned
And walking lame,

Driving throngs
Of butterflies,
That brought it songs
And gave it eyes.

Still they flutter
In the field;

But none will mutter
To the sealed,

Withered senses
Of the corn
Words that fences
Would have torn.

The parents now
Forget their child,
Upon whose brow
Will be the wild

Winds of spring
Forever dumb;
For no men sing,
And no words come.

The stallion uprears,
And softly bethudding the meadow
Beneath him surprises a shadow
That levels his ears.

They, pointing so proud,
Find only the sedulous sun,
Only the breezes, and one
Pursuable cloud.

Never a song
That will tell of the glittering grass
Beyond where the mountains pass
So gently along,

And the father of steeds,
Neighing all day in a bright
Storm of descending delight,
Eternally feeds

On tapering flowers;
Or races with clattering time,
Strewing the slopes he must climb
With the shadows of hours.

Never a strain
Of the song of the pollen that hovers
Close to his flank, and covers
The white of his mane;

No holy bright word
Of the tale of the hurrying dust:
The grains of the sacred rust
His stamping has stirred.

The stallion is lonely,
Hearing no song to his sire.
Slowly he walks to the wire.
The stallion is lonely.

There is no longer any sound
Binding men unto the ground.
There was an arrow flew and took
Its drink of flesh; the warrior shook,
And shook the ground whereto he sang,
Falling while the forest rang.
Then a whispering in his wound,
And the earth whereon he swooned
Whispered up a song of running
Over needles, after cunning
Pairs of foxes that he caught;
Or of stopping with his thought
Deer that trembled, turned, and came.
And up he leapt, no longer lame.

Wind and stars and tongues of men,
And beasts between that talk alone,

You will not converse again;
All your songs are lost and gone.

The sky is singing to another
Sky beyond that none can see;
Man is singing to his brother;
Worm to worm, and tree to tree.

There is no song that all can hear,
Coming from a silent place
Where an Indian slays his fear
With folded arms and lifted face.

Now the Sky

How long have standing men, by such a stone
As this I watch from on this windless night,
Beheld Arcturus, golden and alone,
Guiding Antares and the Snake aright.

The Scales were up when not an Arab walked
On sand that soon was paved with names of stars;
Boötes herded, and the Giant stalked
Past the curved Dragon, contemplating wars.

How many an open eye, bedight with dew,
Over the sleeping flowers has drawn them down:
Andromeda, and Berenice's few
Dim tresses that shall ever flee the Crown.

From such a rock whence greybeards long ago,
Forgetting it beneath them, heard the Lyre,
I watch. But there is something now we know
Confusing all they saw with misty fire.

For them a hundred pictures on a slate.
For us no slate, and not a hand that draws.

For them a pasture-dome wherefrom the gate
Of Cancer led the Lion through its claws.

For them a frosty window, painted over,
Nightly, with flower faces in a ring:
Daisies dancing up, and clouds of clover
Scenting the after way, and phlox to fling

Thin petals left and right till morning lifted.
For us no shapely flame in all the dark;
For us a million embers that have drifted
Since the first fire, and not a sign to mark

Where anything shall end, or which shall go
With which until they both shall die to grey.
For watchers once a changeless face to know;
For us cold eyes that turn henceforth away.

They saw each constellation take its hour
Of triumph overhead, before it started
Down the broad West, whereon the death of power
Was written by the Ram, and nightly charted.

The Eagle and the Swan, that sailed so long,
Floating upon white wings the Arrow missed,
Tilted at midnight, plunging with a song
Earthward, and—as they sank—deep Hydra hissed.

Leo had long been growling in his lair
When Pegasus neighed softly in the East,
Rising upon a wind that blew his hair
Freshly, until Aquarius increased

The stream he aimed against the Fish's mouth,
And all the stars were wet with silent rain.
The Hyades came weeping, and the South
Sent mist to soothe the Sisters in their pain.

66

These things they witnessed, and Orion, climbing
Fiercely with those two Dogs announcing Fall;
Then Winter, with Aldebaran loud-chiming,
Baiting the frozen Bull, that turned to call

The Bears to warm his anger. These they knew,
And knew the seasons with them, Spring and Spring;
Counting the dozen signs the finger drew
That swung the inconstant Sun around the Ring.

Slow Jupiter proceeded as they planned,
Lingering among the Twelve in stately turn;
They touched the breasts of Venus, where the hand
Of Mars's fiery love had been to burn.

The sky was then a room, with people going
Faithfully to and fro, and beasts enchained.
The sky was then a midnight wastrel, throwing
Riches away; and still the purse remained.

But now the sky is broken, door by door.
Strangers in the room obscure the hosts.
The meadow is not guarded any more
By watchers coming lonely to their posts.

The animals are never to be named
That swarm beyond our company of old:
Stragglers from the herd, that we had tamed
Unknowing the recesses of the fold.

Those were no heroes whom we once addressed:
Hercules, Orion, and the Twins.
Unwounded, they were running from the rest
Far there where only now the war begins.

There is a game for players still to play,
Pretending that the board was never lost.

But still the painted counters will decay,
And knowledge sit along to count the cost.

Above the Battle

Higher than hate, and the abused
Stiff bodies of men, and the stiff
Walk, close to the ground, of men not just;
Higher, yes, than the uppermost whipped head,
Than the stiff elbow of the whipper;
High in the unseen air a tree starts waving;
Waving alone, and it says to itself:
                        I know.
Longer, yes, than the uppermost man remembers,
Longer ago than the eyes laid deepest away,
Longer ago than justice, there were trees.
The face of the world was water, and the hair—
Silk at the edge of salt—was waving trees;
But not like these.

             In a slow wind
             They rose and fell,
             Laying them down
             To sleep so well

             That, standing to look,
             They still would sway
             In the bent wind,
             In the curved day.

             With a slant wind
             They fell and rose,
             Slowly, slowly,
             And never a close

             Of the circle of soft
             Unended motion—

Silk at the salt
Stiff edge of ocean.

The low grass at our feet was a forest too;
The wind in it was a snake with indolent folds.
The wind in us was the word the white sky sang,
Sending no more than one slow syllable down.
All of them long are dead, and none remembers.
Not even a root remembers; but I know,
I know what none of the men there huddle and cry.

The salt came,
And talking sand,
And north snow,
And man's hand,

And my slim fathers
Fled and stood
In a coarse fear,
In a loud wood.

We straightly rise,
We stiffly fall.
We do not listen
If men call

On ignorant winds
To set love right.
That was our day.
This is our night.

II ﻌ

Defeated Farmer

Lift as he will a wordless face
To an earless wind, to a sightless sky,

He is not told if meadows lie
Beyond the rumor of the race
He ran and lost; and found disgrace
With common trees that standing die.

He can no more escape the scorn
Of day, that loathes a failing thing,
Than the stripped oak can beat a wing
And fly the wood where it was born;
Falling at night in a forlorn
Contrary wood where mold-worms sing.

Once he thought the wind conspired
With wet and dry and hot and cold
To slave for him. But he is old,
And long ago the year was tired,
And if the wind was ever hired
It bustled off to better gold.

Once he felt the city's eyes
In envy on him as he swung
Ill storms away. But not a tongue
Proclaims him lately weather-wise,
And he has heard towered laughter rise
From throats that in their turn are young.

He still can lift a lidded gaze
And count the mornings light and dark.
So the stripped elm with fallen bark
Receives the days. But not its days.
The greener wood has private ways
That posted death may not remark.

Civil War

The country is no country I have seen,
And no man goes there who is now alive, and no man

Ever is going to leave there. But they try;
Waving a million beards that on pale faces
Blacken with time and spread.
It is a field of bodies of blue boys,
And grey boys, grown half way into the ground.
The wind is dark that sways them;
All of them bending with it, south or north,
All of them straining here; but no one knowing
Of any fellow by who gazes too.
It is a field of legless bearded boys
With bright unnecessary buttons on their breasts,
And skirts of coats that hold them in the sod.
The bodies twist,
The circular, small eyes are mad with being;
A million mouths fly open without sound;
But none can tear his coat up, that must come
With roots and worms or come not up at all.

Away in Carolina, Maine, Wisconsin,
Boys who kept their legs walked long and long.
They set their feet in furrows, or in aisles;
They strolled with girls, were taken, and were fathers;
Had old companionship; and last were covered
Quietly with smooth boards, and grass, and stone.
Stiffly now they hold society;
Forever thus they lie without a want.

In the forbidden country where the sod
Grows down and down, with restless blue roots, grey roots,
In the dark windy land no one can leave,
Separate necks yearn homeward;
Separate hungry shoulders pull and pull.
Wind, oh wind, I did not come to stay;
I must be there tomorrow, not to miss—
But the dark wind is earless, and the day
Is endless, and the grasses hiss and hiss.

The Orchard Ghost

Strictly at noon the mist was there,
Between two pear trees like a web.
There was no other mist abroad,
There was no other hand to grab
And tackle nothing but the sun,
Beneath the blossoms making fun.

He put it safely out of mind,
And sauntered home; but came again
Upon another shining day,
Upon another whitened noon.
And there it was as thin as dew;
And the sun was coming through;

And there were two rows of ribs
Around a heart that shook and glistened,
Like a poppy that the sun
Within a web of beams had fastened.
And there were elbows; and a face
Smiled transparently in place.

He closed his eyes and struck the thing;
He opened them and it was dancing:
Left and right, a little stiffly.
And it bowed, and with a mincing
Gesture came; but he was gone.
They found him lying on the lawn,

And they say that he will never
Leave the door while there is light.
After sunset on the mountain
He can start; though he must wait
And watch the west a fearful minute
Lest it have a spider in it.

Tiresias

There goes the man with yellow eyes
That see within, and see too much.
He was blinded by a god
That he might prophesy and touch.
So he takes a crooked rod
And peers with it as with a crutch.

Propping so his yellow eyes
He can discern the speeding day
Whereon a hundred hills shall fall,
And every city shall decay.
Ask him now and have it all.
Would no one hear what he can say?

They can say, those yellow eyes,
What both a man and woman are.
Since the morning he was cursed
The breasts have shrunk; but not so far
As to forget the teeth they nursed,
As to enfold the bitten scar.

Will no one bid the yellow eyes
Revolve again? Or call the tongue
To witness women in that pain
Wherewith their filaments are strung?
Will no one touch the whirling brain
Of him who is both old and young?

Tiresias, damned with yellow eyes,
Pursue your endless road alone.
What you see beyond the night
Is but a frame of bloody bone.
We were wiser, yet we might
Come never there without a moan.

Man with Globe

In the mornings of my strength
The world is tin upon a table.
Standing from it, I am able,
Fingers firm upon the pole,
To spin the whispering breadth and length
Of its small, rounded soul;
And I am whole.

Then descends an afternoon
Of fallen walls, of panic light.
Staring out, I hear the night
Pursuing seas and breaking land
On spheres too far to cry in tune;
And my once stony hand
Crumbles to sand.

The Disguise

Groper up the narrow landing
Past the invisible voiceless clock;
Then to the left and higher again
Till the carpet ceases, and shadows rock
Of linden leaves on the moon-white floor:
Suddenly stop; for this is the door.

Grasper of club and turner of handle
And prowler as far as a darkened bed;
Feeler of hair; and beater and beater
And beater and beater until he is dead:
Man, descending through the night,
How is it forgotten that flesh is white,

That eyes on a pillow had much to see
On mornings that never are now to come;
That there is silence worse than all

74

When even death is stricken dumb?
Man upon another stairs,
What mask is this your madness wears?

Estrangement

They were not old enough to be
Two musty mows that nothing joined:
Darkening places strange with mice
That never caught a foreign sound.
They were not separated yet
By moldy mortar wrath had set.

They were still a single room,
But longer now than once it was;
And in the middle quiet spiders
Worked unseen on certain days.
What they built she twice removed;
But the third time it was proved.

Each aware of something hung there,
He rebuked it; then was still.
If it stung their meeting faces,
He could wait along his wall.
Neither was old enough to know
How wide and high a web can grow.

The Relic

It is something that he handled;
It is something gold and small
That he dandled

From a button of his vest;
And his fingers never learned
To fall and rest

75

Until they died. But it lives,
Lying on a shaded table,
And it gives,

For me who look, no lie to death,
Though a pale pretence of hands
Is there like breath;

Though a flutter as of fear
Tries to say around the room
That he is here.

Deeper proof of death is none:
That all the ghosts keep abed
Excepting one.

Death

He never had heard of it. Then it was there;
And still he would not talk of anything
Save walking on and seeing; rolling an eye
Right, left, as if there still were nothing there.
And nothing was: that now is what he knows.
He knows that men are walkers through a wood
Filled with a light from nowhere; and the trees
Stand shadowless. He knows them, few and clear,
Companions of a morning no sun makes.
The walkers on bright feet, the happy men,
Forever, until a day, go straightly through,
Or wind a little, swaying as they pass.
Then on a day a shadow falls, and rising,
Stands like a tree; and then another stands,
Twisting the paths of walkers till they falter,
Circle a while, and cease in striped shade.
The trunks are there—thin intervals of light—
But not for mind or foot was that way made.

76

Death is not knowing what is not a shadow.
And nothing is. That now is what he says.

Death of Light

The winter face of wisdom, the slow eyes
Opening never widely lest surprise
Come with the first snow and whitely shed
Whispers where the hard truth should tread;
The grey ears that, hearing, disbelieve
And fallen cheeks all time will not retrieve—
The wary eyes of wisdom are too changed
From the green year when straight the vision ranged
And straight accepted seeing. Then the lines
Led ever on and on, with no designs
Woven upon the world of false or true.
Light was a bird that too much looking slew.
Dropping upon a wire, it sat and sang
And trembled.
                    Only feathers of it hang
For shaded eyes of wisdom to see now.
Safe are the ears, and deep the careful brow
Of wisdom, counting riches. But the tale
Is one of losing, and of lids that fail.

Death of Old Men

When they no longer lean there,
And leer, and hold a sentence in;
When they no longer fix the air
With a grimace, a grey grin;

When they are gone, a stiffness goes,
As if a post were pulled out.
The wire is down, and wind blows
Uncut to where the young ones shout:

Tall and bending, green and free;
Looking up at only light.
But that is not enough to see.
They will weary of the height.

They will say a word for old
And crooked men beneath a cape
Of nights and stars; and for the cold,
That fastens faces into shape.

III ॐ

Mad Songs

I

That chime I hear
And you do not
Is the singing of fear
In the rope, the knot

That I with a knife
Go forth to sever.
You of this life
Through me shall never

Stumble again
In a circle of dust.
The four gates then,
With a crying of rust,

Will equally swing
And will equally pour
Mouths that will sing
In the rain evermore.

And the wind will unsay
That I ever was blind.

78

That was your way.
Now follow behind.

II

You did not come;
How could I keep
Four winds awake
When one would sleep?

I hurried by;
Another slept;
Then all were gone,
And I had stepped

Before I knew—
It was your will—
Into a night
Where, dark and still,

I heard you walking
Round and round.
Not any other
Sight or sound

Until you laughed
And led me back
To touch my brain,
Crack after crack.

Still your fingers,
Pressing tight,
Hurt what could heal
In wind and light

Would you but come
As far with me
As to the singing
I can see.

Philosopher's Love Song

My one love has lighter loves,
And taller ones, and merrier.
Still my love has less than I,
Who having her, have only her.

Having her, who has those others:
Him, and him, and flowers, and horses:
Having her is having sometimes
Jealousies and loud remorses,

Which to punish with her eyes
She turns her head, as if to see
What is to see—and, stepping lightly,
Come those loves more light than me.

Having me that have no other,
She has others; but the sum
Of all her halves is less than my
One that is compendium.

Poorhouse Dream

Death is a tall horse
With large white feet,
Coming on a slow walk
Down the long street,

Nudging with a soft nose,
Opening the gate.
Up you must climb then,
Lest you be late.

Starting on a slow walk
And never looking round,

He moves; and the great feet
Never make a sound.

Soon it is a road
With the houses far between,
And when a farm is there at last
Children come and lean,

Shouting over fences;
But not as if they knew.
And not a word arrives
Of what they say to you.

On beneath a bright hill
Is water in a trough.
But he is never thirsty,
And you are looking off,

Thinking of the afternoon,
Thinking of the night.
But all the sky is green there,
And all the hours are white.

He will never halt again,
And you will not descend.
You will be content there
Without any end.

The Crowd

There were six children in a house,
And there was one across the way;
But when he joined them he was more
Than making seven in the play.
They were six and he was one:
A single flower among the hay.

They remarked the careful stem,
And felt an envy for the face
Of one who, flourishing alone,
Grew out of hurt and rose to grace.
But he among the roughened heads
Bewept his nakedness of race.

He had come as if to cover
All he lacked; for he had lain
Beneath the body of their wind,
And sweated with them in the rain.
But he was white and slender still;
And still they coveted his pain.

The Orphan

In the same moment, child,
With death upon a train,
You walked, and with a wild
Clamor walked again.

I was not by them, boy;
I know not how they fell;
But I beheld the joy
Of you that stepped so well,

And, stepping, never knew
What made us weep to see:
Lightning in the two
Branches of a tree;

Lightning leaving only
Sky above your head,
That still is not so lonely
As the stricken dead.

82

Company Gone

Mountains, stand again,
And flowery hay, put up your head.
They are gone, the ten
Men
That flattened you with nothing said.

Lilac, come alive,
And coreopsis, turn about.
They are gone, the five
Wives
You always shun because they shout.

Rambler, tie your shoe,
And Emily Gray, go on along.
We are here, the two
True
Mouths that move but to your song.

The Dinner

Jupiter and Mercury
Among the Phrygian hills
Envied even sparrows
That picked the window sills.

Not a door was open
To show a table laid,
Till Baucis and Philemon,
Startled as they prayed,

Answered godly knocking
And bustled at the board,
Giving all to strangers
Either could afford.

83

Baucis plucked a salad,
Philemon brought a chine
Of bacon moulded over,
And set it by the wine;

And nodding to each other
They ran—but it was hard—
And slew the only gander
Walking in the yard.

Jupiter and Mercury
Glistened as they went,
And quickly all the valley
Whispered what it meant.

Water flooded inland,
Filling every field,
And everyone drowned there,
Even as he kneeled.

Except in the cottage
Where the four had dined.
That rose up,
And the gables were lined

With a thatch of gold,
And Philemon poured
Wine forever
From a silver gourd.

IV ৡ

Man

Brown as the glade he moves in,
Entering out of the sun, the slayer of eyes,

He walks; and the blind shadows,
Hearing his soundless feet, awake and arise,

Bending with him and parting
The pale hair of ferns, pretending to see;
But while he looks they leave him,
Becoming the portion of earth himself would be.

He still can forget his fingers,
Softly he says—and a toad is there on the moss.
He stoops; and the greyling stays,
Panting, with only half of the rock to cross.

Patiently settling earthward,
One of his hands, unfolded, touches stone:
Rests, and cannot remember
If arms are there or if it is a leaf, alone.

Cold are the rock and the lichen,
Cold are the quieted eyes, and the palm, and the wrist.
Around is a thick stillness—
Save for his suddenly hearing, out of mist,

Waves of an old awareness:
Blood in his hand come back, and bone returning.
Wisdom is underground.
So to the sun again, and the fever of learning.

The Translation

Ant and shrew
And marmot, going
Safely there,
The time of mowing

Comes tomorrow.
Meadow lark

And banded snake,
Then the dark

Sky will fall:
What is green
Above you now
No more be seen.

What is single
Will divide.
And as you run
The other side

Of all the world
Will drop its blue
As if it looked
For none but you.

Toad and cricket,
Worm and mouse,
You will find
Another house

That not a hand
Was there to build.
My own sky
Has never spilled,

Right and left,
And shown a new one.
Night and day
Mine is the true one.

Would it were not,
And could lie
Thus to the sickle
As I die.

Deserted Hollow

This valley sends another sound
Than was delivered of its rocks
When they were seized and set around
The cloven feet of little flocks.
The sheep were taken long ago,
And fences wait a wilder foe.

There is no hushing of the wind
Between the blows of axes now.
No breathless timber-lengths are pinned
And shingled fast to make a mow.
There is not one expectant eye
Upon the purpose of the sky.

It was a race of silent men
That taught the clouds to hesitate,
If only to upgather then
A blacker heaven-full of hate.
Riders up and down divided
Weather since grown single-sided.

Winds that strike upon these stones
Hear not an angry voice among them.
They have smothered their old moans
Against the hairy hands that wrung them.
Boulders, grass, and border-trees
Supinely harken. Fences freeze

And crumble wider every spring;
They will yet be flat again.
There is not a wilful thing
In all this patient mountain-pen.
There is only the dead sound
Of slowly unresisting ground.

Rain All Day

The sky is laid as low again
As once it was when fearful men
Heard the hoarse chime
Of moving time.

Over me now unmuffled feet
Trample the blue, and flatten the sweet
Flowers of day
That sang him away.

As up they sang the distance grew
Between our faces and these two
Merciless heels
My forehead feels.

Space is fallen, time is found,
And we are nothing but the ground
On which he walks,
Mashing the stalks.

Contest

The east wind I worked in,
And endless black rain—
Working with a wet axe
As long as there was wood—
The rain, the wind, and I
Argued which should die.

The chopper never looked up,
Behind him or around;
Only at the wet log
His blade fell and warmed;
Hoping heat would spread
Until the dark was dead.

The wind never looked away,
But, always coming on,
Drove the rainy knife edge
Deeper in and in.
It was the day that died
With blue in its side.

December 22

Noon today, and the earth swings high—
Swing low, you sun whom once she loved—
Noon, and her body is trying to die;
And horses stop, and men go gloved.

Noon in the north, but never an end—
Look far, you sun whom still she knows—
Try as she may, she cannot bend
Backward enough for the eyes to close.

Stiffly at noon now, under the lids—
Look in, you sun, and remind her now—
She stares once more, though her will forbids;
And mice dream on in the darkened mow.

June 22

Up and around as far as her old eyes,
Opening young and warm, can see they swing;
And swing; and swallows
Take them a little farther, daring the wind.
They are off there now, in the quiet,
And here she sits indifferent, playing blind.
One smile she has for all of the rounded day;
One face she turns, and says that this is the time
For sitting and letting the mind go run with the hours.
There is nothing to fear, she says;

In a field so wide and white no body could die.
She smiles and fingers flowers and, lifting her head,
Listens softly; and swallows
Take her a little farther, daring the sun.

Dark Barn

Windows, dying, left for dust
The wings of flies that spiders trussed
And waiting speared. The door is held
With weeds that not a blade has felled,
With vines that thicken since the last
Inlooker shut the shadows fast.
It is a piece of darkness saved
Against the summer, and the waved
Bright hair of harvest, brought to shear.
Nothing will cut the darkness here,
That grows and fills the rafter spaces,
Hangs, and wraps the rusted traces
And blind bridles on their pegs;
Stares between the stanchion legs;
And is the only thing to know
That running mice bear pretty snow
Upon their bellies, which they hide
For joy beneath them as they glide.

The Distant Runners

*Six great horses of Spain, set free after
his death by De Soto's men, ran West
and restored to America the wild race
lost there some thousands of years ago.*
—LEGEND.

Ferdinand De Soto lies
Soft again in river mud.
Birds again, as on the day

90

Of his descending, rise and go
Straightly West, and do not know
Of feet beneath that faintly thud.

If I were there in other time,
Between the proper sky and stream;
If I were there and saw the six
Abandoned manes, and ran along,
I could sing the fetlock song
That now is chilled within a dream.

Ferdinand De Soto, sleeping
In the river, never heard
Four-and-twenty Spanish hooves
Fling off their iron and cut the green,
Leaving circles new and clean
While overhead the wing-tips whirred.

Neither I nor any walker
By the Mississippi now
Can see the dozen nostrils open
Half in pain for death of men;
But half in gladness, neighing then
As loud as loping would allow.

On they rippled, tail and back,
A prairie day, and swallows knew
A dark, uneven current there.
But not a sound came up the wind,
And toward the night their shadow thinned
Before the black that flooded through.

If I were there to bend and look,
The sky would know them as they sped
And turn to see. But I am here,
And they are far, and time is old.
Within my dream the grass is cold;
The legs are locked; the sky is dead.

The Pulse

One thing is sure
When most are not:
That there is cold,
That there is hot.

There is no error
In the frost;
With warmth away
No warmth is lost;

Waves are coming
Of a time
That has been written
In slow rhyme:

Hot and cold,
And cold and hot;
All things may fail,
But this one not.

Though hate and love
And mercy cease,
Under the rippling
Vapor fleece

Of earth goes warmth
Pursuing cold;
And neither is young;
And neither is old.

Pastoral

Fleeing the town where every face
Was long and pale in the lamplight,

He sighed for any simple place
Of minds round as midnight;

And thought he came to such a valley
Westward by a hundred miles;
He sat with Ed, he lay with Sally
Underneath the rooftiles;

Concluding in the autumn, though,
Returning to the pantomime,
That country faces, ticking slow,
Tell too strictly noontime.

Epistle to Town: February

Go to your table, in the lined room
Outside of which four ashmen used to bark.
Go to your table, to the lettered keys.
Send me words quickly, on small hard feet,
Tapping this snow that is too soft and wide,
Dotting this white that is too everywhere.
The trees stand out of it, and bushes blow
Thinly, as if they meant to creep indoors.
Yet nothing moves; all things are waiting here,
And the sky waits upon a dance of words.
Let them say anything, so they are black,
So they come suddenly on little heels,
Dropping like seed upon this table cloth.
Say I am a crow, and have a hungry eye,
Fed now too long upon an empty field.
Think of me hovering. Tell me a taxi
Halted just now and let a lady out,
And she went into Number 45.

Farewell to Fields

Bird, tree, and cloud, and all you creatures going
Under upon four feet, and shadows showing
Of things behind, put so for none to see:
Fold up your pipes, for you are done with me.
This is the seventh summer we have played;
The end comes, and all the sounds are made.
You were the slender instrument I took,
Blowing until the rooted grasses shook,
And the crows cried, and nodding horses came;
But ever now the tangles are the same
Of the mazed steps that once our rhyme unravelled.
There is another wildness to be travelled,
And I have set my feet to go alone.
Over no grass, and by no greying stone,
I now would hunt new music out of bare
Hatred, and quick love, and old despair.
Where I am going men and women go.
Fold up your pipes, that have instructed so.

A WINTER DIARY

AND OTHER POEMS (1935)

SONNETS ੭੭

Sonnets

I

I said: It will not blow this way again;
The branches of my life too soon are old;
The wind is kind to early-withered men
Lest they remember and confess the cold.
I said, and scarcely knew that it was I,
Hanging my leaves there in the springless year.
I said; and did not listen to a high,
Loud sound of March that filled the woods with fear.
Then it was all around me, till at last
Love like a hurricane of hate was blowing,
Bruising me everywhere. Yet I was fast,
And stood among the ruins of his going.
    Only the after stillness came and showed
    These blossoms on me everywhere, like blood.

II

No wonder-deed done in the oldest time
Whose whiteness burns oblivion away,
No miracle of grass, whose muted rhyme
Outsings the dawn and silences the jay,
No fiend's invention, no good man's endeavor,
No other tale of love is so untrue
As this one of my heart, that empties never,
But fills even as you take, and still is new.
It cannot be there is more love to come;
Yet, coming on, love tells me I have lied.
So I must learn to listen and grow dumb,
Believing in a heart that never died:
    Believing then in you, who like a dream
    Draw out of me this ever waking stream.

III

You may grow tired of my incessant tongue,
That loves perhaps too well the work of praise.
You may turn otherwhere, and search among
All men for one who keeps the wordless ways.
This you may do, and I admit the fault
Of loving you too wakefully to cease.
Oh, I have tried to mend me, but the salt
Of silence never brought these lips release.
Still must they harken to the thoughts behind
That form and flow to utter your perfection.
Still must they move before a driven mind
Marching to death in your unchanged direction.
    Therefore at least I bind them with one thong,
    This reticence that wraps a formal song.

IV

As if there lay one other sky beyond
This sky that was enough for any man;
As if the midnight bloomed, and frond on frond
Of blackness waved across Aldebaran;
Or the bent miser, opening his box,
Found double gold; or some most comely youth,
Walking at noon, caught light among his locks,
And the sun paled, impoverished of truth;
So is the love that fills me an excess,
Unlacked before, unwaited till it came;
Unneeded now—but, oh, the mind's distress
If it should lose one letter of your name!
    If nature strolled with her proportioning knife
    And pruned this farthest limb that is my life!

V

No throat had ever told me what I know,
And knowing now so well, pity a lover's
Silence; for the voice of love is low;
It cannot rise to what the heart discovers.
It cannot sing as high as love's own mind,
Which, truant among birds, flies daily back
With a wide restlessness, and looks behind
At everything the darkened house will lack.
Therefore I hold these words inside my heart,
Therefore I tie each thought that would ascend.
They languish, but it is the better part,
And there is sweeter music in the end—
    Unheard by even you, on whom the sound
    Gathers like dew upon the senseless ground.

VI

Chasten your fears, I have not been destroyed,
All that was in me once is living still;
Only I know there was this slender void,
This threading vein through an unconscious hill.
Empty of you, it nourished every part
With nothingness, and I was none the worse.
Filled with you suddenly, it is the start
Of older riches than I can rehearse:
Joy like a hidden river that no stone
Ever is worn away by where it runs;
Peace in the darkest passages of bone,
And buried light as from a hundred suns;
    With tolerance, that sweetens as it flows
    This blood whose red remembers late the rose.

VII

That you were there to see before I saw,
Midway the range of old day-lighted things,
That you were there, and so by vision's law
The truth of you went off in widened rings;
That you lived ever in such early time
Is past my understanding, save that now,
This evening, I have seen the day-stars climb
Down step by step of darkness; and I vow,
No more than you they needed night between,
No more than you they watched the world away—
As here upon no earth I stand and lean,
Loving your light that is the end of day;
    With no beginning after, for the dawn
    Was grey, and I am glad that it is gone.

VIII

When I am called by Love to give account
Of the one thing that holds me unto you,
I will obey him to the strict amount;
One nameless thing I know, and it must do.
I will tell Love how first you looked at me:
Head down, and something level in your eyes;
How still you stood and looked; and I could see
Half-risen modesty, to rule surprise;
How then you spoke, and how your voice was low,
And how your arms hung perfectly await.
I will ask Love himself to pause and go,
And look, and understand my changeless state:
    Rooted again within your level gaze,
    Eternal now across the evening ways.

IX

All of the steps that our slow love has taken
Were your own steps at last, who led the way.
I was too fixed—or like an oak was shaken
That has been marked to fall yet never may.
Never unless you taught me had I known it:
Love must be advancing or it dies.
You found each resting-place, but had outgrown it
Before I too was ready to arise.
Love is a journey to no end, except
One traveller, halting, cannot journey more.
When I awoke you had as wisely stepped
As the sole fox across a forest floor;
    So I would always follow you; and will
    To the last hedge upon the highest hill.

X

The time not spent in kissing you is chaff
Gone windily away; is desert bones;
Is the lost acorn; the discarded half
Of ore from which were plucked the golden stones;
Is air beyond our breathing; is the dust
That rings another world, nor brings it rain;
Is worse than nothing had: the final crust
Was there, and it was fatal to refrain.
So have I said, yet it was never true.
Poor talk, you had your uses all the while.
Slow words, between your pauses hung the two
Far eyes I had forgotten, and the smile.
   Not that I had forgotten; but the heart
   Grows blind if it too seldom holds apart.

XI

Where is the wit that I could sometimes wield?
And yours, for you were happier than I?
Where is the hand that held the tapered shield,
Daring the sharpest arrows to let fly?
My wrists are down, I am without defense,
And what is worse, incompetent to wound;
My regiments are sleeping in their tents;
My talk at last is gentle and untuned.
And yours, for you were readier to strike,
And sat upon the swifter-coming horse—
Now do you understand what love is like?
I think he cannot even feel remorse,
   This mischievous small killer in the dark
   Who cuts two living tongues out for a lark.

XII

I disagreed, and you misunderstood,
And the sick moments dragged their wings along.
What matters, though, one worm within the wood,
What matters one rude note within the song?
There still is all of time, wherein this hour
Will sweeten as it ages and be relished.
Love is no love that lacks the bitter power
With its own ugliness to be embellished.
There still is all of song, that will enclose
These wounded wings and heal them till they lift,
And the worm sleep, and the musician doze—
Swooning to hear a melody so swift
    That no one there can guess the happy hand,
    Save you and me, who both will understand.

XIII

Come with me, Love, and listen all the while,
And warn me if I say too much again.
She cannot see that I am bare of guile,
Or that there grow as many loves as men.
She cannot estimate my love is me.
She takes me as I am, but it should alter.
It should be tentative, observe degree,
And in a kind of greenness never falter.
So come with me and watch my ripened tongue,
For I am willing now that she be suited;
Let her believe that I am only hung
With blossoms that so heavily am fruited.
    Then in good time she may accept my words;
    Unless the worms have had them, and the birds.

XIV

I was confused; I cannot promise more
This morning than to keep these miles between us.
I can do that, although the heart grow sore
And the night weep for ever having seen us.
I can do that; but I will not engage
To come and slay this love before your eyes.
Let it die here, without the extra wage
Of torture that would shame us everywise.
Let me come afterward, however long,
And say to you I love you none the less.
Nor will I speak of any righted wrong.
Let it be dead, and let us both confess
    With laughter how we fasted forty days
    In the kind wilderness of time's delays.

XV

Should this end now it were the end of light,
That would no longer reach an earth receded;
And the grey death of odor; and a blight
On taste and touch, with every sound unheeded.
I could no longer count the falling days,
Nor weigh an ounce of sorrow out to pain;
It were the end of knowledge when the ways
Of feeling are as reason to the brain.
Should it end suddenly—but I am wrong.
Nothing so invisible can shatter.
Our love is not an object, like the long
Cold hand of time, that is the purest matter.
    But that is something different, and slow,
    And closes gradually, as the senses go.

XVI

Leave me not overlong at this remove;
In the half-darkness, Love, I see too well
My shortness when some measurement shall prove
How far below her hope I always fell.
Keep me no longer, Love, for there is that;
And this, which is more dreadful to attest:
Out of the dusk I have been staring at
Her face is gone that was my only rest.
My dwelling-place, her eyes, cannot be found;
I look, but see as little, coming home,
As the long voyager whose only sound
Is sighing when he finds the ocean foam
    Still hung to make a curtain high and dim
    Between the house of his true life and him.

XVII

When I came back to your unlifted eyes,
And spoke to you, inquiring how we did,
And you looked up without the least surmise—
Then the old music, that so long was hid,
Sounded; and I knew it was to pour
Forever while we lived, with no abating.
The unskilled players were unskilled no more,
And every string had sweetened by its waiting.
There will be nothing now but one clear tone,
Of which we shall not tire; and when it pauses
We shall exist upon love's faith alone,
That knows all silence to its deepest causes;
    And comprehends the ever devious ways
    I still must follow as I sing your praise.

XVIII

I would dislike you if you used an art
To make me love you more than this, the most;
For it is only downward that the heart
Could move from such an eminence. Poor boast!
Each day I am confounded, for you give
Each day the wheel of love a little turn;
And I go headlong with it, lest I live
Henceforth one arc behind; and never learn
There is no going downward in our love;
I could not fall and lose you if I tried.
There is no under here, and no above,
But round and round; and distances have died.
    Nor am I ever giddy, for love's air,
    Like this of earth, turns with it everywhere.

XIX

How can I prove that I have undersung,
Like you, the written air of our affection?
You do not sing at all, but keep among
Dark words that tell of love by indirection.
And have I sung too high? It is not so.
I rose, but it was never to be reached—
This simplest note that any reed could blow;
Yet not my voice, however it beseeched
Bird, sky, and grass to lend their happy skill,
And every buried lover all his art.
They laughed; and he advised my stubborn will
To cease within the silence of your heart;
    Which I would have it do were I as wise
    As one who had not listened to your eyes.

XX

Let it be always secret what we say;
And where we meet, be that our world alone.
Nor think us ever guilty, since our day
Is one on which no shadow-bands have shown.
Shame is a shadow that will never fall
On us who have cut down the trees of pride.
Let the world darken past the garden wall;
The space within is conscienceless and wide.
Nor think us ever weary, or in need
Of company to bring the night at last.
Love is a lonely and contented deed,
Done in a desert that is sweet and vast;
    Where neither of us turns a timeless head
    To see the world behind us that is dead.

XXI

As the blue fringes of this flower desire
Comparison; yet even this old glass,
Wherein some workman hid the sky afire,
Is not the same; and so the mind must pass,
And look along the world, and never come
To the pure hue repeated—thus I range
Through the live chronicles that tell the sum
Of love's known history; and each is strange.
No love is like our love beyond the start;
Two look upon each other, then we lose them.
They whisper to each other, but apart,
In a wild shade, and we can never use them;
    Likening ourselves to nothing more
    Than two late comers as the long day wore.

XXII

Sometimes I fear that I too soon was mastered.
Sometimes I think that you would have me still
Untaken—not like any crippled dastard,
Here with my hands up and my useless will.
Yet I must run the risk of being sure.
I tell you I am captive, every inch;
And was so long ago that I am pure
Even of the memory that pride could flinch,
And look away, and dream of being free.
I tell you this, and ask you then to know,
Nothing so well could prove my high degree,
Nothing so well declare the worthy foe.
    I am no more ashamed to kiss the rod
    Than the king was, acknowledging the god.

XXIII

What golden spider warmed himself and spun
This web that is the flesh upon your bones;
Warming himself beneath a spicy sun
That caught the winds and let their little moans,
Like woven music, enter every place
To hide until love's fingers should be near?
What artisan was singing at your face?
Who wrapped the rest, that too will disappear?
For time, that made the spinner, lets him die.
He will be long in leaving, yet he must;
So every moistened thread of you will dry:
At first to lace; but then a little dust.
    And I— Oh, time will take my desolate hand
    And sift it on you, letting it be sand.

106

XXIV

I carry in me always, since you live,
The devil of an uncontrolled delight.
He is my hidden master, whom you give
No heed, for he has seldom come in sight.
No passer-by may know I am possessed,
And even you will never learn his power.
The host himself is helpless when the guest
Sits on and on, and, smiling hour by hour,
Spreads darkest joy that round him ever flows
Like a sweet, bitter poison. So I keep
This fellow of the smile, and no one knows;
And so it only seems to be asleep—
  My laughter, that the world forever misses;
  Yet here it is, like sun upon our kisses.

XXV

Oh, I could talk forever, and as smoothly
As angels, were I farther from the fire.
I am the coal, and so I say uncouthly
Less than I mean, and more than you require.
Or if the distance widens on some days,
And I am for the moment swift of tongue,
A sudden sword will stop me on the phrase,
And every sentence after be unstrung.
Or if I once again am well contained,
And cool, as though I grew in watered ground,
The green with which my branches have been veined
Runs red, and I am rooted in the sound
  Of blooming under earth, and blowing cold.
  There is no single way it can be told.

XXVI

My fancy is less cruel than it is kind,
Though cruel it is to bring your spirit here,
Letting it seem your body; for I bind
No arms within these arms when you appear.
They know, and my eyes know, you have been standing
Most of a summer's day beyond the door.
But they have not the magic for commanding
One solid proof: a shadow on the floor.
Your lack of so impalpable a thing
Convinces me at last you never came,
And stood, and looked upon your underling;
Or if you did, my reason was to blame:
    Refusing then to recognize in you
    What such an afternoon might filter through.

XXVII

The earth is full of spirits once again.
Maidens in the marshes, bearing light,
Laugh the old ones up, the little men;
The ground remembers goblins day and night.
For every standing tree there is a face
That, somewhere hidden, soon must flicker home;
Each mountain side is rippled with the race
Of night-returning devil-face and gnome.
The thought of you is everywhere. It rises
Sometimes like a fiend and stares at me.
I am the helpless savage who devises
Charms; and knows he never will be free.
    Never shall I walk another wood
    Than this of your fixed eyes and pointed hood.

XXVIII

Never to be renewed or to increase,
And never to be changed from what it was:
The love that was the maker of this lease
Was love-upon-first-sight, whom all the laws
Of happiness obey, and kingdoms coming
Choose to be the glory of their thrones.
He is the oldest love, he is the humming
Of these incessant bees among my bones;
He is the senses' king; my youngest thought
He molds before I know it has been born;
He is the flesh's despot; the inwrought,
Deep joy; or in my side the sudden thorn.
    Oh, strange that on that day I was so strong,
    Bearing him all at once; and now so long!

XXIX

This book declares my love is a condition,
Determined in the tissue; but it lies.
I banish the impertinent physician;
I must refuse to credit one so wise.
Or if there must be fables, let them tell
Of wounds that were inflicted from the flank;
How once we faced each other, and there fell
Swift arrows out of nothing, and they drank
My blood, and put a poison in its place;
My courage, and refilled me with desire;
How then the tincture spread, till into grace
I stumbled, and the punishment of fire—
    Unending, for no heart in all that heaven
    Recovers from a wound the god has given.

XXX

The longest hour is swifter than I thought.
It is more cruel, having a sharper end.
So time is my close foe; yet I am taught
Some safety by this fear that is my friend:
This fear of eyes that if they ever used
Their utmost power would then I think destroy me;
This awe of something not to be abused,
Lest the world break, and love no more employ me.
For such a fear it is withholds my hands
At the last greedy instant; there I wait,
Lowly, as the shaded hunter stands
And lets the shining pheasant pass in state—
 Something that is too beautiful to miss;
 Yet the dream holds me while the sickles hiss.

XXXI

These things I say, no one of them can reach
The roundness of the sphere that is your truth.
They are but lonely segments, they beseech
Environment and complement. Time's tooth
Devours even while I write; though did it starve,
I still would stand too far from either pole.
Had I eternity, I could but carve
Inscriptions that were partial to the whole.
Not even all together would declare
This roundness, that more swift than words can follow,
Grows, until the mind is thin as air,
And what is most compendious most hollow.
 Better that I should cease, and so re-enter
 Love's little room, revolving at the center.

XXXII

Not pride it was that made me say so much
Bearing on my own mind in these, your songs.
Intended for your praise, they did but touch
Idea, where your beauty best belongs,
And straightway thought was active, bringing proof,
Here in my heart's possession, of your power.
These but effects; the cause remains aloof;
There is no certain entrance to the tower.
If any gate were open I would climb,
Life-long, and reach your verity at last;
And sing—Oh, I can hear the happy rhyme
Break upward, I can see the overcast
    Part swiftly, and can lose the final sound.
    Alas! I never heard it from this ground.

XXXIII

My only need—you ask me, and I tell you—
Is that henceforth forever you exist.
You are not mine; I may not ever bell you
Like an owned animal for night and mist.
My only need, whatever darkness take me,
Whatever tears close now my separate eyes,
Is that you live, and let the knowledge make me
Immortal as the day that never dies—
That, swift and even, turns into the sun,
As turns the after-shadow down to death.
Let neither then my night, my day be done;
Let them both swing in silence, with no breath
    To call you from the distances you keep.
    Would they were little; would that my love could sleep.

Growing a Little Older

Growing a little older is suddenly
Standing a little still;
Then forward again, with something learned
Of the slow skill
Of skies,
Where motion dies.

Growing a little older is holding
One day a question back;
Then letting it go, with something seen
Of the faint crack
To crawl
Twixt nothing and all.

Growing a little older is hiding
Shivers of sudden fear;
Then letting them work, with something guessed
Of the deep spear
Of joy,
That too will destroy.

Why, Lord

Why, Lord, must something in us
    Yearly die?
And our most true remembrance of it
    Lie?
Until the pure forgetting
    By and by.

Why then must something other
    Come and grow?

112

Renewing us for nothing, save the
  Slow
Upbuilding of this bed
  Of needles, so.

Why is the soil not bitter
  Where we stand?
Whose, Lord, upon our roots
  The sweetening hand?
For so it is: we love
  No shallower land.

Joy Cannot Be Contained

Joy cannot be contained.
I know, for I have seen
The stricken eyes; and strained
To hear the blood's machine;

Have watched awhile and listened:
Terrible the stillness!
Then the eyes have glistened,
As from illness;

Then the heart has sounded,
Breaking in the dark;
As if the seas, impounded,
Had set again to work.

Fate Comes Unswerving

Fate comes unswerving like a frightened horse
Sky-maddened on a white mid-afternoon.
Fate comes unseeing, and the blinded hooves
Drum a shrill thunder to a noteless tune
That dies into the forest, where an owl
Returns it to the midnight and the moon.

113

Lean neither way, for nothing can escape.
No walker in a field knows whence it comes.
Only there is an instant when the dust
Whirls upward and the round horizon hums.
Then the feet loudest, and the final leap.
With afterward no dream of any drums.

Wit

Wit is the only wall
Between us and the dark.
Wit is perpetual daybreak
And skylark
Springing off the unshaken stone
Of man's blood and the mind's bone.

Wit is the only breath
That keeps our eyelids warm,
Facing the driven ice
Of an old storm
That blows as ever it has blown
Against imperishable stone.

Wit is the lighted house
Of our triumphant talk,
Where only weakly comes now
The slow walk
Of outer creatures past the stone,
Moving in a tongueless moan.

Praise

Praise is no crust of snow
That fell long since and formed,
And now one day will enter the shut earth:
Stale wine, and warmed.

114

Praise is directest rain
That comes when it is needed:
Cool in its newness, and descending where
Desire has seeded.

Praise is merest water:
Nothing, but enough.
Nor makes it any choice of how it feeds
Smooth ground or rough.

Praise falls on both alike,
And is at once beloved.
There is no good that is not prospered then;
Nor evil proved.

Pity

Pity is a naked sin,
    And a stripped weakness.
It does not wear the long clothes,
    The proud clothes of meekness.

Pity drops as suddenly,
    And is as frightening,
Entering the white breast,
    As streakèd lightning.

Pity comes, pity goes
    With a great rudeness,
Having not anything to do
    With love or goodness.

Meekness After Wrath

Of all perfected things,
Man-made or devil-god-made; yea, or both;

115

Nothing so undefective is, and fine,
As thundered wrath.

Nothing! save this mute
That follows like a lamb beside the udder,
Gesturing, when the mind—except it burst—
Cannot grow madder.

Nothing so pure as this:
The after-meekness, lacking any tongue;
Nor anything so powerful, though it lives,
Poor child, not long.

The Tower

The greater world is water,
The lesser world is land.
Out of moving vastness
Promontories stand.
Out of undulation
Heaves the firm sand.

The flood of moments, flowing,
Bears desire away;
Returning unto wideness
Distributable clay.
But not the hill of reason,
The mind's high play.

The greater world is water;
This little world is rock.
Beneath it subterranean
Sinews interlock;
And round it, silent, silent,
Wheels the invisible flock.

How Can Man His Stature Know

How can man his stature know,
   And so far grow?
How be incapable of less,
   Or of excess?
How can man the image find
That shall be matter to his mind?

How can man be like the least
   Clear herb or beast?
How be faithful, cold or warm,
   To his own form?
How can man as plainly be
As the sure mole, nor ask to see?

How can man contrive to borrow
   No more sorrow?
How return what he has taken?
   Nor be shaken,
When he wears the world no longer,
By the simplicity of hunger?

Never to Ask

Happy the mind alone,
Dissecting the body's mesh;
Happy, until the bone
Is there in a flash.
Happy this thing of knives
Until it arrives.

Better that it divide
Waves, and the ruly winds;
Let it go deep and wide
In the alien lands.

117

Let a plow quit the loam
When it comes home.

The moving whole, and the heat,
And the nine-day fever, love;
How the cracked heart can beat,
And eagle turn dove—
Let it be wisdom's task
Never to ask.

The   Confinement

Whence, whence this heat of the brain?
I know, I know, he said:
The sleeplessness of continents and stars,
Rivers, and oily pavements, and old wars
Across too small a bed.

Whence, whence this fever-sight,
This still inflamed research?
I know. It is the press of the last sphere
To shrink its mighty pride and enter here:
All heaven in a church.

Whence, whence this burning bone,
This furnace in a skull?
Listen! I have heard the chafed complaint
Of thrice too large a cargo, hot and faint
Within too weak a hull.

Whence, whence this little fire
Whereon no fuel is put?
But it is fed with Africa's great groans,
And wrinkle-deep Aldebaran's live moans,
Recessed within a nut.

As from Arabian Ashes

As from Arabian ashes
A dustless bird arose;
And still the purple body
In a vast spiral goes,
   Envying the sun,
   The unrenewing one;

As from this waste of changes
There is a mind can fly,
And sail beyond confusion
In a fixed sky;
   But still it will remember
   Maytime and December;

So I, that now am starting,
And am so faithful-sworn,
Almost repent the voyage,
Almost am unreborn,
   Foreseeing, over the foam,
   The phoenix circling home.

The Bystanders

Who is this host of folk this fair spread day?
And who these few that stand and do not run:
Watching the others only, in the way
Of the dark stars outside the circled sun?
Strange, but the less are greater; only they
Have number; here the many are the one.

Strange, but the host is single, like a beam
Of noon that folds its particles inside.

Strange, but the few are many. Yet they dream
Of darkness, and of standing unespied,
Watching the rabble current—envied stream!
One river! though it is both deep and wide.

Here on the shore, in an imagined night,
They stand and wrap their arms; but on each face
Falls the dead flush of a reflected light
That fringes their aloofness as with lace:
The memory of a multitude's sweet might;
The flowing, and the union, and the grace.

The greyness all around them is old mist
Engendered by the chill of their contempt.
These were the few that labored to resist,
And the flood set them, separate and exempt,
Here on the windless shore. But now they twist
With a new longing, and the frail attempt,

Returning, to go smoothly once again
Down the sole river where the lashes close
And the eyes, sinking, dream of dancing men.
Yet here they stand in their uneven rows,
Superior forever—until when
Death lifts a hollow socket-bone and blows.

Why Sing at All

Why sing at all when the parched
Throat gives forth, unwillingly, dry sounds,
Wing-withered, that ascend
And rustle between the skull's deserted bounds?

The dim bone valleys there
Lie long and are unvisited by rain.
This dust, this music, rising,
Deepens the grey ground-cover, spreads the stain.

Why sing? But the tongue's attempt
May startle the chambered silence, and awake
Some spring whence joy, thin-flowing,
Trickles awhile; then rivers; and then a lake;

Then green, then sunny waters;
Then grass, and a bird-live forest moist with shade.
Why sing at all? But a sound
May serve, and a hopeless wasteland be unmade.

Oh, the long, toneless drouth!
Oh, the sunk pathways, shrivelled of their gladness!
Somehow the end arrives:
Drouth's end, with intermittency and madness.

Oh, the sweet run of rain!
Oh, the fresh floods, how carelessly they fall!
So will they have their end.
Yet sing! Or they will not come, not come at all.

Return to Ritual

The mother of life indulges all our wandering
Down the lone paths that narrow into peace.
She knows too well the gradual discovery
And the slow turning round until we cease:
Resolved upon the wide road once again
Whose dust hangs over day and mantles men.

Here is the drumming phalanx, here is the multitude;
Listen, and let us watch them over the stile.
We that remember clean moss ways and the tamaracks,
Let us be timorous now and shudder awhile.
We shall be early enough, no matter when,
Mother of dust, O mother of dust and men.

How time passes, here by the wall of eternity!
Even so soon we summon her; we are prepared.

121

Already these feet are lifting in a wild sympathy;
Who can remember the cool of a day unshared?
Mother of marches, mother, receive us then.
Listen! The dust is humming a song to the men.

Now This Joy

What was that life I led?
Answer, dumb wit that out of darkness clambers.
More yesterdays than now this joy remembers
Had I a liar's heart, pretending glad?

How could I think deception when the seated
Circle of old and young ones knew me wrong?
The multitude was hopeful of my tongue.
Was I the fool, and waited?

Was I the vain one, wanting
All a loud world to marvel upon my truth?
I do remember now, I heard them both:
My own still voice and that one, hoarsely chanting.

Was it too rough for rightness?
Answer, my new-found wit, and bid me know
Every wild tune by night, without one flaw,
And whether I lose by lateness.

Another Music

The harmony of morning, and a thrush's
Throat among the sleep-deserted boughs;
Expiring mists that murmur all the day
Of a clear dusk, with music at the close;
Wind harp, rain song, night madrigal and round:
There is no word melodious as those.

Rage of the viol whose deep and shady room
Is sounded to a tempest by the strings;
Sweet keys depressed, swift rise upon a note
Whence all the narrow soul of music hangs;
The lifted flute, the reed, and horns agreeing:
Words in the wake of these are scrannel gongs.

In them another music, half of sound
And half of something taciturn between;
In them another ringing, not for ears,
Not loud; but in the chambers of a brain
Are bells that clap an answer when the words
Move orderly, with truth among the train.

It Is a Moveless Moment

It is a moveless moment, with no wings,
No feet to bring it flying. There it stays,
And there it would be always, like the dead,
But that we turn and find it on some days.
The merest turn; the neck would hardly know;
Then the sky dips, and all the landmarks go.

It is the moment when we understand,
Relaxing every effort to be wise.
It is the moment of our boundary's fall:
Proud stone, that we had armed against surprise.
It is the merest moment. Then again
We turn and are distinguishable men.

This Amber Sunstream

This amber sunstream, with an hour to live,
Flows carelessly, and does not save itself;
Nor recognizes any entered room—

123

This room; nor hears the clock upon a shelf,
Declaring the lone hour; for where it goes
All space in a great silence ever flows.

No living man may know it till this hour,
When the clear sunstream, thickening to amber,
Moves like a sea, and the sunk hulls of houses
Let it come slowly through, as divers clamber,
Feeling for gold. So now into this room
Peer the large eyes, unopen to their doom.

Another hour and nothing will be here.
Even upon themselves the eyes will close.
Nor will this bulk, withdrawing, die outdoors
In night, that from another silence flows.
No living man in any western room
But sits at amber sunset round a tomb.

On Such a Day As This One

On such a day as this one, time and sky
Flow round our shoulders mingled past division;
Past asking which, past hearing, for on high
One silence broods: the ultimate elision.

Such a day as this one lifts the seas
And loses them in air—as blue, as thin.
Yet not the seas; there is no current moving;
Not anything translucent, wave or fin.

Such a day as this one is the end;
Or would be if there were no shoulders listening.
Nothing but their question saves the world;
And that high sun, upon the silence glistening.

Phenomena

He thought some things were not to be compared.
They sprang from their own seed, that once had dared,
Dropping from several stars, to sow by night
One half of earth with unexplained delight.
Then morning came upon her equal feet,
And levelling her voice denied the sweet,
Sharp difference; she was not to be confused
By novelty of names, and form abused.
So noon and afternoon saw nothing strange.
Only at twilight did unreason range,
And only now by night is wisdom had
In a spun world of which the name is mad;
Only through darkness will the meaning shine
Of things that are but planets fallen fine;
Only the black meridian declares
That old descent from big and little Bears.

Laboratory Still Life

This apple now, and this smooth block of wood
That long ago forgot the watery tree—
The round red thing remembers in its wet heart,
The patient cube is mindless and immortal—
Set them on the table and declare
Their density, position, form, and mass.
Bring the slim brain that walks on calipers—
The little bow legs caper while you wait—
Bring the ruled retina, and pads of paper,
And take the sharpened pencil from its sheath.
Now weigh them well, the apple and the wood;
Let the mind's least antennae touch and write,
And writing, not remember what they touched.
There will be only figures at the finish,
Bodiless worms that if you stoop and peer
Cross-edgewise of the chart you will not find.

125

It is a flight of moths from skull to paper,
And back to the bone again, the hollow room.

Whereas the deep eye innocent of numbers,
Moist eye moving in a world of shapes,
Warm eye wonderful in child or man,
Sees only a bright apple and a cube.
The deep eye looks, and there is nothing more
Than a red apple with a watery heart,
Than a blank face of wood that has forgotten.
The deep eye looks, and not a word comes forth.
Nothing is here for counting or dividing,
Nothing to understand; nothing to add.
Only the red round face grows redder, rounder,
And the six flattened cheeks widen a little,
Complacent of their enduringness indoors.

Time and Water

The humped back of the beaver, and the four
Curved teeth that bring the poplar splashing down—
There in the lake it lies, and the silver branches
Turn, in the day, in the night, to a watery brown—
The upthrust and pond-dividing whiskers
Say that the world is wet, and seasons drown.

Swimming in darkness, nearing his willow dam,
Pausing before he climbs to the dripping sticks,
He is eternally far from hills and deserts,
Roads, and the odorous barns, and the drying ricks;
The beaver is only credulous of meadows
A rising river enters and moistly licks.

Diving in darkness, down to the lily roots,
Turning and paddling off and rising slow,
The beaver descends again and finds his burrow,
Rises again and is home, and he says: I know.

126

Water is endless, time is an undulation,
Water is all there is, and seasons flow.

Spread, Spread

Spread, spread, November rain;
Sleep-bringing river, widen so
That every meadow takes the stain
Of rising death's first overflow.

Instruct the trees that are adorned
Too bravely now, and drown their blood.
Leave not a sunwise slope unwarned
Against the white, the final flood.

Invisibly the banks of time
Give way; the unseen river reaches.
The mist of change begins to climb
And slide along the grassy beaches:

Sliding until no further drop
Of dryness lives in any vein;
When even change will, flowing, stop,
And stumps no more remember rain.

The Other House

The leafless road midwinters by itself,
And the slat gate, wired open, never swings.
Should the loop rust, and weaken in the wind,
Two posts will join that now are separate things;
Forgetful how they guarded the little space
One entering coat could fill, one entering face.

We spoke of strangers happening to pass,
And wondered if such openness were wise.

But the posts know; they have not felt each other
Since the high sun was shaded from their eyes.
We spoke of footprints; but a sparrow's track
Is all that diverges in and circles back.

Even a look from us so distant here,
Even a sigh might leave its line on snow:
Up the still road and in, then round and round;
Then stopping, for we must no further go.
Let the line pause mid-yard; there let it end,
Lest the sad chimneys smile, and smoke pretend.

She Is the Youngest

She is the youngest of the wood,
Yet is there many a newer thing.
The hemlock with the ragged hood
Droops in everlasting spring.

Above the snow, or when the leaves
Lie well around her, safe and dead,
Not a wind but lowly weaves
The delicate spine; deflects the head;

Picks up the green and greyish cape
That all but flowed into the earth.
Grave, grave the maiden shape,
Out of love awhile with mirth.

Sad, sad, but it is well:
How she looks upon the ground
Cures the melancholy spell
Of age and coldness all around.

Sad, sad, but what she means
Is that the world is old and strong;
Indulgent still to one that leans
On youthful sorrow overlong.

128

Somewhat More Slowly

Somewhat more slowly, lengthener of days—
Oh, you that pull the crusted nails of winter—
Somewhat more slowly work. Within is lying
One who would not hear too soon the splinter
Of wrapping-boards; nor see too soon your light
Enter and like a thief put out the night.

Lay down your hammer somewhere in the snow,
Deep snow and dark, and drop your chisel after.
Sleep there upon the wind, as far away
As April, and be deaf to this my laughter:
Muffled in the linen of a box
Upon whose lid Time comes, Time comes and knocks.

But comes not yet if you lie long and dream,
And, wakened on a morning, doubt your eyes.
Look then for those you lost—you will upturn them,
Cold beneath the snow—and slowly rise,
And slowly make approach. I shall be rested;
Nor is death then unwillingly molested.

THE STORY-TELLER ೩೪

What Is the Hour

What is the hour, how loud the clock,
When the heart knows itself for rock?
Or is it ignorant? Does the rose
More silently than centuries close?
Perhaps no man so long ahead
Predicts the flint, proclaims the dead.

There was the year it opened wide
And tore a hole in his calm side.

Strange the petals' hingèd strength,
Staining, staining all his length
With wasted blood; until they shut,
And he forgot the flesh's cut.

There was the day it stirred again
And straightway stopped; and chilled him then.
There was the fear his pain had ceased.
But it returned, and it increased;
There was a rose within him said
He must be happy while it bled.

Is there no rose inside him now?
Is there no vein to disavow
This rocky stillness? So he stands,
Exploring silence with his hands;
Wonders, waits; and leans to hear
That valvèd sound of yesteryear.

He Was Not Wise

He was not wise to dally with the curves
Of earth and set his fancy continent-free.
The game at first was merry, and he smiled;
He was at home with aliens, land and sea:
Stoking a fire with bullies west by south
In the same hour that Persia curled her mouth.

He felt the flame, he tapped the pearly teeth;
He blessed himself and nestled to his kind.
But then he scudded further, and beheld
Tall men of China chatting as they dined;
Flew on, and by an island strange of name
Struck sail; for now the terror of it came.

One porch too many, folding in its shade
Some brow unseen, some lip, destroyed the count.

Here was the death of number, the abstract
Mute reckoning—how dim the pure amount!
How far desire, how close the little space
Encircling every watched and silent face.

The Escape

Going from us at last,
He gave himself forever
Unto the mudded nest,
Unto the dog and the beaver.

Sick of the way we stood,
He pondered upon flying,
Or envied the triple thud
Of horses' hooves; whose neighing

Came to him sweeter than talk,
Whereof he too was tired.
No silences now he broke,
No emptiness he explored.

Going from us, he never
Sent one syllable home.
We called him wild; but the plover
Watched him, and was tame.

The Hermit

On a grey hill above the talk of streams,
Where not a risen rock repeats the wind
And no tree groans with standing, and no grass
Rustles upon itself, the still feet stay.

Here no hidden deity, bespoken,
Utters a thunderous answer ill or good.

131

Only the feet are here, and these straight hands,
And one pale mind, sending its column up

Of silence. It is silence that he says
Will wash the earth below him of its pain.
Words are but fire we pour into old wounds
That long ago wove blood into the sky.

So the white column, rising, spreads and comes
Down softly midst our sounds, and we are soothed.
He says the sky is healing, too; and hears
Some day the whole world dreaming under snow.

Memorial

If nothing else let this poor paper say,
Outwhitening time and those subduing voices,
How once a black-eyed doctor drove away,
After she died, behind his dappled horses.

This shall not be memorial for her,
Nor him, the black-eyed man, nor for the dappled
Shadow upon two breasts; but as they were
That morning, let each word of them be tripled.

Within a room she lay, and they were going—
The bright defeated man and those long faces
Slanted upon the wind—and time was snowing
Forgetfulness already, as he uses.

And still he would, had not this paper power,
Holding the four together, to remember.
These hungry hooves will not outstep the hour,
Nor the dark eyes come ever home to slumber.

Going Home

His thought of it was like a button pressed.
Far away the figures started going;
A silver watch ticked in a sleepy vest,
And on the porch an apron string was blowing.

His thought again was like a fly-wheel cranked,
And circular machinery set gliding.
The little town turned truly, as the banked
Brown houses followed in and out of hiding.

His travel, once he went, was like the troop
Of farmers in an autumn to the fair.
All year the field was flat, but now the coop
Of turkeys and the horses would be there;

People moving everywhere and nodding,
Little boys with birds and yellow whips;
A person at a counter would be wadding
Rifles, and the girls would hold their hips.

His coming near was like the soft arrival
Of gods around a thing that they have made;
And will again forget; but long survival
Saves it, once again the trance is laid.

Highway Ghost

The gravelly road is gone.
Old people, whirled behind a windy wheel,
Huddle their coats about them and remember
How they went proudly once;

How the eight ringing feet
Flung gritty pebbles into the grass,
And how the four high iron tires
Sang in the sand.

133

Old men, silently borne
Where now the way goes black and wide
And smoothly like a river into the wood,
Old men, saying nothing,

See a white horse come curving,
Swinging an empty buggy round the hill.
The white feet fall without a noise, approaching,
And thin wheels lightly follow.

Spokes flicker by,
And grey heads, nodding at each other, turn
To see between the curtains what is there.
Nothing at all is there.

The gravelly road is gone,
And dim eyes, drawn around a bend forever,
Have in them only history, and the fall
Of a slow shadow.

Old Tune

The words of this old woeful song
Float so merrily along,
Out of ages that they sweeten
Though the hearts of men were eaten.
This old tale of souls that brake
Falls softly on us, flake by flake.

He raised the knife;
She spread her gown
And begged for life;
But only a frown
Got ever that wife;
Got ever that wife,
Hey derrikin down.

This tune that came so long a road
Has shed the sorrow of its load.
Though its burden will endure
The air is merciful and pure.
This bitter tale of one that died
Leaves only honey in our side.

> The knife it fell;
> She spread her coat
> And made a well
> Of that white throat.
> She made a well
> For him in hell,
> High dollikin dote.
> So merrily float
> With him in hell,
> High dollikin dote.

The Story-Teller

He talked, and as he talked
Wallpaper came alive;
Suddenly ghosts walked,
And four doors were five;

Calendars ran backward,
And maps had mouths;
Ships went tackward
In a great drowse;

Trains climbed trees,
And soon dripped down
Like honey of bees
On the cold brick town.

He had wakened a worm
In the world's brain,

And nothing stood firm
Until day again.

Recognition Scene

From many a mile the son,
From a third of the earth the father;
Each of them bearing his sign
Of kinship high as a feather.
Dusky the hour, and late;
What shall we do that wait?

We shall not quit the grove,
We shall not rise and scatter.
Something deep as the grave
Holds every heart in a flutter.
Dewy the night. No bird—
There! Who trembled? Who heard?

Who spied him, tall in the west?
Old is the night, and bitter.
Far in the eastern waste
Who caught a faint hoof and a clatter?
Now closer—now here—he draws—
Oh, insupportable pause!

To a Friend Hesitating Before Change

Shatter the moldy glass
Wherein you look too long.
The arm of time is ready,
And trembles at the gong.
Nod and let it fall,
And stand outside the wall.

136

Such suddenness of sound
Will loosen every tree,
And though your house is broken
The mountains will run free
With frosty colors, new and fine,
Set upon each curvèd line.

Or else—and who can say?—
Darkness will be there,
With danger at its heart,
And teeth about to tear.
Even then I tell you change;
So it be strange.

The Friendship

It was so mild a thing to see,
People saw it silently.
Such peace was in it people said
It would not alter with them dead.

None knew the difficult design
They worked to follow, line by line,
Nor in the sending of a glance
How much was art, how little chance;

Nor how that courtesy was kept
Wherethrough no step was overstepped.
There was no hazard in these hands
That wove a set of silken bands

Binding honor unto praise,
And tying tenderness, that lays
No single burden on a friend
As far as to the tethered end.

Not a disagreeing word
Between the two was ever heard.
But when it ended with them dead,
Buried bones got up and bled.

The Unwanted Lonely

Make way for them, who nothing see
Beyond the shadow of their eyes.
Make way for that—the sharpened cone
That shoots before them now as flies
The pointing night of an eclipse,
Wherein a day's triangle dies.

Make way for them; they lost their hope
Longer ago than faith can heal.
They walk condemned, yet think to find
Some face perhaps that still can feel.
But let them pass you; be not one
Transfixèd willingly with steel.

Make way for them, and turn your head
Perhaps with pity; yet be strong.
What they can penetrate you with
Is thin and poor; but it is long,
And will not break. It is the fear
Of light's dislike; and is not wrong.

Laugh Not Too Loudly

He said that we must thank the gods
For vanity, which like a wheel
Whirls a man or woman now and then
Till the soul bulges, and a giddy heel
Is pivotal to something oversized.
He said the vain were vases under seal.

"Opened, though, there's nothing there."
Admitting this, he only smiled.
"As barren, top and bottom, as a tomb;
Not even filled with future, like a child."
He said this too was true; but must insist
That vacancy not always be reviled.

"They are the sacrifice," he said,
"So that a miracle can be.
The soul, that is invisible, becomes
A something then which anyone may see.
Laugh not too loudly, for the gods translate
Only the brave, the wild. The rest go free."

The Philanderer

It was the very innocence of love;
Though words were whispered that have toppled walls
And taken sleeping lives, he was a dove
Nesting in little gables, whither his calls
Brought momentary mates to share the dim,
Sweet dawn along the eaves, and strut with him.

The nearness of the morning was what saved him.
He never would have dared the naked night;
And they were such as never would have braved him
In the true dark. It was a pretty fright,
A flutter of alarm beside a door;
Then the sun came, and there was nothing more.

It was delicious doom to be suspended
Thus between having and not having them.
What never had begun was never ended,
Save that some tried a deeper stratagem
And flew to him at midnight. Then he ran,
Lest now he be possessed as proper man.

He ran, and they were glad that it was so.
It was their doom to play at the surrender.
Having themselves again, they still could go
Remembering the eyes of this pretender;
Leaving a lonely portion of them there,
Under the soft eaves beyond the stair.

Antipathies

Item, the man by whom he was reminded
Of the dead calfish days before the rope
Broke, and he ran till he was tired of running;
This fellow, staring here and snorting hope,
Dangled the ancient tether past a wall.
Right there it was. Had he come thence at all?

Item, another one who knew too well
The paths that he had come by, if he came;
Who shrank the middle distance till it sat,
A small divided desert, full of tame
Four-footed memories, that by day remarked
His face with little coyote eyes and barked.

Item, the newly known one with the brow
That wore a different wisdom from his own.
What loss in that, he wondered? Yet he saw
How each comes only once, and comes alone;
And asked the wind if many wandered off
In a sheep's night, missing the wether's cough.

Modern Sinner

He was of an old mind,
And so would have preferred
Consciences less kind

Around him when he erred:
Darker wires to bind
The scarcely cagèd bird.

Such wings as now he wore
Delivered him in vain
Without a narrow door
To take him in again,
And shut, and hide the sore
No probing would explain.

For still he could be healed
And try another flight.
Now all was sunny field,
With never a stroke of night.
So wearily he wheeled
Into the endless white.

The Bore

He was not helped by knowing well
How cold he made us, and how weary.
He must have told himself at last
He was not saved by being sorry.

Better than anyone he saw
The stealthy turn, the trained escape,
Or if he came too soon for these,
How frantic courtesy could wrap

Desire to fly with skill to stay—
A twitching wing beneath the feather;
How within a greying eye
The kindest agony can gather.

And did he witness this too well?
Was then the knowledge but the cause?

141

Long time we looked, but could not find
A way of learning why he was.

Partitions

She fled into herself before the sun.
When the wind rose her thoughts became a thicket,
Drawing her in, while firmly one by one
Thin leaves behind her laced the final wicket.
None of our voices ever got so far
As to the trembling center of that maze.
We found the margin easy, but a bar
Of shadows lay across the deeper ways.
Sometimes we waited; then a face would peer
Half woman through the laurel, and half deer.

She was afraid of openness and act.
A deed would tear the bravest barrier down.
She loved the lone partitions where she tracked
Green fancies never trampled into brown.
We called to her, extending our still hands;
She only stared and smiled, and we could see
No meaning in that brow, or in the bands
Of fear that tightened, tightened quietly.
Safe in her lanes she wandered. Was she wise?
The answer is dead leaves upon the eyes.

The Photographs

The person on the sidewalk is possessed
Of a loud secret, capable of crying.
This haster among the many holds himself
Like a mute man that presently is dying.
And yet there is old age for him—and those
In the pressed parcel he would be untying.

142

His children's faces, wrapped against the sun,
Sing low between the still sleeve and the heart.
This holder of his tongue sends more than breath
Invisibly ahead of him: sends part,
Sends all of him, advancing as he goes
To a frail music, soundless at the start.

He hears it there and hardly may contain
His joy that Time can sing so young a song.
He follows it, prophetical of days
When the grown burden suddenly is strong.
Thereafter—but his smiling is confined
To the live moment, mercifully long.

It Should Be Easy

It should be easy, letting the small feet go;
Quick should it turn, the necessary knob;
Empty this porch of any following eye
Fixed upon waves wherein a head shall bob
Now up, now down forever; till it rises,
And floats and disappears among the mob.

We should be sure the shoulders will return,
And the hands reach and click the lock again.
We should be thoughtless, occupying days
With a new ritual modified to men.
We should be proud and let a trumpet say
How close the waters welter about the den.

And solitude would soothe us, were it not
For the slow sound of breakers near the door:
Reminders of the many farther out,
Of the lost many, nameless evermore,
That young with pride set seaward long ago,
Leaving the grey alone, the mother shore.

143

It would be easy, letting the cap depart,
And the small face that never looks around;
But the firm coast line—suddenly it bends;
Suddenly it follows, and the sound
Of hopeless cries is heard; until the waves
Wash once again on straight and silent ground.

The Monument

Swift cruelties to children are a pyramid
Built of soft stones that harden under time.
They were not quarried, they were not shapened craftily,
They were unconscious then of granite or lime.
They were not planned at all. But they have altitude;
They are too high for memory to climb.

When memory is merciless, and labors,
Gaining the topmost cube, and lingers there,
The view is of an undivided wasteland
Down from the breather's height through darkened air;
Nothing familiar now except the still voice
Bidding him measure deserts if he dare.

Better the climb untaken, and the guilt
Forgotten, could the mind go clear around.
But the long way is endless, and the stones
Are numberless; immovable the mound.
It is our own memorial, and stands
In front of us wherever we are bound.

Simple Beast

With rope, knife, gun, brass knucks, and bloody laws
Earth everywhere is noisy; not with paws
Of leopards silent, not with saber-toothed

Long tigers paced all year upon and smoothed.
That was the age of hunger, when the taken
Fourfoot with a moment's dread was shaken;
Then the slow-closing eyes; then over stones
Time's scattering of the picked, the cleanly bones.
This is the age of anger, when the hail
Beats corn and rose alike, and leaves a trail
More sluttish that it tells man's appetite.
This is the age of gluttony and spite.
With lash and bomb, blue fire and bayonet
Earth everywhere is littered. Earth is wet
With blood not drained for drinking, earth is loud
With sounds not made for hearing, earth is plowed
By steel that will not reap it. Earth is least
Like what earth was when beast was simple beast.

Strike Then the Rusted Strings

Strike then the rusted strings.
Pound, pound the sluggard voice.
And bid deposèd kings
With our poor selves rejoice.

Hang branches from the rafters;
But where the doors have been,
Hang thorns to prick the laughter
Of lost ones coming in.

Pour liquor that will widen
The skull's already smile.
The darkness we have died in,
Let it be red awhile.

Let it be white, and burn us
Unto the finest ash.

145

Let music be the furnace.
Let every fiddle flash.

Ha! and now we gather.
Ho! and now we part.
Let every bone be lather,
Next to the fiery heart.

Let every arm, upswinging,
Be melted as it goes.
So, to such a singing,
The stoniest sadness flows.

Be still! for they are letting
The last poor devil in.
Now shut the door! forgetting
Whatever deaths have been.

Ha! and now we gather.
Ho! and now we part.
The last one dances rather
Stiffly at the start.

Epitaphs

For Two Men

When these were idle shouting boys
Their mouths could make an equal noise.

When these were young and earnest men
One managed all the talking then.

When he grew famous he forgot
The other one that here doth rot.

But which is now the louder dust
The eyeless worms have not discussed.

146

For One Unburied

Stranger, do not think to find
The banter here of parting bones;
We let the desert wind unbind
His flesh, and scatter it like stones.

He was impatient with the jest
Of eyes enlarging underground.
So his are open to the west,
And day diminishing around.

There all the pieces of him lie,
Too far apart to understand
The comedy of ribs awry
And sockets filling up with sand.

For a Maiden

This girl was not to go
Until two shoulders cast
Shadow upon her snow,
And melted it at last.

The warmth she had within
Still waited to be found.
The coverlet is thin.
Be curious, cold ground.

For a Fickle Man

Two women had these words engraved:
The first and last of whom he tired.
One told the other, while they lived,
The thing between them he desired.

What now it is they do not know,
Or where he seeks it round the sun.
They only ask the wind to blow,
And that his will be ever done.

147

For a Jester

The things he used to do, and laugh,
Are blown along with other chaff.

Never to rustle and arise,
Here the kernel of him lies,

The solid portion of the man.
And this we count; but feel the fan,

And lift a sudden far-off look
At what the wind of harvest took.

For Two Brothers

Let no man say that either mind
Heard willingly the scythe behind.

The edge was on them ere they knew,
With that undone which words could do;

And now is done upon a stone
That time has not come back and mown.

Until it tumbles, brother and brother
Understand they loved each other.

REPORT OF ANGELS ॐ

There Is No Language

There is no language that the heart learns wholly.
One thing it fails at, though it deeply tries.
It cannot ask a question; it is only
Skilful in surrenders and replies.

Most eagerly it answers, and most softly
It gives the needy asker surest proof.

But when itself is doubtful comes the dumbness.
What most is meant remains the most aloof.

The heart is never childlike, though it stammers,
And half the words it weeps for are refused.
The ancient one can do no more than answer;
It cannot beg, as once the young one used.

Report of Angels

"Nothing for envy there"—
Folding their dustless wings—
"Nothing, beyond this pair
Of impossible things:

"Love, wherein their limbs,
Trembling, desire to die;
And sleep, that darkly swims,
Drowning each brain and eye.

"Nothing is there for us,
Who may not cease to know;
But heaven was merciless,
Fixing our eyelids so;

"Whereon no tide may run,
Rolling its night ahead;
Where love is a labor done,
And death long since was dead."

Always Evening

You eyes, forever west of afternoon,
And, oh, you setting-sun-descended hair,

Make every day of absence die more soon
Than minutes, that it may be evening there
Forever, shadeless eyes,
Wherein all distance dies.

Forever be the hour that is the end,
The hour that blackens daytime and the grass.
O eyes, it is the moment when you send
Hither most heat, as through a burning-glass;
Hither excessive light,
Love's lie against the night.

Be always spicy evening, my love's mind,
Contracting to yourself the deaths of roses.
Gather into an instant every kind
Of fragrance that the waste of time encloses,
Letting the long world shrink
Into one drop; and drink.

His Lady Lacks Not Anything

His lady lacks not anything
Save a beholder:
Wiser born than was the king,
Yet noway older;
Young and wise, and fit to sing
What none has told her.

Say it quickly to the queen:
How she dissembles,
Letting only that be seen
Which time resembles;
How at the rest, the ageless green—
How my verse trembles.

Tell her nevertheless I know;
And am suspended

150

Here between an ancient woe
And one unended.
Music fails, as long ago;
Nor can be mended.

They Were Good Fortune's

They were good fortune's maid and man;
The gift of love between them passed
As lightly as the snow comes,
And silent to the last.

They talked, but not of what was given;
There it hung, by chance descended;
Each but held a hand out,
And exchange was ended.

So colorless, so soft a thing,
So free—they would not name it love;
It was but whitened wind-fall,
Slanting from above.

So painless, it was not themselves.
They never knew that flesh can tear,
Suddenly, as boughs break
Upon snow-heavy air.

The Willingness

The willingness that Lucy wears
Becomes her like a fitted gown;
Nor is there any seam to see
Until the thing is down:
The whole of it, as if a lone
Young tree had cast its crown.

Those leaves that make so loose a ring
Will never again be hung together.
The flying bird does not regain
A single drifted feather.
So Lucy stands forever now
Unlaced against the weather.

The willingness that Lucy wore
Was nothing to this naked side.
And yet the truth of her is both;
The raiment never lied.
Desire without, desire within:
So is love simplified.

The First Blow

Embrace it, though it be
A salt new inland sea;
Make the most of such a pain
As never now can come again.

It is the first, and quenches
Even what it drenches;
Heart, too soon you will outgrow
This unremembered overflow.

You will grow wise, and lose
Black honey from a bruise;
Anticipate this weeping while
The drained, inevitable smile.

Let Not Your Strictness Vary

Let not your strictness vary;
Be less, be less than just;
In a mild January
We miss the frost.

I have a store of wood in;
The windows well are stopped;
I sleep a sleep that sudden
August would interrupt.

Let not your coldness, going,
Leave too well prepared
One whom years of snowing
Have into virtue snared.

Let every May-fly slumber,
And in deep holes the fox.
Nor will I lie and number
Centuries to equinox.

The Difference

Day after day, for her, the sun
Drew semicircles smooth and high.
A week was seven domes across a desert,
And any afternoon took long to die:
Rounding the great curve downward not too fast,
Not falling; not a shadow ran awry.

His day was two thin lightning lines
Pitched here one instant like a tent;
Then night; and there was neither afternoon
Nor evening to be witness how they went.
His day was but a burning at the top;
Then the steep fall, and every spark was spent.

They lived together only thus:
One tick of noon their common day;
And many a noon, so meeting, each would ask:
What found the other past the middle way?
But neither he whose leap was like a star
Nor she who curved and swung could ever say.

She Said Too Little

She said too little, he too much.
She drooped; he could not droop enough.
Between a sigh, between a song,
Simplicity defeated both.

He was importunate with proof,
But undervalued then the pause.
She was judge of something else,
Something silent in the blood,

Something destined to be loud
If only words could fail and wait.
She never heard it; or explained
What sound is deeper than the throat.

They were not different save in this:
He paused too little, she too long.
But each was farther at the close
Than all northwest, and spreading storms.

First Alarm

Nothing could be stranger
Than this silence was.
There never had been danger
Until the sharpened saws
Of pride cut in and in,
Unbuilding what had been.

Nothing was the matter,
Except they barely talked.
The end had come of chatter.
They whipped it, but it balked
At climbing the two hills
Of their awakened wills.

154

There was a time, perhaps,
When they would do with stillness;
But now it seemed relapse
Into a worse illness
Than any mending lover
Ever got up and over.

I Passed the Sleepy Ridges

I passed the sleepy ridges
Whereon my love had looked.
Her house was by the bridges
Where the slow rivers crooked.

Many and many a morning,
As the white sun would rise,
The darkness, at her warning,
Flowed down upon her eyes,

That took it in and saved it;
Oh! there was room and more.
With her own tears she laved it,
There by the turning shore.

There were two crooked streams there.
Heavily went they round.
Now darkness only seems there;
And dewless is the ground.

By Their Own Ignorance

By their own ignorance I knew them,
And the tall way they stood;
Denying she had ever wandered through them,
Entering that wood.

By their indifference I proved them,
Those high old border trees;
Pretending that no thunderbolt had grooved them:
Each heart at ease.

No lesser lie could they be brooding:
A football had not died.
The truth, I said, was weaker praise; intruding
No more upon that pride.

HERE THEN HE LAY 🐦

Here Then He Lay

IN MEMORIAM
C.L.V.D.
1857–1933

Where mild men gathered he was half at home,
Though none of him was there in hostile guise.
Yet even then the swifter half went on;
And still it goes, and still the curving skies
Contain the soundless footfalls of a man
Whose moving part our obsequies outran.

Here then he lay, and stationary flowers
Were like the words of good men come to see:
All pure, all nodding whiteness; final proof
Of wonder—save the last, the far degree.
Already, while the compliments uncurled,
He gathered with the dark ones of the world;

Came noiseless up, and shed the afternoon
Like a thin shoe behind him; so he stands
Eternally in twilight, and the rest
Acknowledge nothing alien in his hands,

That hour by hour acknowledge nothing there
Save the full dusk and the sufficient air.

It was the eyes that brought him; so he stays
Despite the something different in his walk.
Round, round he moves among them, and each one
Is different: more the panther, more the hawk,
More the slow-treading dove; yet no disguise
May alter their unburiable eyes.

Both sun and shade are in them, pair by pair,
Both everlasting day and boundless dark.
This is the field to which the few have come;
These are the visions death could never mark.
There was no way to deepen such a gaze
Save with this dusk, abstracted from all days.

There now his feet fall silently, and now
He is both old and young, his hope the same:
Ranging the mild world, sowing it with pride,
And leaving not a meadow of it tame;
Praising all men that have the quenchless eye;
Yet loving the unlustred who will die.

We praised him for the kindness of his talk,
And a meek heart mortality had kissed.
We might have sung the justice of a glance
Wherein not even littleness was missed.
Then, then we should have added his desire
For the great few and the unburning fire.

We told a tale of charity, and hands
Long practiced in the banishment of pain.
We knew his mind's ambition, and his tongue's
Swift temper, and his wisdom to refrain.
We should have known how nothing held him back
From the great dusk and from the trodden track.

He treads it now, and he is never tired.
There where he goes, intensity is ease.
No strict requirement but of old was met;
The world at last is single that he sees.
All one, the world is round him that he saw
When he looked past us, innocent of awe.

from

THE LAST LOOK

AND OTHER POEMS (1937)

I ੨ঌ

Axle Song

That any thing should be—
Place, time, earth, error—
And a round eye in man to see:
That was the terror.

And a true mind to try
Cube, sphere, deep, short, and long:
That was the burden of the sky's
Hoarse axle song.

Improbable the stoat,
The mouse, toad, worm, wolf, tiger;
Unthinkable the stallion's trot,
Behemoth's swagger.

Unspeakable; yet worse—
Name, look, feel, memory, and number:
Man there with his perverse
Power not to slumber.

Let things created sleep:
Rock, beast, rain, sand, and sliding river.

159

So growled the earth's revolving heap;
And will forever.

The Ecstasy

For he so loved the world today
That he fell down like dead, and lay,
His left arm dangled at the sofa's side,
Smiling inanely.

You would have said he searched the rug
For signature of pin, of bug,
Of sunbeam. But the silence of his eyesight:
That explained him.

That was the symptom: nothing seen,
Yet a whole world washed dark and clean
By his acceptance—oh, a mile away
Horses were grateful;

Curveted, and clipped the ground,
While here, relaxing from all sound,
He let the mohair heft him: light as wheatstraw,
Harvested lately.

Inarticulate

The morning flashed like mica,
And the tendrils stretched
Like dawnrays: every leaf a little sun.
A wind flowered out of nowhere,
And the birds inwove
Bright walls of air with streaks of curving song.

The horses fed like angels,
And the pasture spread

Like tidegrass: greenness foaming over all.
The fencewire dripped with dewdrops,
And the rabbits sat
High-eared across the never parching ground.

He wandered, he the lost one,
And his tongueless joy
Made gestures: bending rib and dancing bone.
Felicity is limbless,
But an inward joint
Grows flexible, and hidden liquors flow.

He would have sung the season,
And his fiery joy
Flung upward: towers of tune, and bannered words.
He would have hymned the wholeness;
But he paused and heard
Part after part thin-piping in its place,

And knew the day concerted;
For his ranging joy
Still counted, adding choristers to these.
So he discovered dumbness,
And his humble eye
Found duty, and he glittered, tall with tears.

No Faith

What held the bones together? Not belief,
Not anything he could probe, no ligament god.
Why was the world so one for him yet many,
So woman and yet so speechless? Then the odd,
The furtive, ashamed security. We wondered.
But there was no faith in him that sang or thundered.

There was no understanding in this man
Of his own simplest secret: of the way

Earth's air kept warm for him, and how there shone
Always another light outdoors of day.
He would have chosen darkness; he denied
What was so strange, so palpable, inside;

He said he could be unhappy. But we knew.
There was this sweet continuum, this flesh;
There were these bones, articulated so:
A web they were, with music up the mesh,
A frame of hidden wires too deep for tone,
A skeleton wholeness, humming to him alone.

He must have heard the harmony, but he swore
Time talked to him in separated sounds.
He took them as they came and loved them singly:
Each one, he parried, perfect within its bounds.
As for the burden's end, the tune's direction—
He smiled; he was content with disconnection.

Yet who could smile and mean it? Who could rest,
As this man did, midway the million things?
Who else could be serene at truth's circumference
When only the known center of it sings?
Who else but he?—submissive to each part
Till it became the all, the homeless heart.

The Good Fates

I see the dun, low western house,
I see the propless porch,
I see the grass and cherry-leaves
That a June sun would scorch;

While flies buzzed through the broken screen—
I hear one in the room,
I hear one settle on the plush
Past the piano's gloom.

Then silence in this forward part;
But there are doors and doors,
And deviously the clatter comes
Of middle summer's chores;

Of deep pots simmering on the fire,
Of strainers dropping juice;
Of knives; though most of all I hear
Three tongues upon the loose:

My aunt and her warm daughters there,
My cousins, whom I stand
Long years away and listen to
Across a changing land.

There is no sound has sung to me
Since then so rich a song;
So reticent of injury,
And yet so laughing strong;

So stopless; for the afternoon
Hangs high above us; waits
While their lost voices hum to me
Across these seven States;

Hum busily above the pans,
Unconscious how I hear
What he and she and Charlie did
In that fine cherry year.

The Cornetist

When the last freight, dusk-musical, had gone,
Groaning along the dark rails to St. Louis,
When the warm night, complete across the cornfields,
Said there was nothing now, no motion left,

No possible sound, we heard him:
Rocked on the silent porch and heard the low notes

Leave on their level errand like the last sound
Ever to be man-blown about the earth.
Like the last man this sentry of the switches
Blew, and the mournful notes, transcending cinders,
Floated above the corn leaves:
Floated above the silks, until arriving,

Arriving, they invaded our warm darkness,
Deep in the still verandah, and we laughed:
"Why, there he is, that pitiful lone devil;
There is the Frisco nightingale again,
There is our mocking-bird-man"—
Laughed, and said these things, and went to bed.

And slept; but there are nights now when I waken,
After these years, and all these miles away,
When I sit up and listen for the last sound
Man will have made alive; and doubt a little
Whether we should have laughed;
Whether we should have pitied that poor soul.

You were too sure of being there forever,
And I too soon was leaving to be wise.
Not that his horn had wisdom; but at nighttime
Man has a need of man, and he was there,
Always; the horn was there
Always; and joy, I think, was why we laughed.

And slept; for there is many an hour of drearness,
Many an hour unloud with lips or brass,
When I lie still and listen for the last note
Ever some lung has blown; and am self-envious,
Thinking I once could laugh;
Thinking I once could pity that poor soul.

At Last Inclement Weather

At last inclement weather.
After a month of death—
Of holding it and staring—
Day grins; blows out its breath;

Grimaces; and, deep-growling,
Furies the bated air;
Of which the lack-love atoms
Had fainted pair by pair.

Now in the wind's excitement
They dance a tumbled round:
Their first and only madness,
Their single rage of sound.

Invisible the clashing;
Unheard the little cries;
Save that in us they echo;
Our particles uprise—

Dimensionless, dark pieces,
Yet are they fiery strong—
And sting us with their whirling,
And lift us high and long;

And threaten us with flying
Like cannon balls apart;
Save that the skin is thinner,
And tougher next to the heart.

Animal-Worship

Once on this ancient plain there fell the shade
Of a great loping hare who hid the sun;
Who darkened the high sky; and has not made
Another unearthly visit since that one.

Even that day is dead; no solemn eyes
Remain of those that watched him down the North;
Or those that feasted yearly, Indian wise,
On the small furless copies he sent forth:

The timorous rabbits, ancient on this plain,
Who now no more bring messages of cold;
Sons of the great mild hare whose dozing brain
At the world's upper edge grows dimly old.

In a sunk nest of snow he lies and dreams;
Down a grey depth he slumbers, long from here;
While the plowed plain forgets him, and the teams
Trample, and fatherless rabbits shake with fear.

No longer does their blood remember time,
No longer do they feel their far descent;
As the loud valley crows cry out and climb,
Sky-highward, where the one great raven went,

So long ago, so darkly through these hills,
That the last man is buried who was told;
That the last wing is mildewed, and the bills
Of once deep-knowing birds are green with mould.

So the loud western crow wings flap and lift,
And sagely now the beaks consider corn;
But none of them remembers here the swift
Vast body whence their images were born.

Past a blue mountain, westernmost of all,
He floats among the mist-pools, round and round;
And meeting the Hawk, floats on; no feathers fall;
For they go by, those gods, without a sound.

There is no beast or bird too delicate now
For man's vain understanding; no shod feet

Veer shyly from their pathways; no heads bow
Benignly when a man and serpent meet.

No creature upon four paws, in field or wood,
By rivers or by runways, stares and wins:
His muteness meaning wisdom, and his hood
Some heraldry of old where birth begins,

Where truth, where secret might, where sun and moon,
Where song and words of song, and what to pray.
There was a time when foxes set the tune;
And tigers; but it is another day.

It is the beasts' oblivion, when they run
Uncounted unto cover; when they shrink,
Denying their tall origin; when one
Trots lonely in the dew that he will drink;

When two by two they wander, with no word
Between them of the Hawk, the burrowed Hare;
The Raven, or the Bullock, or the herd
Of tempest-laughing Stallions, or the Bear.

One only of earth's animals is proud;
One only of its movers can be still.
Man only sits at rest and sees the crowd
File curving by, deflective to his will;

Sits on and sees, with nothing spread above,
No weird ancestral wing, no hovering mane;
Sits loftily, too certain of self-love
Ever to see a world upon the wane:

His world and theirs, the strangers whom he knows
Forgetfully, from their own selves disguised.
Man is time's fool, who withers the wild rose
Of that young day when gods were recognized.

Millennium

The dream of this new man upon the earth
Was not of angels walking, their bright hair
Day-dusty, and their feet a little slowed,
Their litheness dimmed a little in dense air.

Nor was it of wild hunters strayed away
From an interior forest, the gold hides
Sun-tarnished, and the flying leopard-tails
Wind-ravelled, and a shadow up their sides.

Nor men in rusty mail, nor passion-struck
Lean lovers, nor the tall ones in a grove,
Bare-shouldered, who dispute the evening down;
Nor saints in cells; nor loafers round the stove;

Nor farmers in the field; nor clever eyes
Pale-squinting into clefts of a machine.
The dream of this new man upon the earth
Was new of its own self. No brain had seen

What he saw when he scanned the coming day.
Square-headed then the heroes; high-oblong
The faces, and the ankles stiff with strength;
Heels hobbed; the insteps braided with a thong;

Caps eagle-beaked, and sooty overalls
Steam-blown as, pouring forth in swarthy pairs,
Their shoulders like Leviathan, their hands
Good-humored, like the idle paws of bears

Down-hanging, thumb-and-fingerless, they strode,
One giant by the other, up the world.
And over them the angular steel tubes
Joined smoke to smoke, and jagged sparks were hurled;

And lines as straight as lightning led the way
To a foretold horizon, whither stamped,
Unending, file on file; and tireless sang
One song; and shook the mountains as they tramped.

The Last Look

The great eyes died around this room;
Died everywhere; no matter what wall's blankness,
He printed a pair of circles on it; filled
All four of them; surviving with a rankness

Terrible now to us, the livers-on;
The more so that we loved him for his quiet.
He was a man most delicate: not loud
Like this, like these round eyes; like this gaunt riot

Of spent, unsmiling gazes; for at the last,
Trying to smile farewell to us, he could not.
So it appeared that day, I mean. We now
Think otherwise. He looked at us and would not.

Why? But if we knew this, we had known
The other man, the man before the illness.
Now that he is a stranger—studying back,
We were unjust, loving him for his stillness.

That was the least of him. The great eyes prove it,
Lingering on these walls, and hanging fire
With the same truth we buried in the box—
Subdued then to the sermon and the choir,

Yet louder; for the concert here of walls
Is music's self, the sound of someone staring
Utterly, at all things, till they spoke.
This man alone was capable of sharing

Ultimate name and number. This is where—
Yes, this is where he lay, and where the ceiling
Said his last word for him; and where his eyes
Still wander past us, listening and feeling.

II &

Private Worship

She lay there in the stone folds of his life
Like a blue flower in granite. This he knew;
And knew how now inextricably the petals
Clung to the rock; recessed beyond his hand-thrust;
More deeply in, past more forgotten windings
Than his rude tongue could utter, praising her.

He praised her with his eyes, beholding oddly
Not what another saw, but what she added,
Thinning today and shattering with a slow smile,
To the small flower within, to the saved secret.
She was not his to have; except that something,
Always like petals falling, entered him.

She was not his to keep—except the brightness,
Flowing from her, that lived in him like dew;
And the kind flesh he could remember touching,
And the unconscious lips, and both her eyes:
These lay in him like leaves, beyond the last turn
Breathing the rocky darkness till it bloomed.

It was not large, this chamber of the blue flower,
Nor could the scent escape; nor the least color
Ebb from that place and stain the outer stone.
Nothing upon his grey sides told the fable,
Nothing of love or lightness, nothing of song;
Nothing of her at all. Yet he could fancy—

170

Oh, he could feel where petals spread their softness,
Gathered from windfalls of her when she smiled;
Growing some days, he thought, as if to burst him—
Oh, he could see the split halves, and the torn flower
Fluttering in sudden sun; and see the great stain—
Oh, he could see what tears had done to stone.

Winter Tryst

When the Atlantic upsloped itself
Like roofs of higher and higher houses,
To the great ridge, the foaming shelf
Whereon no dolphin ever browses;

When the wild grey broke into white,
And ships rose endward, crushing mountains;
When it was thus, and icy light
Poured up from phosphorescent fountains:

When it was thus, at winter's crest,
A vessel arrived; and the annual ocean,
Faithfully setting her down in the west,
Repented awhile of its furious motion;

Subsided; but only until that prow
Was pointed again, and a passenger, waving,
Wept in the channel, reminded now
Of eleven months, and the duty of braving

A spring and a summer, and longer fall
Till the month of the year that was set for returning;
Then the grey slopes; and the port, and the tall
Still lover—O time! O bitter adjourning!

When the Atlantic upheaved its whole
And the bottomless world dared keels to try it:

171

Then was the season; this poor soul
Only that month kept longing quiet.

Only that month: most difficult,
Most dark. Most loveless, and most unable.
Yet is was hers. And time's result
Is love's most fair, most speechless fable.

The Letter

You will not doubt I loved her,
You are too wise, and know
Too well that love is little,
Too well that love is low.

Or may be. Mine was groundward.
Confession is content.
How could there be idea
Where all was accident?

I mean I loved her forearm
Just as it lay to see.
What she was least aware of
Is what she was to me.

I mean there was a tired way
Her ankles crossed the floor.
And there were sleep and sweetness
In the slant cape she wore.

I mean that I remember,
Now she is gone awhile,
Nothing about her forehead
Save that the hair could smile;

Nothing about her bosom
Save that it could be still;

172

Her very breath was patient,
Climbing that slender hill.

Intelligent her waist was,
As though both heart and brain
Lived there along with silence,
And with them love had lain

So long ago I learned it
Almost too late, I fear.
At least I do remember
These things, and you must hear.

The Whisperer

Be extra careful by this door,
No least, least sound, she said.
It is my brother Oliver's,
And he would strike you dead.

Come on. It is the top step now,
And carpet all the way.
But wide enough for only one,
Unless you carry me.

I love your face as hot as this.
Put me down, though, and creep.
My father! He would strangle you,
I think, like any sheep.

Now take me up again, again;
We're at the landing post.
You hear her saying Hush, and Hush?
It is my mother's ghost.

She would have loved you, loving me.
She had a voice as fine—

I love you more for such a kiss,
And here is mine, is mine.

And one for her— Oh, quick, the door!
I cannot bear it so.
The vestibule, and out; for now
Who passes that would know?

Here we could stand all night and let
Strange people smile and stare.
But you must go, and I must lie
Alone up there, up there.

Remember? But I understand.
More with a kiss is said.
And do not mind it if I cry,
Passing my mother's bed.

How Such a Lady

She waits in a grey high house, this lady, and waits;
Morning upon loud morning no one ascends.
Daytime is cobble-clamorous down by the gates;
Daytime or nighttime, nobody comes to her hands.

She does not keep them folded across her knees;
She is not sitting and waiting, or even saying:
I am alone in a grey high mansion, and these
Are the sign of my pride and patience who am dying.

She lives by an endless labor of going and turning
And losing the count of corners, and measuring walls;
Or sits, in a gilded chair not made for mourning,
Mending the ancient lace with the mouse's holes.

How such a lady can keep her wristbands flying
Never a man may guess. No man is there.

174

Yet it is true she waits. Her hands are praying
Suddenly to be his, and quiet as air.

Proper Clay

Their little room grew light with cries;
He woke and heard them thread the dark,
He woke and felt them like the rays
Of some unlawful dawn at work:

Some random sunrise, lost and small,
That found the room's heart, vein by vein.
But she was whispering to the wall,
And he must see what she had seen.

He asked her gently, and she wept.
"Oh, I have dreamed the ancient dream.
My time was on me, and I slept;
And I grew greater than I am;

"And lay like dead; but when I lived,
Three wingèd midwives wrapped the child.
It was a god that I had loved,
It was a hero I had held.

"Stretch out your mortal hands, I beg.
Say common sentences to me.
Lie cold and still, that I may brag
How close I am to proper clay.

"Let this within me hear the truth.
Speak loud to it." He stopped her lips.
He smoothed the covers over both.
It was a dream perhaps, perhaps,

Yet why this radiance round the room,
And why this trembling at her waist?

And then he smiled. It was the same
Undoubted flesh that he had kissed;

She lay unchanged from what she was,
She cried as ever woman cried.
Yet why this light along his brows?
And whence the music no one made?

Neighbor Girl

You do not know me then, she said.
Well, it is what you asked.
I went away ten thousand miles,
And altered me, and masked.

Your son has never been so safe
As when I heard you cry:
Rather than he be country wed,
Oh, I would see him die!

And has he lived, and has it gone
Forgetful-well with him?
And have you found another face,
And is my own so dim?

But listen! It is doubly gone.
I came to bring you word
How both of you are safe from me,
And if there be a third,

She too may smile and slip to bed
And never glance around;
I am so changed from what I was
I make no earthly sound;

I do not stare like that great girl
Who foddered her father's sheep.

176

I am more thin than thread—and look!
How listlessly I creep;

Yet not too slowly, going hence,
For if you laid a hand
Like this, like this upon me there,
You scarce would understand.

You do not know how far I've been,
Nor why this patch of white
Like frost upon my forehead grows.
Good father-in-law, goodnight.

Is This the Man

Is this the man who multiplied,
Divided, added, and was quick
As any wizard to subtract,
As any conjurer to trick
Love's innocent numbers, love's eleven,
Love's unswift arithmetic?

Is this the man who hung the air
With spangled syllables all day?
And was indifferent if wind
Bore every word like webs away?
For there was more that he could spin;
Such love was infinite to say?

Is this the man who carried fire
And left a radiance all night?
Undid the shadows and released
Some old incarcerated light?
Some moldy beam that lived and spread
And was to love as second sight?

Is this the man? For it is dusk,
And he is standing dark and still.

For there is silence; not a sound
Weaves out of him against his will.
For he is awkward; he has lost
Even the memory of skill.

Even the memory of love—
Oh, inarticulate, betrayed!
Oh, this the man for whom the world
Was honor-bright and cleanly made.
Yet here he stands, as darkly dumb
As love's first guiltless renegade.

Something Acrid

Giving him up, she kept the art
Still to engreen his desert part;
His conscience's high inner hill—
She saved the strength, she nursed the skill
To climb and climb and in that clay
Plant what never can blow away.

The top was sandy to desire;
Knew only wind, loved only fire;
Would have been barren of a shoot
But that she found the ancient root:
Felt moisture out, and creeping thence
Created meadows far and dense.

So memory covered him, and killed
What still were healthy had she willed.
He could have withered into friend
Had she accepted verdure's end.
He now is enemy: the spoil
Of something acrid in the soil.

A Different Avarice

It is a different avarice
From any a shadow hides.
Ambitionless in daylight
And without craft he rides.

He is another miser
Than night's old closet knows.
Inhabitant of highways,
Nodding, he comes and goes.

He is a man still grieving
For his small house's heart.
Never again to beat there,
She was the muffled part,

She was the sum not counted,
That now he goes to find
In a wide world and friendly,
In a deep world and kind.

She was the breathing total
That now these numbers build:
People in other houses,
Morning and evening filled—

Oh, numerous, oh, nothing,
Oh, dry and soundless days,
That only set him weeping,
Remembering her ways,

And how their mingled rhythm
Beat time and love in one.
What no one measured, living,
Is infinitely gone.

The Cockerel

You are my grandson's bride, she said,
And a dark stranger here.
Sit close, for now my cloudy head
Is by some magic clear.

What I forgot more years ago
Than you have had those eyes—
Sit still awhile! He is below,
And his fox ears are wise.

It has been well with him and me;
I heard him tell you so.
And grin. Nor do I disagree;
Only, before you go,

Sit close, and hear me say the name
Of one that walked the world
More beautiful than he; but tame—
Oh, tame, with feathers curled;

With plumes that never stood again
After I went and wed.
Nor have I missed him in my den,
Making a fox's bed.

I have been thoughtless; yet this day
Turns me a moment home;
To the green lawn, and to the way
The sun gilded his comb.

Beyond Compare

All he can hope for is that hills and children
In a sky-eyed conspiracy will say:
"There he goes now, the old one; but the young one—
Ah, she was lifelike; she will not waste away.

180

"She is as fair as then; and it is years now
Since anyone saw her forehead under a cap.
There never was such another worn by woman:
One of the signs and secrets, like her lap.

"When she was in a low chair, tired of talking,
Something about her there denied the rest.
Something about her sitting was not weary,
Something in her was motionless and blest.

"Yet she could move, and then all things went with her:
Neither too swift a harmony nor slow.
Children upon the highway will remember.
All of these hills were there, and they should know.

"This is the bare beginning; she was endless.
There is no number named that would enclose
Each of her clear particulars; abstraction
Dies in the deed, as language in a rose.

"There was the way she had of answering questions:
Not with her lips alone; the shoulders tried;
And the dropped hands succeeded. But how tell it?
Truth is a deep oblivion, and a wide.

"Let her not live in sentences. She merits
Memory, and is anterior to sound.
Let us forget these lines that we have spoken,
Lest they be steel and bind her to the ground.

"Let her be what she was, unpaired, unequalled;
Centered within the circle of her kind.
She is alone there"—patiently he listens,
Hopeful of death when light shall be defined.

III 𐑸

The Bundle

He was too tightly bound—
The faggots pressed like one together—
For the bright wire to be unwound
And he be loosened to the weather.

There was a kind of day,
The air almost dissolving bones,
When he could wish the knot away,
And he distributed like stones:

Keeping their hardness still,
So they be scattered soft apart;
Space between them like a hill,
And time discovering his heart.

There was a kind of eye—
His children's, tethered at the rim—
Oh, he could even wish to die
If death could make them free of him.

Oh, he could be dispersed,
And the lean sticks grow fat with ease.
But he was fearful of the worst—
And panic then was his disease—

Lest the first break be last:
The wire a serpent in the air;
Fragments of him flying past;
Then all at once a nothing there.

Many the milder ways.
He scoured the world and counted, so.
But not for him the vagrant gaze
And the light-minded letting go.

Not for him the field—
Though he could watch across the wall—
Where the bones danced, and children wheeled,
And songs ascended at nightfall.

The Invasion

Know thy good self, he said,
But if it be
Permissible, physician,
Know not me.

You have been swift enough,
And tramped as far
Already as to my sentries:
Sons of war.

Know thyself and them:
Count up those fears;
Lead off those joys—lifelong
My prisoners,

My dwarves of thought, fair slaves
By me deformed.
Then rest; there is a room
Not to be stormed.

I shall breed other watchers
For the walls.
Take these and march. Minute
Be their footfalls.

The Runaways

Upon a summer Sunday: sweet the sound
Of noon's high warmness flowing to the ground;

Upon a summer Sunday: wide the song
Of strengthless wings that bore the sky along;

Upon a summer Sunday: strange the power,
Inaudible, that opened every flower;

On Sunday, in the summer, through the white
Mid-world they wandered, meditating flight.

With every boundary melted, still they ran,
Still looked for where the end of earth began;

Still truant; but, dissolving far ahead,
The edge of day as effortlessly fled,

As innocently distanced all they were
Of quick-eared dog and fat philosopher.

On Sunday, in the summer, down a field,
Leader and led, alternately they wheeled

Till the great grass possessed them, and the sky
No longer was a map to measure by;

Till round and round they floated, lost and small,
Like butterflies that afterward will fall

But now between the great sky and the ground,
Sun-tethered, dance all morning meadow-bound.

Upon a summer Sunday, when the light
Of perfect noon was everywhere and white—

Pure death of place and color—then the pair
Grew sudden-silent, hungry for home's air;

Paused, turned; remembered shadows in a yard;
And had again their own high wall and hard.

The Little Doctor

The little doctor with the black
Ambitious eyes had giant horses;
High the reins and loud the splash
Along those muddy country courses.

Black the harness, black the eyes,
And black the phaeton's new fringes.
Dappled, though, the necks and flanks,
And foaming white the fetlocks' plunges—

On and on, a winter's day;
Warm the sudden south-wind thawing;
On and on the doctor watched
Rut after rut with water flowing;

Guided the eight, the silver feet
Proud into pools; and heard the utter
Puddle and plash; received the sound
Most deep, most eloquent to flatter;

Loosened the reins, allowed the hocks
Through flooded grooves to speak his greatness;
Whence the black ambitious eyes
Saw now in everything a fitness;

Saw the hide of dappled rumps,
How it cross-wrinkled with the straining;
How the great backs forward sloped;
How in the manes the wind was moaning.

Yet the straps outsang the wind,
And yet the hoof-spray drowned the grasses.
So in that lost, that country time
The little doctor ever presses.

On and on, a dateless day,
Down sunken roads where death has prospered,

185

Black-eyed breezes still can blow,
And private glories still be whispered.

The Music-Box

When they were almost there his skinny fingers
Tightened upon some secret, and he said:
"You are deceived, there will be no more silence
Than ever;" and licked a knuckle and knocked his head.

"This tilted, motionless bone above my shoulders,
This seedless gourd, this tomb whereon your locks
Shall click—it is a maker of far noises,
A many-times-removed loud music-box.

"Not loud to you, though; so it scarcely matters.
Save that you are deceived. There will be sound.
It is my mind that makes it, as it rushes
Like a fresh wind across the risen ground.

"Like a small animal parting the tops of grasses,
Like a bright face with feelers, so it goes.
It is my mind at work remembering objects;
It is the earth remembering what it knows.

"Till then each piece of matter, each grey sliver,
Sleeps; until I arrive; then upward springs!
Oh, the wide cry, the crackling! Oh, the music!
As my still thought runs rustling over things."

When they were there, relaxing his long fingers
He smiled upon them, fastening the door.
"Peace on you then," he said; "but on your planet
There never will be silence any more."

186

The Meeting

It was no intercourse of palms;
Or foreheads, mutual-bowed;
Or tongues, returning courtesies;
It was so far from loud
That one of the two hears only now
The rustle of a shroud;

Hears only now, by thinking back,
And pressing fact before,
A corridor's white vacancy;
The darkness of a door;
And how the other, secret there,
Looked out; and looks no more.

The eyes of illness make for sound
The scratching of a pen—
Oh, every inch of pallid wall
Is traced again, again;
Unceasing; but a deeper sound
Looks out of dying men.

So on that night, unknown to him,
So in that thoughtless hall,
So round him clung a whispering
Half hoarse, half musical.
So round him rang the silence's
Mute break, and shadow's fall.

He hears it only now, and knows
How tight the vision drew;
How longingly the other looked;
And how he merely threw
His cape across his back; tripped down,
And whistled over dew.

Tantrum Wings

Rather than ups and downs,
Now here, now high,
Rather than tantrum wings he would have known
No skill to fly.

Rather than lightning joy—
His will and theirs
Sky-wedded—he would lubberly have moved;
Been caved with bears;

Been lame upon a ledge;
Refused the top:
So evenness be in him, and cool blood,
And motion stop.

Rather than he be else,
Be juster, though,
They took him as he was—they loved him more
For high, for low;

For doubtfulness all day,
For noon, for night.
The average of this man was burning cloud,
Was thrashed sunlight.

Exaggerator

The truth for him was like a tree,
Was like a funnel; like a fan;
Like any point from which a cone
Spreads upside down until the span
From base to base across the top
Cannot be guessed by any man.

The truth for him was not the seed,
Was not the apex, handle, spout;

188

Was not the particle or germ,
Or what grew thence so wild and stout;
Was not the great, the upper end.
It was the joy of starting out:

Of feeling something in him rise
And widen instantly; and swell,
As if the wind and he were one,
And blew upon each other well;
As if the sky and he were single:
Clapper there and flangèd bell.

The truth for him was hearing quick
The cordage whistle, and the whine
Of wakened metal; something bronze;
Something moaning thin and fine,
Something low; until it burst,
And all was plangent with word-shine.

The truth for him was leaving earth
Between two beams that sloped and rose;
And never joined—the angle's bound
Was all of distance at the close;
Whence he descended, narrowing down
And resting gently where he chose.

Mimic

Summing him, we subtracted
The men he acted.
Yet he was not contained
In what remained.
Still must he overflow
Lest numbers know.

All that ourselves could be
Is what you see.

189

Starved, unchangeable stuff
Was task enough.
But not for him, whose feigning
Was girth and gaining.

Wit-wonderful, he discolored
Himself to dullard;
Ceased, and as soon began
More god than man;
Descended, and was the least
Articulate beast.

Nor have we yet divined
The one behind;
Save that the many have told
Of water and gold;
And how such clear excess
Is lastingness.

Wind-Cure

Coming up here to mend, she picked this window,
The big east one, the clear one, so that lying,
Our sister, like a broken lily stem—
Twice broken, waist and breast—
Her careful eyes could feed upon the low lawn,
The trees, and over walls a mile of meadow.

With the still house behind her as she watched,
And the dark west, that waited at the corners,
The whole west, that never spoke a word—
But waited there, and swelled—
She lay upon her soft side, expectant,
Trusting the loved east, the planned October.

Then round it rushed, that devil there behind her,
Both ways, and put the sun out like a breath.

It only was the third of her sweet mornings—
One, two, three's a charm—
When half the world came warlike round both angles,
When there was wind from nowhere, so that stone walls

Wimpled, and the maddened grasses pulled,
Insane of root, their forelocks everywhichway
Diving, and the maple trees, leaf-wounded—
The first high leaves to fall—
Bent sudden-double, dazed, as up the roadway
One dust-whirl met another whirl descending.

Or then the gales agreed, so that a music,
Single but heaven-harsh, whined overhead
Straight onward, stretching hours upon a note—
Hours, evenings, days—
Till each of us grew fearful, and went tiptoe
Thinking to find her mad. But she lay smiling,

On her soft side lay smiling, turning upward
No longer a tired eye, no longer strengthless.
Beyond the glass she listened to that fury—
Gazed at it, wild again—
Then whispered to us, bending for the low words,
"Oh, you and I, wind, you and I forever!"

The Breathing Spell

The black share-cropper, grizzled in his prime,
Night's face grown frosty-grey with terror's noises—
Six children on the floor pretend to sleep
While white men prowl outdoors in dark disguises;

Level their guns, and laugh; and then the pause
Till crack! two holes high up, and plaster flying;
He does not duck, the croucher by the stove,
He does not catch what this new sound is saying—

The black share-cropper, deafened long ago
To the discord of misery, half-dozes;
Hears no more hunger now; ignores the banged,
The dispossessing door; drowns all those noises,

Dreaming. He is bent beneath a dream
Sky-tall and windless-wide, with rivers running
Waveless, and the smoke above a train
Cloud-stationary, distant, over fanning

Elm trees that he counts along the line:
One, two, and dipping three, and arched eleven.
It is a mile of quiet he has found,
It is a township's peace that he is given.

He moves among the low weeds, mute as they.
The wrappings of his feet are gauze on gravel.
And when the white, the black men pass him, slow,
The greeting of each eye is round and civil.

Even the moment's battle, and the storm,
And the down pitch of timbers—even the falling
Forest is no roar against his ears,
Time-tempered, and the wounded are not wailing:

Stout bodies that collided as in mist,
Rock-hearted trees descending there like feathers.
By the cold stove he drowses, safe from sound,
While midnight clears its throat and morning gathers.

Incorrigible

We never could see it wound him, the tipped weakness
That flew, oh, deadly often, while a twang
Like music with a plume of malice in it,
Like sorrow's rawhide, sounded in his ears.

192

But not in ours. We only heard, harmonious,
The outer song, the one he wrapped it with.

He never could believe they were immortal:
The bowstring there behind him, and the sprung
White wand that let the feathered arrow fly.
He had lost count of subtlety's directions;
Supposed the compass rounded. But his back
Somehow was always magnet, for it came.

Meanwhile he faced us, hopeful of his cure.
If that was all the poison, he was well.
He had outstared the circle; so he faced us,
Smiling, and we could envy such a man:
So wise against his weakness, and so ready.
So ready until tomorrow wheeled around!

His very hope exposed him; and his effort
Never again to doubt of proving good;
And his long list of victories—it wanted
Only one more, the next. But he would win.
And that was when we missed him: when he lay there
With the last barb—he knew it—through his spine.

He knew it, and a month of song succeeded.
Now he had finished mending, now was whole.
The quiver had been dropped where moths, inside it,
Measured the print of arrows; while green leaves
Fell calmly and were drifted to the mouth;
And while he sang, flesh-innocent, his song.

It was a song of moths and sleeping needles.
Under some glass an arrow never swung.
All of the norths were numbered; the wind rested;
Under some cloth a heart beat still and clear.
Under some song—oh, then it was the earth shook,
Shifting an inch, and feathers flew and flew.

Foreclosure

So he sat down and slowly, slowly
Worked at his Christian name;
Watching the gold and halfway smiling
As the last letter came;
Till the whole sound was there, and shouted,
Suddenly, his shame.

Between this word then and the other—
His and his father's too—
He stared at the pen as if its handle
Were a great horn, and blew;
Then lowered the point and quietly labored
Till the last ink was through.

So he got up, and through the wide silence
Wandered; and song began.
Not the old tune, for that was buried
Where the slow writing ran;
But remnants, hung in the wind awhile,
And impotent to scan.

There was the bell that once had brought him,
Frightened, across the field;
There was the mad white shepherd's barking,
And the hurt child, unhealed;
There was a hen whose brood came piping
To the red worm revealed.

There was quick trampling on a stairway,
Until doors sealed the sound.
There were the drums of winter booming
When the lame boy was drowned.
So his lost land went with him, pulling
Its tatters close around.

Ordeal

Sir Eglamour has limped a mile
And left his blood on forest leaves.
Here he must rest himself awhile;
Looks round the hut; undoes his greaves;
Falls down like death, and cannot smile
At thought of plumes or banded sleeves;

Cannot remember now the wine,
The lances glittering in the hall,
The goblets lifted at a sign,
The ceiling dusky over all,
The waiting trumpets, and the nine
Young nervous minstrels by the wall.

Sir Eglamour is not to die,
Though blood is dropping from him still.
It is to cease; for in this sty
There waits another test of will.
Strength conquers wounds, but straw may try
How much of knighthood it can kill.

This dampened heap whereon he lies,
These rafters, songless and obscure,
These rotted shingles, and the flies
Whose country buzz he must endure:
What thing among them knows him wise,
Who now will name him bold and pure?

Without a lady by his side,
Without the proclamation's din—
And then a door is opened wide,
For now the king is coming in—
Without their praises, how can pride
Feed on itself and not grow thin?

Sir Eglamour, how can your fire
Feed on itself and never cool?

How will you pray when this poor mire
In its indifference thinks you fool?
So far from pomp is there desire?
Can flesh remember every rule?

Old Landscape

There was some kind of safety in the feathery
Forest rising leftward from the lake—
The lake no more a mirror, and the shadows
Deepened in a frame of time, of dust,
Of slumber—there was safety in the ageless
Trees a hand once painted, plume by plume.

Across the tarnished waters, on a level
Waste, a blackened lawn, the castle towered,
Its windows morning-darkened, like an ogre's
Eyes that have been dreamless year on year;
Its moat no longer glittering, and the country
Carts all mired with time, the fetlocks fouled.

But there was safety leftward, by a faded
Bridge that in the foreground leapt the stream—
The stream no longer lustrous where the timbers
Fell on it like shadows. There his eye
Found comfort, and his feet imagined movement,
And he entered, and he mounted toward the grove.

And there was safety for him in the shaggy
Ceiling of dusk leaves, of lofty down
A brush had swiftly painted—thinking only
Of sloped masses, maybe; yet the hand
Might well have fancied feathers, and the under
Breast of what great nameless brooding bird.

So anyhow for him, who now in safety
Glided through the silence, and who heard

196

Soft beatings overhead as of a heartstroke
Muffled from the world, and from the carters
Struggling at the moat, and from the lake
Whose poisoned waters glittered under change.

IV ॐ

Young Woman at a Window

Who so valiant to decide?
Who so prompt and proper-active?
Yet each muscle in her brain
Relaxes now; is unrestrictive;
Lets her lean upon this dark
November night wind; lets it work—

Oh, lets it ask her if she thinks,
Oh, lets it whisper if she knows
How much of time is like a stream
Down which her headless body flows;
How many answers, proudly made,
Will be like minnows overlaid

With inch on inch of glossy black,
With depth on depth of sliding water;
Lets it dare her to predict
Those floods of silence coming later;
Till she melts, and leaning long
Is only conscious of wind-song.

Who so valorous of voice?
Who so staunch upon the ground?
But wind-and-water-song at work
Stops both her ears against the sound
Of someone here she used to know;
Of someone saying: It is so.

197

She leans and loses every word.
Her loudest wisdom well is gone.
But still the current of the night
Comes with its foaming on and on;
Pours round the sill; dissolves the hands;
And still the dreamless body stands.

Night's End

Young man of many sorrows, do you know
How narrow the sweet night is, and how soon
This hemisphere above you will be split,
Letting light in, the monster; letting clear waves
Shatter the scented cloud? Do you, the feaster,
Know the great air as tasteless on the tongue?

You cannot measure smallness; you believe
Still in the darkened stature, you are rounded
Still with all color's thickness, you can count
More sorrows than the night was numbered for.
You groan. But what of sunrise, and the white time
Coming? What of the voice lost round the sky?

Do not so much as listen to me asking.
Keep to your little dome, whereof the sound grows
Nightly: throat and dusky metal joined.
Keep to your little darkness, where the rose thorns
Pierce the rich heart of odor, and the eye
Is opened upon soft shapes, and sorrows flow.

Never look up, anticipating night's end.
So near the limit is, so low the ceiling,
Almost a glance would lift you. Or the mind would.
Let it keep home awhile, and miss the high
Wide-swinging waves, the coolness, the great clearness.
They are another joy, not spread for now.

Through the great oneness over you—so high there,
So far, so all around, that even earth shrinks,
Even the world is one dropped poppy seed—
Through the glass-white immensity go flashing
Ages of light criss cross; the soundless beacons
Wheel, and the great air sparkles, blind with time.

Young man of the dense sorrows, you will rise there;
You will cast off, delectable, this load.
You will be wind and sky-ray, you will thin there
To the pure beam, transparent, self-denied.
Yet will your tongue not taste; nor will that presence
Sing in your ears, like this one, all day long.

Young Blood

After so many blushes,
And stoppings at the heart,
How it recovers—rushes—
Stings every part—
And pauses; for these lovers
Are sluggish movers.

Experiment of fingers,
Faint breathing in and out—
Enough of something lingers
Lest passion doubt;
And flames; for in these children
Is flint and cauldron.

Yet there is time for burning,
And many an ashen place.
Let them be; they are learning
Fear's courteous face.
Perceive. The hands of these lovers
Are delicate rovers.

Changeling

This woman is bewildered,
This mother of a son
Cries out upon imposture:
He's not the one,
He's not the hunger-helpless,
The clamorous one.

Where is the other hidden?
And if he still is fed,
Why has he grown ungrateful?
Is famine dead?
Is foolishness? No answer;
No curl of head.

She nourishes a stranger,
And knows it by his wish
For anything but dainties.
Untouched the dish.
Unshatterable the silence.
Undone the leash.

The Widower

The little fellow—partly fool—
Remembers perfectly his mother.
Nobody better understands
There never will be such another.

His pretty sisters, said the man,
Are not so wise with all their wit.
For them already she is saint,
So they improve her as they sit,

Recalling only she was cool,
Remarking always how she smiled.

And this is rare and touching-fine;
But truth is with the coarser child.

He has not ceased, when he is wrong,
To hear the angry volume close,
And tapping step: to him the thorns
Are real as petals down the rose.

The flower is firm; gone slow to bed,
He gazes suddenly and grins;
Pulls bare his neck for her caress;
Recites the goat's, the parrot's sins.

But then tomorrow he will run
Like any thief to miss the wrath
Of someone coming tall and red:
It is herself upon the path.

It is herself, and nowise changed
As late with them, the weeping pair.
They have the spirit, he the flesh.
And either sight is sad to bear.

The Vigil

Young Walter keeps all winter
In a high land and cold.
Nor has he any fortune,
Save that his blood is gold;
Save that his eyes have riches,
Deep-woven, damask-old.

I hear that round his house there
The mountains crack like ice;
But he has bread, with buckwheat
Honey upon each slice;
And cats that range the kitchen,
Killing the famished mice.

I hear there is a woodlot,
And that he daily tramps
With birch and alder cuttings,
And heaps the hearth, and stamps;
And by their flicker nightly
Reads late, disdaining lamps.

I hear that farmer people,
Who lived here once and died,
Left rows of witless volumes,
And that young Walter cried:
"They will be buckram coaches
Wherein my fancies ride!"

I hear that he goes through them;
Blows off the dust and lint;
Finishes every chapter;
Is faithful to the stint;
And that his mind has gilded
Some tales as in a mint.

Young Walter is not coming
Like other heroes home.
His wars are solitary,
His shield the honeycomb;
His hostages the fire-log,
The tabby cat, the tome.

This Is the Boy

This is the boy that rode nine hundred
Miles. And did the porter,
Bowing to you, feign and find you
Seventeen or older?

Was there a lady down the aisle
Looked up and smiled; decided

It were a pity if a child—
So were you then invaded?

Or was the double seat and bag;
The narrow glass, the bell;
The polished berth above you—boy,
Were these your own and all?

Whence if you turned a quiet head
You saw the country spin,
Nearby more swift, far off more slow,
And humorless horses run?

Whence if you leaned you saw the pillows
Propped in a slumbrous row?
And the shut eyes? And did you shiver,
Suddenly? And sway,

Ecstatic, lonely, on the plush,
To such a rhythm, rising,
As only flange and rail produce,
Past copying, past praising?

Exploring forward, did you pause
In the loud gale and clank
Of vestibules? And spell the names—
Plum Valley, Onderdonck,

Septentrion, Minervaville,
Darius—did you walk
Through Glendon to the dining car?
And did you careless take

That leather seat, high, single there,
And blink in silvershine
As now the sun poured in to please
The veteran of the train?

203

Noisy China

The forty acre oatfield,
The hedge fence, the raincrow,
The silence—the boy said:
Sound, sound? it lies so
Forever, sweet and dead;

Forever with its head down,
Sleepily and sidewise,
Cheek upon the warm grain,
Dreamily, and dove's cries
Never leave a stain;

Never may corrupt this,
The silence, the sweet sun,
The low breath—the boy leaned,
Guarding his horizon
Against the loud fiend.

Half around the bent world,
Even then, in Peking,
Even then a boy said:
Sound? it is a fierce wing
Forever overhead;

Another wing, a thousand more,
A swift flock—the quills whirr,
The feathers beat, and gabble falls
Like droppings where the dews were,
Like hail along the walls.

Sound? it is a cracked voice;
The pigeon men will never die:
The starlings, ravens, jackdaws.
The little maid that used to lie—
What is she now but crow's caws?

Spectral Boy

I told you I would come, he said,
I told you with these very eyes.
Be not ashamed. The grave is deep,
And terror in it dies.

If in these circles that you see
There is the old, the child's alarm,
It does not live to startle you,
Or work the pulse's harm.

It was not gathered underground,
It was not freed upon a day,
Except that something might come home
Of the whipped soul, and stay.

Except the fever, all is here.
My deathless part, my fear, returns.
Be not ashamed. The grave is cold.
Nothing in it burns.

I have not suffered since I died,
Though I have lain with eyes as round
As when you fixed them; but enlarged,
Some days, from lack of sound.

And so there fell to me an hour
Of utter quiet; then I rose,
And am revisiting old Time,
Before his close.

Was I not washed and buried well?
Why this desire, why this research
For time and wrath? Be still, I beg!
What now? This twitch and lurch—

You would escape me, but I swear
I was not sent to punish you.

I came alone, that fear might form
Once more on me like dew.

No longer groan and hide your hands.
This thing I seek is chill and sweet.
Be not ashamed. The grave is pure.
No horror now. No heat.

Sin of Omission

He will remember this; the cunning Fates,
Seeing all seventy years laid flat ahead—
The spring-tight coil of days unrolls for them,
Their little and deep long eyes forewatch the dead—
The mouse-eyed Fates can number the known times
He will remember this, the thing unsaid.

Only to say it now would soothe that man,
His father, come to sound him in his room;
Most friendly, but the stairs are still acreak,
And the boy, deafened to another doom,
Says nothing; he is guilty of desire
For the mind's silence, waiting to resume.

What it was filled with, he the least of all
In a far day will know; remembering then—
So the Fates reckon—how he ran and called,
Hoping to bring the shoulders up again;
But only called half-loudly in his pride,
And in the pride of him the best of men.

He will remember this, and loathe the hour
When his fair tongue, malingering, stood still.
He will rehearse the sentences not said;
Pretending that he climbed the lonely hill;
Pretending that he met him at the top,
Articulate, and cured him of his ill:

His need to know, so innocent, how sons
Read in their rooms the dark, the dear-bought books;
How in his own good flesh the strange thing grew,
Thought's inward river, nourishing deep nooks,
Dyeing them different-green. The boy will feign,
Concealing his long sighs, his backward looks—

Will fabricate warm deeds and laughing words,
His hand upon a chair, his cheeks alive;
Instead of this cool waiting, and this gloom
Wherein no starting syllable can thrive.
He will remember even as he runs.
The Fates run too, and rapider arrive.

Boy Dressing

There lies the shoe, picked up a minute past
And dropped when something struck him, and he paused,
Eye-rigid, fixing daylight on the door:
Thin daylight, that a careless clock has caused

And windows have conspired with. So his hands,
Conscious of nothing leather, float to work
At buttons on his breast, and at the tie—
He fumbles round it; finishes with a jerk;

Stops dead again, his hair in timeless tangles,
Obedient to a moment that will end—
Bang! Doors downstairs have doomed it. But the shoe.
Remembering, his back begins to bend,

His knee comes up, his fingers at the instep
Play with the knotted laces. Leave him there.
Be tolerant of trances. For he feeds
On time, and drinks the milk of mother air.

207

Home from School

Here they come, the paired brief-cases
Cutting, port and starboard, the waved street;
Their thought all smoke, their laughter the white whistle
Of steam as two slim funnels tilt and meet.

One vessel these, the minds well mingled
And the gay hull oblivious where it goes:
Set homeward, but the helmsman is a dummy,
Drifting them safe whatever folly blows.

One purpose theirs, that no one listens
Down the long tide and faintly overhears.
The sidewalk only billows, and the indifferent
Spray of their footsteps floats and disappears.

At four o'clock arriving, and slowing
Suddenly round and down, the satchels swing.
While the waves wash, and lap at them a little,
The serious white heads together cling.

Then a quick puff—their scheme escapes them,
Splitting aloft and thinning into air.
Divided now the vessel, as each portion
Enters a separate house and climbs a stair.

Only tomorrow, clean and early,
Will they be one again and sail away;
Their end almost forgotten; but no matter;
Innumerable the islands down the bay.

Like Son

Your stillness here at evening, with the shade
Wide up and both your hands beneath your head—
I see. It is the same as when I lay,
Just so, and watched the window-people tread:

208

Our neighbors, at their little squares of glass
Come suddenly to eye, then off again;
Extinguished in the frame until that boy,
That watcher, worked his magic on them then:

Stared, hummed, and brought the dressing gown, the sleeve,
Brought folded arms and faces, brought the smile.
But not for him. For no one. This he knew,
And knows it now with you a whispering while.

See? Neither of us here can be imagined.
They stand as if alone; and how they seem
Is how the planets find them: row on row,
Night-blown, and candle-brief as in a dream.

No More Different

The random eye mismates them,
So bearish is the man,
So like a tender goatling
The boy is—and ran

Like this, beside his father,
As long ago as earth,
As long ago as evening,
As bird time, as mirth;

As any mountain old one
Moved with a leafy cry
For music to his loudness,
And with a palm to lie

Like this one in the cavern
Of his too granite hand.
But they are no more different
Than hour-glass and sand;

209

Requiring so each other
That one gives up his rage,
And one gives up his sweetness.
Divine the average.

Men and Children

What moon presides when mosses grow,
What sun when celandine, may know
The courteous name of one dark star
That comes where men and children are,
But comes most rarely. For it rules
Dusk-suddenly, and none but fools
Foretell it. None but fathers' eyes
Look for it round the evening skies.
Let them not look. They cannot bring
What makes identity to sing
In man, in child—in them as two
Drops of the selfsame merry dew.
They shine together for a while;
Too wise for speech, too clear for smile;
Too unremembering for doubt,
Too blissful. Then the star dims out.
Too single were they to endure,
Too indivisible and pure;
As water may not water be
Longer than there is light to see.

V &

The Moments He Remembers

The moments he remembers? They are those
In the dog part of him, the sleeping nose,

The animal awakened in him once—
Decrepit the old hound, yet how he hunts

Through the moist lands of youth! Or then he did—
Remembering what time almost has hid:

The hour at sunset when the ball and glove,
Hot with the play, exhaled a leather love,

And his left hand, withdrawn to wipe his eyes,
Sweetened the whole air with musk surprise:

The sweat of horses, tempered with his own,
And the rubbed oil that lingered on alone.

The animal, awakening once more,
Almost can live; except his bones are sore,

And the sunk valleys of his mind can save
Only a few more moments from the grave:

As when the boy, in January wind,
Ran till his face was nipped and scarlet-skinned;

Then stopped, and all of winter like a bell
Rang in his nostrils, soundless. Or the spell—

He can remember, suddenly, his trance
When feet upon the lawn had ceased to dance,

And his small cheeks, enamored of the bruise,
Lay pressed in grass the way sky-witches use,

Straining upon earth's arc, to enter in.
He entered it, the odor—now so thin,

So struggling now, so faint across the ground,
To the old man and the near-sighted hound.

Uncle Roger

When he was eighteen autumns old,
With Indian hair and wiry waist,
He says America was a map
Whereon a boy and engine raced.

It was a field of moving fires—
The sparks uprushing, and the red
Of open boilers; and the green
Of signals floating far ahead;

Or else a wild, a lonely plain,
A waiting desert, where the howl
Of locomotives miles away
Was ghosts awalk and beasts aprowl.

What all it was he will not say;
How beautiful he cannot tell.
Yet in his chair I know he hears
The cry of steam, the starting bell.

I know he sees himself asleep
In prairie clover, while the clank
Of couplings on the Danville freight
Is music to him, sweet and rank.

So stretching many a cooler day
On gravelly weeds beside a grade,
He hears the whine of coming wheels,
With desolate whistles overlaid;

But feels the rumble in his bones
Before the loud, the nearer sound;
And all the history of a line
Reads out of rumors in the ground.

He can remember a wet dawn,
He can remember a stopped train

In Pennsylvania, and the hoarse,
High notes—again, again—

That tore the mountain walls apart,
That split the cold, the dripping oaks;
And still he hears the lean yell,
And still the dewy engine smokes.

Far in the west a water tower
Leaks in the sun and dampens sand:
The only circle that is dark
In many a mile of desert land.

Yet by the Gulf an endless swamp
Gurgles beneath the trestled ties;
And he has waited on a bluff
To watch the Mississippi rise;

And crawled behind the going flood
And tested bridges, beam on beam,
Until a signal waved ahead
Brought the great wheels, and swish of steam.

He loiters in the branching yards;
He climbs a cabin red with rust.
Those polished engines puffing by
Are doomed like this one unto dust.

He tries the throttle; it is fast;
Corroded gauges cloud his eye.
So this is growing old and old,
So this is what it is to die.

Then Uncle Roger, coming to,
Sits in his chair and nods and smiles;
And clicks his lips through seven years,
And lives again ten thousand miles.

Two of You

I know you after sixty years;
They have not changed, she said:
Those incombustible black stones
High in your ashen head;
Those coals that, as our passion blew,
Outlasted my poor dread.

Those eyes that I so lowly feared
For their unstopping gaze—
I may not fancy even now
That on my snow it stays;
This level whiteness of my life;
These warm, forgotten ways.

I have come back to look at you,
I have come back to find
The incorruptible straight stalk,
The rod within the rind.
And I can wonder if time erred,
Proving so rigid-kind.

He has made two of you, I say.
Does either of them hear?
That dark one rising inwardly?
This other one—this sere,
This whiter one that snows have singed,
Piling the faggot year?

But not the first, the ageless man.
I see him where he stands,
Stiff prisoner inside the glass,
Contented with smooth hands;
Condemned, erect, and total-deaf
To the sweet run of sands.

From the swift song of change, my love,
You long ago were locked;

A young man in an old man's hide,
And both of them are mocked;
Unless you listened, one of you,
When my crisp knuckles knocked.

Bailey's Hands

The right one that he gave me—
I could have shut my eyes
And heard all seventy summers
Rasping at their scythes.

The left one that he lifted,
Tightening his hat—
I could have seen the cut groves
Lie fallen, green and flat;

Or seen a row of handles,
Ash-white and knuckle-worn,
Run back as far as boyhood
And the first field of thorn:

The two-edged axe and sickle,
The pick, the bar, the spade,
The adze, and the long shovel—
Their heads in order laid,

Extending many an autumn
And whitening into bone,
As if the past were marching,
Stone after stone.

So by his hands' old hardness,
And the slow way they waved,
I understood the story:
Snath-written, helve-engraved.

215

Woodpile

The high heap that now and then,
When the wind thumps it, settles—
The breathing space decreases for the grass
Beneath it, and the nettles—
Will lie, when April thrashes,
Compacted ashes.

Not here, not like this mountain, tossed
From the saw's teeth all fall;
Not here, but humbly leeward of the house,
And ghostly small.
Nothing, after this winter,
Of sap or splinter.

There will be nothing of the difference,
When grass grows again,
Nothing between the big and little mountains
Save two unfrozen men:
The blood in them still running,
Lukewarm and cunning.

For such as them this pyramid
Must pass, becoming flame—
All but a little powder on the ground there
That no lit match could tame.
Lest their poor lives be finished,
Bulk is diminished:

Shrinking until a room expands
To summer under the snow;
Melting away though earth is solid iron,
And ice-flakes blow.
Perhaps itself should stay.
Yet who can say?

His Trees

Only when he was old enough, and silent:
Not breaking-old; time-coated; that was it;
Only when he was dry enough: but seasoned;
Time-guarded against all weather-warp and split;
Time-roughened, with years of ridges down his bark:
Then only grew he worthy of their remark.

They did not move; but watched him as he came,
Man-tired, and paused and peered among their shade.
No magical advancing; each emerged
Only as slow acquaintance thus was made:
The oaks and he confronted, that was all;
Save that his leaves of ignorance could fall.

They fell, and filled the temperate aging air
With a crisp rustle, flake on flake descending;
Till in some month it ceased, and trunk on trunk
Acknowledged him, in rows without an ending.
The lesser with the greater shadows wove:
He there with them, companions of the grove.

The ash was proud to show him in its side
How narrowly and coldly time had cut:
A flank of iron; and how its sharpened leaves
Stood out too stiff for any wind to shut:
Stubborn; yet some antiquity of grace
Still kept it king, still proved the priestly face.

That maple there, the old man of the wood:
Shaggy, with clefts of shadow in its rind;
Like a deep-bearded deity, becloaked,
Shed down upon him, slowly, what of its mind
Went floating: lightly, lightly; though of late
Time pressed it under centuries of weight.

He touched them all, and moved among their shapes
Like a blind child whom giants might despise.

Yet he was their true copy; so they leaned,
Indulgent to his autumn; met his eyes;
And uttered as much, responding to his hands,
As ever a second childhood understands.

Old Whitey

Old Whitey is not met with any more.
There is no farmer left has heard the tale.
No word of him runs swiftly round the store,
Past tea and twine, past lard and candy-pail.

It is not long, not many men have died,
Since the last dodderer insisted here:
"I saw him! Not a dapple on his hide.
Pure white he was, and clean from rump to ear.

"It must have been at midnight; that's his hour,
And never has he come a hair behind.
There suddenly he trotted, pale as flour;
And silent as a paddock in the mind.

"But he was there, not here"—he tapped his head—
"I saw him in the darkness, making three.
I saw the fetlocks falling, and a dread
Of so much softness falling seized on me.

"I whipped my two, I kneeled against the dash;
I did not look, if looking were the cause.
He only trotted faster, and the splash
Of eight feet grew to twelve without a pause;

"Except his hooves were noiseless—that I knew;
And clean; he watched the others, dark with mud.
He had come here from pastures dripped with dew,
On weightless feet that, falling, tried to thud.

218

"Oh, then it was I pitied him, and looked.
But he was proud, Old Whitey; he had gone."
It is not long, with finger stiffly crooked,
Since the last bent reporter babbled on.

Yet time enough to prove him doubly dead,
This horse that once was flesh and then was cloud.
Now nothing. Even pity for him fled
When the last man remembered he was proud.

The Dismissal

I have not found it strange, she said,
Though it took strength to bear,
That you came back to me so young,
Even to curly hair.

Even to pouting: you whose years
Lengthened to stoic grace.
Something is less impossible, then,
Momently to face.

Momently I listen now
For the stiff alien stride
Of him that was my second rock,
After your father died.

He would not see you if he could,
Nor would I yield a part
Of this that has come back to me
Out of my earliest heart.

You must be ready, my small son,
You must be quick to go;
As when—but it is forty years
Since I stood frowning, so,

219

And opened the unwelcome door,
And pushed your shoulders out.
You must obey me, now as then,
Whatever the slow doubt.

It will be easier, pale boy.
A word from me, and walls—
Oh, these unlit and noiseless ones
Will swallow your footfalls.

Three backward steps to match those three
That brought you where I lay—
Oh, it is hard that company comes,
And that you must away.

There Was a Widow

There was a widow had six sons,
Door-high and gone away;
Not one, returning, but must duck,
Must laugh to hear her say:
"Come in, come in, the room is long;
Lie down, and sleep, and stay.

"Lie down, my tall one, and pretend
Time still is young and clever:
Can make you think, as once you did,
This is your house forever;
No silver key to let you out,
Never, never, never.

"Sleep here, my high one, and observe
How slow the ceiling moves:
Time's meadow, turning round and round;
Invisible the grooves;
Inaudible the engine; dim
The chickadees, the doves.

"Lie still and let their minute-notes
Weave hours and months and years.
It is a net so loud and fine
I will unstop my ears;
Though I have heard the tearing sound
Of one that disappears.

"Time's meadow, tall one, even now
Whirls rapider—is rent!
Were you my own son coming home,
Dear ghost, or demon-sent?"
Then silence; and not one of them
Was laughing when he went.

No Ghosts

The sorrows of this old woman taper
And come to a pitiless, come to a sharpened
Unbearable point. Her dead, her lost ones,
Susan and Jasper—oh, she has harkened
Many a midnight, many a morning,
Many a moon's hour, when the darkened

Barnway and goatshed dropped blue shadows—
Oh, she has watched, this woman has listened,
But neither of those two dead and gone ones
Ever will haunt her. Oh, she has fastened
Shutters and windows, and nailed the doors,
And then she has combed her hair, and hastened

And jumped in bed, in the middle chamber
Safest from thieves. But not from spirits.
For they are wilful, and one that flouts them
Never is certain. Down from garrets,
Up from cellars, or through some crack
They may come anyway, like ferrets,

Growing to something great and slender—
A friendly son, a pale-haired daughter—
Growing for hours. But, oh, not Susan,
Oh, not Jasper. They besought her
Never and never to forget.
But time runs by like clearest water,

Cloudless, childless, and she moans
Because of all her deathly losses
This one, this one must be last;
Because of all night's ancient uses
This one, this one long is withered.
So she wipes three kitchen glasses,

And she sets them by her bed
For three to drink if throats be dry;
Half believes herself asleep;
Never opens hand or eye;
Prepares to tremble. But the twain
Are too considerate still, and shy.

The Visitor

Something about her hair among these low hills,
These small, odd mountains she never had looked upon,
Something about her hair I say was strange;
For the pure whiteness suddenly was gone.

What in its place was there I scarcely know.
Not grey, not gold, not anything fresh or younger.
Something the other side of whiteness, maybe,
Matching an old thought, minding an ancient hunger.

She had come, she said, contemptuous of mountains;
She was born in a level land—and let her eyes
Go following the valley to its limit;
Then steeply among the ridges let them rise.

Now in an alien moment she made out
A people once all moulded to these shapes.
Her people, too; all moulded; and returning
To the hunched land this side the misty capes.

Without our help she knew which way to look
For the grey range that hid the working ocean.
With her white head she gazed, until the sky
Closed, and the valley sides were soft with motion;

And the hills heaved, and mothers called their children
In a slow, wandering voice to come and sleep.
She had grown doubly old remembering mountains,
And all dead time dropped round her in a heap.

Nothing But Death

Nothing but death could do it,
After the world had tried.
We living ones were powerless,
Knowing that pride.

Knowing the stiffness in her,
And dreading such a tongue,
We grew immediate greybeards;
Never were young;

Never, until she altered,
Knew wanting or delight.
Then it was death that taught her
Something of appetite.

Then it was friends and husband,
Ceasing where they had been,
Made her so ancient-gentle;
Let mercy in.

Nothing but death so doubly
Could have been winner thus;
Leaving her sometimes pensive,
Pitying us;

Leaving us low and helpless,
Robbed of our proper prime;
Nothing but death the gambler,
And two-faced time.

We Were Not Old

When the whole valley whitened and the wind split,
Tearing both ways, demolishing direction;
When snow blew up the mountains—but confusion
Tumbled it down again, and whirled its whiteness,
Blinding each dizzy looker—then the dark house
Vanished across the meadows, then the old man
Danced in our minds, a mote, and we could see:

Each of us here could pierce the windy distance,
Each of us here could pity him, surviving
Ages of days for this; all time for now.
He should have died, we said, some pretty summer,
He should have lain down gently in June's lap.
Why should the old back bend another cold inch?
Why should a blizzard whip him who was tame?

Each of us here could think this, and be wrong.
We could not see for snow; and something darker.
We were not old. We had not loved the winter;
Loving its meanness, too, and taking lashes
Hot from the hangman's hand. We were not ancient.
We had not loved, we had not lived with anger.
We had not learned to measure life by blows.

We could not see him smile at all this fury.
We could not see him welcome one more wind—

Sticking his head out secretly and saying:
"Ho!" and drawing it in again, and going
And writing another year down in some book.
Those needles in his brain showed where the page was,
That pricking at the hair roots—that was time.

So while the valley whitened and the sky cracked,
Letting the twofold gale in, and the fourfold
Slither of tossing snow, and the icy voices,
We in our warm bay window pitied the old one.
This was too much, we said. We did not know.
We could not see him crouch beneath the nine-tails,
Grinning and counting the strokes, and crying "Ha!"

After Disorder

In the clear land he went to after noon,
After disorder, after the growing stopped—
The live root is reluctant, and some soil
Still with scorched leaves is littered where he cropped—
In the cool barren land there were two curtains:
Two days a year oblivion down-dropped.

And lest he choose between them each was all,
Each was enamelled glass on everything.
One hour it was pure autumn, and he smiled;
But then that other suddenness, the spring—
Each was entire, betraying nothing under
Of the veiled bone; of time's remitted sting.

To him the fall said nothing of spent sap;
It was no three-month husking, no high-piled
Good harvest; it was color, and it fell
As if the sun's own shadow, gold and wild,
As if the sky's old wine had dripped and spread,
Painting the round-cheeked earth a russet child.

225

Not even May was younger. Both were born,
There in that shining land, without true cause;
Both without use or warning; save that history
Slept the long sleep, and time was free to pause
Twice yearly, with a pack upon his back
From which then grandly spilled these bright gewgaws.

Youth's Country

The little god sat bright across the board:
Man, you could almost see him: and both played—
Oh, both of you in moving swept the files,
Both took and lost, both laughed and were dismayed.
The rooks in place, the pawns upon their meadows—
Old man, it was clear evening when you played.

The country of your dotage was clean lit;
Walls ran both ways; time-sharpened were the squares.
It was a pretty land, a promised garden,
With no hot wind to whirl your snowy hairs.
You could forget the lightning and the rain,
And how your feet once pressed among the tares.

You could forget the mistiness, the danger,
And how at sunset horses rubbed the dusk.
But that was long ago, another country,
Of the wild weeds, the fetlock and the tusk;
Of the uncertain fences, and the way
Thickets at night exhaled a threat of musk.

That was another contest, and the odds
Were huge against you; beautiful the loss—
Oh, beautiful your smallness and your stillness,
Waiting upon the thunder of a toss;
Beautiful your eyes, that could not read then
Even the print of day, the riddle's gloss.

Even at noon the board was big as earth is,
With the far trees like islands tilting past.
You did not sit and smile, you did not measure
Meadows that still were shapeless; and the vast
King's voice, you never knew it as a chuckle—
"Check!"—with someone mated at the last.

The End

I sing of ghosts and people under ground,
Or if they live, absented from green sound.
Not that I dote on death or being still;
But what men would is seldom what they will,
And there is farthest meaning in an end
Past the wild power of any word to mend.
The telltale stalk, and silence at the close,
Is most that may be read of man or rose.
Death is our outline, and a stillness seals
Even the living heart that loudest feels.
I am in love with joy, but find it wrapped
In a queer earth, at languages unapt;
With shadows sprinkled over, and no mind
To speak for them and prove they are designed.
I sing of men and shadows, and the light
That none the less shines under them by night.
Then lest I be dog enemy of day,
I add old women talking by the way;
And, not to grow insensible to noise,
Add gossip girls and western-throated boys.

AMERICA'S MYTHOLOGY
(1939)

These Ancient Walkers

America's great gods live down the lane;
Or up the next block blend their bulk with stone;
Or stand upon the ploughed hills in the rain;
Or watch a mountain cabin left alone.

Gigantic on the path, they never speak.
Unwitnessed, they are walked through every hour.
They have an older errand; or they seek
New sweets beyond the bound of mortal sour;

Or love the living instant, and so minded,
Bestride the lesser lookers—who can say?
There is no man has seen them but was blinded;
And none has ever found them far away.

America's tall gods are veteran here:
Too close for view, like eagles in the eye;
Like day itself, impalpable and clear;
Like absolute noon's air, unflowing by.

They are the first of all. Before the grey,
Before the copper-colored, they were moving

Green-brown among the deep trees: deep as they,
As curious of the wind, as tempest-loving;

As shaggy dressed, as head-proud; and in summer,
As lazy. So they lived. And so they still
Live everywhere, unknown to the newcomer,
Whom genially they watch. And so they will

To earth's end, feeding on their ancient grain,
Wild wheat tips, and barbed rice tops, and the meat
Of mast whereover richest leaves have lain;
Although they pick the tame fields too, and eat

With fathers at the heads of merry tables;
And sleep on beds for change, and sit with talkers.
Whence all their lore; for man's least deeds are fables
To these old-natured gods, these ancient walkers.

Porch God

And there is one with somewhat pointed ears
And new-moon-whitened eyes, and a thin grin;
Which, widening, is witness that he steers
The rocker talk of wives and takes it in.

All afternoon, past the wisteria sprays,
He listens while they tip and tilt and fan:
Their minds the turning mill from which a haze
Of dust drifts over goddess, maid, and man.

It is the dust delights him, thickening so
The air on which his memory travels back
To the first courtship, and a lofty row
Of eyelids arching high for the attack.

It is the past arrives for him; or now,
With sunset gone and midnight in the vine,

It is the clockless moment when his brow
Deep-wrinkles while young secret fingers twine

And two warm heads come closer. Not a word.
No thought of ear-tips here, or sickle smile.
It only was eternity that stirred;
Only a leather cheek that winced awhile.

Driveway God

Where the two mows divide and green hay hangs
Like hired man's hair, wind-parted in the middle,
He sits and listens while a wet door bangs,
And is to them as fingers to a fiddle:

Playing upon their plough-wit while the rain
Drums gustily on grey boards; drowns the chicks;
Puddles in holes, and drips upon the mane
Of the wild workhorse, hobbled against her tricks.

Shower-livened, hear them laugh: the men and boys
Who all a sultry morning mewed their tongues.
Now elbow-loose they loll, that outer noise
Sweet music to their ears; while brains and lungs

Breathe lustily the tune the jester calls.
His body fills the driveway, beam to beam.
His heart among their heartbeats lifts and falls.
Yet none will know him, even in a dream.

Even when they doze he will be nameless,
This antique cider-mind of gods and men.
Shower-drunken, see him sway and pour the tameless
Liquor into Bill, Dave, Mack, and Ben.

Strange Town God

He is the one that meets us where the first
Small houses, dark and poor, lead into light;
And tells us how the features, best and worst,
Make something like a face in country night.

He is the only townsman who would know.
For the lean rest it is familiar chaos.
His love is older; is a breath to blow
Strict lines from curb to roof till patterns stay us:

Till pausing by the dusk hotel, we count
Street lamps, store fronts, red jail; and farther on,
The first white house again, where the maples mount
That high east hill our road goes up—has gone

Each night like this since who knows when? Who'll say?
The sprawled god never answers in his pride.
The question is enough. And shows the way
To hot hamburgers, coffee, and thin fried.

Cherry Leaf God

A dark sky, the wind waiting;
Ladders motionless, and heels
Of pickers vanishing, house-high, among the leaves;

Pails dangled, cherries dropping;
Twigs snapped; and there a limb
Bent low to breaking as a boy, too bold, forgets.

So seems it from the ground; so goes it
Here in the long grass whither he,
Never descending, peers between the green, the red:

232

The hanging leaves, the dripping hearts
He flutters while he swings beyond—
Huge picker, yet he lies, more light than robin's leg;

Lies; leans over Johnny there;
Swings over Nell; and topmost now,
Swings up and out, heigh ho, as seven pickers climb.

Sickbed God

His body wreathes the room like draughts
Of air, of tender air, and wafts
Both pity in and envy: both
The terror and the nothing loath.

This weakness, the uncertain eyes,
The back that will not rest and rise,
The fingers—they are strange as fear,
Though he has practiced it all year;

And would have faltered at the heart
Had he but known the helpless part;
Had he but mastered how the breath
Refuses what it can to death.

The wonder bends him to a cheek;
To the seen bone, and to the bleak
Burned-over forehead. Then the stare.
At which there have been days the air

Sorrowed with him, and the scent
Of older weeping came and went;
And he lay visible, as though
A current should forget to flow.

Garden God

He is the sun-white one that loves
High noon in the bean rows, or as you tie
Gourd tendrils fenceward comes like doves
And will not let your memory lie:

Pecks it till it lifts and wings
In bright near circles by him; floats
Like fire above your forehead; flings
Thought-atoms down, minute as motes,

In front of your eyes, that mingle green
With brown for study, and sift the clods
For such clear answers as are seen,
Not heard. So goes it with the gods.

So too with gardeners when the sun
Pours silence past them, and they hoe
Like men of old. Young though to one
Who still was older, and would know

Why all at once, nobody by,
They smiled and pulled it, or at the bend
Of some hot corn row looked on high
And frowned, reflecting; then the end.

Compass God

Which way this forest faces;
How sharp we angled there;
When the wind struck us, came it
Slantwise or square?

At home now is it certain—
The hay door—perfect west?
Our cousin in the spare room:
Will he rest?

234

He said he had it backwards:
Due south for simple north:
Turned full around, no matter
How he went forth.

There is a tall one watches
And pities our poor eyes:
Except that some are knowing;
Are needle-wise;

Were eastward set when Phosphor
Whitened the oldest dawn;
And are the eyes he blesses,
In babe or fawn.

Crowd God

He is untouchable, or he would cry
In the close press of bodies; he would tower,
Knee-tortured, numb, until his wrath must try
Some awfulness against our herded power.

He is invulnerable, and so he moves,
Unfeeling and unfelt, through what of space
Our lungs and elbows leave him; whence he proves
How alien is the day, how rank the race.

Time was when two or three upon a hill
Came tall together if he framed it so.
He was the lord of meetings, and his will
Was merely that they happen wise and slow.

And still they happen nightly; still at noon
Four walkers in a high wind hold apart.
And still he listens; haunted by the tune
Of half a million others heart to heart.

Horse God

They are new comers too, the bent-necked
Pullers, the head-high starers, the stampers
Of flies: new legs, new tails in the hay.
So he picks a red foal as it scampers,

Breasting the flowers, and all a wet summer
Follows its misty feet; till cold days
Flatten the grass once more; till frost
Barrens the world; till bones of the old days

Show in the sod, and a wind reminds him
Of animals lost and gone. Yet ruffles
The coat of his rusty yearling; blows
All morning between the two, and muffles

The whinny that was a meadow's music;
Mingles the fencewire's hum with a neighing
Shriller and farther away. So he blinks
And follows the hoof-thuds closer, staying

Warm by a flank, wind-tossed at a foretop;
Turns, and approves the eyes. Then wanders,
Free of his charge, all day. But whirls
At sunset to that sound again, and ponders.

Bird God

His study is the way we stand and peer,
Foot-lifted, toward a thicket where the shade,
Sewn suddenly with needle notes, declares
The wing most wild, the feathers most afraid.

Or openly at evening when the swifts
Cut the same blue as ever, when the crows
Rip the last hour of silence and subside;
He watches how we listen, and he slows

236

To a last clumsy pity; leans and waits;
Leans closer still. But still our birds are strange.
Still are we distant from them, and no arm
Of any wishful man can wave exchange.

He walked among them, numbering their beaks,
When the first forest shed them to the sky;
When the first eagle spiralled, and the owl's
Aimed silence wrapped a midnight mouse's cry.

Finches from his wrist looked down for seed,
And dropping to the grass heads picked and ate.
As long ago as ravens—but he pauses,
And pities once again our after date.

Posy God

Wherever a still apron,
Free of the stove awhile,
Descends among the rising
Sweet Williams, and a smile

Inhabits all the sunstrip
Betwixt woodshed and wall;
And then the rapid fingers;
And then the beetle's fall;

Wherever posy fringes
Keep time and darkness back:
Beyond the pump, the smokehouse,
Hotel or railroad track;

Wherever white and purple
Bring a brown hand to swing,
There is a hooded watcher,
Higher than hawk's wing,

Who folds his arms and listens,
Shady in morning shine,
To what he can remember
Of hum and bee whine

When flowery land was larger:
The center brilliant too;
All daisied, and all buzzing
Betwixt sun-up and dew.

History God

The young eyes leave the volume and stray out,
Weeping for greatness gone, but half in pride
That they have been the witness; they alone
May estimate the blank since wisdom died.

They wind among the water towers and pierce
The many moonwhite roofs, like gravestones laid
On courage; one far sepulchre of souls.
The city is long silent; not a maid

Expects upon her window any more
The tap of steel, the leather-handed love.
She has gone in forever; nor do clouds
Burst into fiery grief and clash above.

The eyes return, and words march on again
With the proud tramp of yesterday's green earth.
Brown are the branches now, and spent the sap
Of the well mind that guessed the body's worth.

So one across the room, observing, smiles.
And sleeps; for this is how the creatures grow:
Dim months of pain from out their little past;
Then lighted strength; and then the letting go.

Black Night God

No further doubt now. He is near.
When your throat filled he was the fear.
When though you screamed you made no sound,
He answered, binding you around
With bull-voice echoes. Still they roar,
And when they weaken he has more.
Yet he may pull the quiet in:
The utter quiet, like the skin
Of bat wings beating; or may pause
While you imagine bludgeons, claws,
Snake-bellies, tushes, whetted teeth,
Dew-lapping dogs, and venom sheath.
It is the time he wakes and plays.
His nights, he says, are to your days
As man to son: earth-wiser, older;
And not to be afraid is bolder.
But have no horror now, no doubt.
Keep walking, slow; and when you shout,
Take comfort in his thunder crack.
It is an ancient talking back:
A god that gambols, never knowing
How on your head the fears are snowing.

Tall Tale God

If there were sound, the slapping
Of his reminded thigh,
The chuckle in the treetops—
As old, as high—
Would publish the true ages
Of our best brag and lie.

The colt that jumped North Mountain,
The macaroni dance;
The time we heard the breathing

239

Of boulders in a trance;
Midnight's lost meridians
Wheeling home from France;

The names we roared to rascals
Met on the back-hill road;
The insult at the picnic,
And how the children glowed;
The mica tree; the minted
Dollars in the lode—

He, long ago delighted,
Laughs now a double laugh:
At these, and at the wing-strength
Of so much dust and chaff;
The truth, he says, flew farther,
But not so high by half.

Anger God

Report of thunder words arrives
Full minutes later than the flash
Of powder touched along a vein,
Of muscles whitening to ash.

Inside their clothes he scents the wrath
Like hackles risen; feels the flood
Move like a wall to where the heart
Will not acknowledge it for blood.

It is their hatred holds him close
And sweetens afternoons with gall:
He may not be transformed so soon;
He cannot be wrath-changed at all.

His judgment lighting on a fool,
His heart exiling drone and knave,

His glance corrective to a leap:
No one of these is half so brave.

Nor half so transient; that he knows,
And can predict the clasp of hands;
But sighs a little for the bruise
Of anger tightening its bands.

Haunted God

There is a kind of man can bring
Bystanders round him, one by one
Slow-risen in the dropping dark:
Litter of dead day, husks of the sun.

Bystanders merely, there they shade
Cold eyes with evening; lift no foot,
Advance no heel, as if the night
Broke into stems at its toughest root.

Expecting nothing, there they hang
Long arms like leaves to the finger pods;
As if the twilight were a plant
To step and pluck, and these the gods.

But these are growth of none but man,
Who reaping so, sees not the vast
Mild-shuttered lids of one that must
Himself be harvester at last.

However lone his greatness here,
He too will turn; is turning now;
Is motionless: his tallness ringed
By sudden others come to bow.

Wheel God

Amazement never leaves him,
If gods can be surprised:
The ponderous swift stillness;
Center realized;

The whirling yet the slumber;
Circumference in act.
It is the only plaything
Primeval meadows lacked.

The sun and moon for circles,
A turning arm for spoke;
And lily leaves; but never
This lightness at a stroke:

This over, round, and over,
This oneness till it stops;
Then hub and ray and felloe,
Distinct—whereat he drops,

Distracted, by the mover,
The man with patient hands;
And begs another going,
And barters forty lands.

Schoolroom God

Knowledge here will overgrow
Desk, aisle, and door, and tendril-running,
Climb the haystalks, loop the streets,
And cast an ocean round with cunning.

Knowledge here has outmost leaves,
And cannot live unless they flourish.
Far or near it is the same:
The end must the beginning nourish.

242

Except, he says, there is no end.
Nothing here but news of going.
Nor does green come round again
As comes the circle of his knowing.

Nor if it came would it be his,
That never starting, never finished:
Earth encompassed all at once,
When growth was not; nor since diminished.

Nor since made greater, for its arc
Lives at the limit, past all reaching:
Past all green; past thinnest blue;
Past even white, that time is bleaching.

Burial God

He is in love with patient death
That comes up here so slow and often,
Belling the mourners past the pine
Whose boughs are music to a coffin.

Set it down now, here is the place,
And let a man's words bury man.
But there are two, kind death and he,
Can say what sound nor silence can.

Among the many they declare
How none so upright but will come
The slow way also, through the gate
And underneath the needles' hum;

Up in sunshine, then the halt,
And then these two that no one hears:
Man is everlasting grass
Whose every fall renews its spears;

243

In this box a single blade
Descends to darkness, nor will rise;
And wind is rippling through the rest;
And day is on them shadow-wise.

Music God

He does not hear the struck string,
The stretched voice, the blown brass.
The sudden start, the sweet run
Of notes are not for him, alas.

Then what the measure, what the pitch,
Whereof he is acknowledged lord?
What the laws for less than sound,
And whose the silence whence a chord?

He will not answer save with eyes
That feed on distance all the while;
With more of pleasure here than there,
But most at some remembered mile

Too far for count, or so we say
Who cannot number save with ears;
Who cannot stand with him and see
Triangles perfect after years:

From grove to grove the singing base,
Then on to where two rivers cry;
Or so we say of three clear tones
That in eternal quiet lie.

THE SEVEN SLEEPERS

AND OTHER POEMS (1944)

OUR LADY PEACE ౭ఌ

Our Lady Peace

How far is it to peace, the piper sighed,
The solitary, sweating as he paused.
Asphalt the noon; the ravens, terrified,
Fled carrion thunder that percussion caused.

The envelope of earth was powder loud;
The taut wings shivered, driven at the sun.
The piper put his pipe away and bowed.
Not here, he said. I hunt the love-cool one,

The dancer with the clipped hair. Where is she?
We shook our heads, parting for him to pass.
Our lady was of no such trim degree,
And none of us had seen her face, alas.

She was the very ridges we must scale,
Securing the rough top. And how she smiled
Was how our strength would issue. Not to fail
Was having her, gigantic, undefiled,

For homely goddess, big as the world that burned,
Grandmother and taskmistress, field and town.

We let the stranger go; but when we turned
Our lady lived, fierce in each other's frown.

The Single Hero

This man kept courage when the map of fear
Was continents, was paleness to the poles,
Was Jupiter milk-white, was Venus burning.
The very stones lay liquid with despair,
And the firm earth was bottomless. This man

Could walk upon that water; nay, he stamped
Till the drops graveled, till a sound returned
Of pillars underheel, of granite growing.
This man, alone on seas, was not afraid.
So continents came back. So color widened:

Bands upon blankness. So the other men,
The millions, lifted feet and let them down;
And the soil held. So courage's cartographer,
Having his globe again, restored each mass,
Each meadow. And grasshoppers sang to him.

Christmas, 1941

The millions at this solstice
Who cannot see the long,
The white days coming:
To them no song

Except the death of others,
By bullet or by ice,
In dark Malayan waters
Or where the North Sea mice

Eat hawsers, and a howling
Wind from pole to pole

Brings minute word of bleeding,
Of the surrendered soul;

Of agony that nothing
Is song enough to soothe
Except of million others
The strong death news.

Total War

For the grey temples, for the slippered feet
That bounded such a life as, bent to grace,
Looks brittle now, looks breakable, the word
Nevertheless is shatter; the shocked face

Must fly on other errands, the pale shins
Must brown, must bruise themselves, and all that trunk
Be fragments; the cohesive thought be shrapnel
Peppering cold skies. The sands are sunk

That pedestaled our figure, that as one
Mock granite sounded echo to our soul;
Whose end is now this grit, these million grains
That star a blackened heaven, where no whole

Ever again may shape. Yet, gentlemen,
Be shivered. What was habit now is myth,
Is mumbling. Let it go. A hunger form
Waits round the world: man still, and monolith.

The Lacing

This danger that like wire
Ingathers all to one;
And every morning shortens,
Cutting in and in;

247

This noose about mankind's
Huge waist, that not till now
Felt bondage, or had bled
From anything but blow;

These stays that never stop,
As if an ogre pulled
Whose foothold was the moon,
The merciless, the chilled:

When will that tightness be
As nothing? Or as form
Henceforward to maintain,
To feel as grace's germ?

As closeness to be loved.
Then, when the figure clears,
A sweet incurving line,
Ageless, among stars.

Invincible

Rain, that wets powder,
Slows axles,
Blinds bombers,
Gurgles in grass roots too, and clover;
Steadies the knees
Of flowers, of trees
That soon will surround
A burst battleground.

Rain, that delays
Far meetings,
Fierce onsets,
Thickens the old hide, doubles the armor
Of earth, that will bleed
No more than it need

248

When man the newcomer
Seizes his summer.

Rain all the while
Stores noiseless
Provisions;
Tangles the meadows, jungles the woodlots;
Mixes a meal
Of rust for steel;
Is quartermaster
Against disaster.

The Little Wars

The million little wars
Of peace: the sharpened word,
All night the grassy rustle,
All afternoon, absurd,

The games, the leather shouting,
The white lines to cross;
All over earth the tinkle
Of silver win and loss:

The billion little battles
Of peace are like a sea,
Are like a field that ripples;
And so it still would be,

Save for the one, the War,
The hawk wing that reaches,
Suddenly, and stops
Bravest breath; and teaches

No one now to move,
No one here to mar

The death peace, the waiting
On one, the overwar

That would not have us glisten,
That loathes the little waves,
The trillion, the green trembling
Peace returns and saves.

Halt

Halt, commanded bombers,
Stand where you are, said the brown
Shoulders hunched and coming,
Said the hoarse throat of war.
But the world's people, balanced
On bitter feet, grew sore.

Hobbled, they heard the aching
Bones in their own arches;
Heard them angry together,
And guessed the consequence:
Some day, and soon, regardless,
The interdicted dance.

Some day, and soon, resuming,
Some day, and high, the lift
Of heel and toe, of lightfoot
Shuffle; and then the click
Of forward, backward bodies
As earth relearned to rock.

The Loud Hour

Two vessels of his heart converged in wish
For the loud hour of peace: the bells, the pounding

Of the free blood again, the ears reopened
After such hush, after such lull of sounding.

But left and right they differed; one received,
One sent the stream of longing. So, and sinister,
One hope was but for silence's cessation:
At any cost an end, though death be minister.

But the right side said no, endure it yet,
And let it be our shout that splits the quiet.
Victorious, we live to swell the singing,
And the top note is ours; nor shall we sigh it,

Sister, as now. The music to be made
Is yours and mine, so be you fresher, fatter
In courage, and tune all your strings to toughness:
Like mine, against millennium's long chatter.

What Now to Do

What now to do on such an earth
As bombs belief and bullies mirth?
A hint of more, a laugh at less,
Brings in the torturer whose dress
Is tin and bullets; and his pride
Counts merry millions who have died.

Yet think and risk it, in the way
Of the first will. On such a day
Men toppled mountains, and their grin,
Outlasting light, still lets it in
If faith is under; and upstands
Mind's old muscle, made with hands.

Conquerors

It is a kind of love, insisting
After pursuit upon surrender;
After defeat the willing death
Of everything but woman's gender:

Woman if it is hers to dote,
Rising to receive again
The palm that felled her; were it woman's
Blood that blesses regimen.

Believing so, the angry thrust
Repeats itself; and grows more wild
As something on the ground refuses,
Red, to be with horror's child;

Bruised, to be the happy bride
Of bludgeons, of affection's fist:
Insanely falling as the man,
The woman, and the babe are missed.

Not to Fear

What is it, not to fear?
What is it some can see
Beyond the battle's edges,
Distant, cool, and free?

It is a thing not altered
By what will happen here.
Whoever bleeds, that body
Blessed is and clear.

That person—for its wounding
Were no less grief than ours—

252

Keeps interval: remoter
Than Thrones, Dominions, Powers.

And cannot die; which opens
This alley to our gaze
Wheredown the foeman, startled,
Sees nothing but moon maze.

Epidemic

Panic has feet to fly with, and the ground
For purchase; no lost motion as it mists
All the low-lying places. It is the first
Infection, and most terrible. The bowels
Are close above, and comfort every growth.

Yet all the while another link prepares:
From head to head, solitary, the winging
Of one free thought, corruptless, with no power
To enter the sick region. It is weak
With cleanness, and with beating the white air.

Then, miracle of reason, the dry lines
It drew through lucid space become a web
That the heart loves, the strong one close below;
Which heaves to it; and hears the nether curse
At courage's contagion, no more slow.

Headquarters

Bleak order, and impromptu
Quiet: the made hush
As telephones intensely
Listen, and files flap;

As on their hooks the papers
Straighten, gravity's yawn

Relaxing the bent word:
No prisoners taken;

Smoothing to a smile,
Erroneous, the warning;
Or to disaster's placard,
Death window in a wall.

Who knows? Not they, the orderlies,
Not he, lieutenant-colonel
Of cavalry; who whistles,
Meanwhile, to far horses.

Adjutant, he sends them,
Anciently, the high cheer:
The Regiment; and taps out
Courage on a cold desk.

Crisis

Now that the seas are limed
With fire, and a fathom under
Water spouts prepare,
In the salt cold, their thunder;

Now that the land is warm
For the due rain, for the seed,
But war birds, dropping sulphur,
Drone, and the borders bleed;

Now that the ways are strangled,
Now that the best has been,
Where lies the hidden pathway
Verity walked in?

Still hidden; as when blue peace
Clouded no other sky,

And would not name our death dates,
Nor answer how and why;

Nor happen along these pavements,
Lightening with news
The feet wherewith we stumble
Still, cursing our shoes.

Status

What would I have then
Who fear the great change?
Domino centuries?
Children less strange
Than these are: identical
Lambs of the range?

What would you have,
Who implore the disaster?
Looms to be locked
When the right thing is master?
Selvage all fixed?
The coloring faster?

Neither could bear it,
Catastrophe's loss.
Look far enough,
There is nothing but moss.
We would shiver like geese,
With no graves to cross.

The Doomsters

The difference they prophesy,
If utter, disappoints the fear;
Apprehension only starves,

Staring at too far a year:
Feeding upon too changed a woe
From any that time's children know.

If relative, a law decides:
From this to that, so many causes.
Whereupon the fear grows fat;
Then midway of its feasting pauses:
Recognition stales the fare
Sooner than panic can prepare.

Too strange, a blank; too known, a foe
Familiarity refuses.
Experience lies down with doom,
That sleeps again, as history uses.
The difference they weep and sing
Is nothing, or is everything.

Cycle

What shall be said of the lucent, the going;
Then of those that come in, swart swine from the fog;
Tooth-fronted and terrible: See? their hindquarters,
Not to be seen yet, say danger is young.

Danger is young yet, but haunches will form
And hind hooves have purchase in, hard, the daylight.
What shall be said then of shoulderblades going:
There! At the boundary! The small of their backs!

Fine-waisted, they taper, they burn in the sunset.
Slow they go out: afterimage of grace.
But, swift all the while, this breasted inbruising
Of mist hogs who froth because flanks are not free.

But they will be. Is that what is said? Is it cycle?
These in their turn to be goers, be pearl,

256

Be clarity fading, millenniums on,
While other forequarters, and hairy, foam through?

How Far to Heroes

How far to heroes from this spindle stretch
Of scrub that leans together, looking in:
Ostriches to storm, except for sand,
For darkness; all is blinking and sun blind.

Continents of sapling save for scorn,
For promise; all atilt, all mutual pleased.
How many scuffling leagues, how many pits
Of years until the selvage of sweet wood,

Of horn, of hardness, separately old:
Oh, organ tall the harmony none hears.
Within there is but each, and each more hoarse
Than others: heaven's pillars, groaning on.

How far and deep to heroes where the touch
Is not of neighbor skins but sky and ground;
With night between, the perpendicular,
The splendid, lightning cicatriced and sound.

Defeatist

He is so proud, recalling
An assignation once
With Utter, and Impossible,
And him that hunts
Pure Death out where it corners
Accident for dunce.

He is so pleased, approaching
Those torturers again;

257

It is a second confluence
With regimen;
And last, if Chance's courage,
Dark, dies in it then.

He is so cool, arriving,
This master of despair,
That he can miss the hectic
Whereat they stare:
The burning cap, in an angle
Empty except for air.

Myopia

Pity for them, the coasters
Past premonition's reef
Who then but toss and shudder
In shoals; whence their belief
That all the sea is shallow,
And only sand is grief.

Who coming near, can measure
None but the present threat;
Who do not see the high ground,
The grimmest danger yet:
The tower that must be taken
After the waves forget.

Pity for them, the tremblers
Too far away from truth
To know its drought and hardness;
Indifferent, uncouth;
And how not to have tried it
Crowns all other ruth.

Holiday

For this one day much thanks, and for
Its wetness, spreading east from war
To where the rains rise, orient cool
Against the hectic. Man and fool,
I dip and splash, I tangle feet
In knots of sorrel as I greet
Pure greyness coming, on and on,
And do but think it is our dawn
Against the fever's black and red.
I drench my knees, I hunch my head,
Banishing all bruise of sound
Except this whisper, mound to mound,
Among the grass roots: "Man and child,
Woe upon him in the wild
Noon and midnight still to be;
It is not over, finding me."
Nor do I say it is the end.
Not yet, my freshener, my friend.

Pond in Wartime

So far from sirens and the fear of wings
That fold not, so content with the one foe
Whose hunger, not whose anger, flexes plumes
And hovers: how explain it, the cold luck
That keeps five trout I know forever gliding,
Ever in weedy corners hunched and hiding?

I see them there as though the summer still
Kept green for me and warmed the vacant fields
They knew not, spreading sideward from their pool.
Nor do I have it now, the crossing land,
Nor can I bend, arriving, and count backs
To the slim fifth, the sluggard, the late born

Who dreaded me too little, and I laughed.
He would not know it now if I should name him
Lazy; no one crosses the brown stretch
And shadows winter water. Even if there
I shouted, they are dozing, the deep five:
Safer than luck interprets, and more live.

God Sends a Cheerful Hour

Most terrible the time, with nations falling
In bloody clusters, blameless. For what man
Wanted such woe? What imbeciles of might
Hunt in the heavens, torturing sweet space?

It is no time for icicles of tales
Tinkling our curiosity, for death
In little, for detective voices narrowing
Evil and good to footprints in fine snow,

To sediment in goblets. Yet it may be.
In the saved hours of Saturday, what harm
In miniatures, in frost work on one pane,
One mirror no more window to lost worlds?

For so man sees himself there, by a fire,
Preferring the old law, the immemorial
Fragment, and of those that love it still
The victory. What hurt if heaven dreams?

New York Unbombed

Pray never. But if no one hears,
And noise is coming, and cold tears,
What highest cornices elect
Will weep them? And does stone suspect?

Patience, quarried and set there,
So far from ground, so poor in air;
But then so proud among the gulls
And the white steam that puffs and lulls;

Patience, vain of its keen edge,
Will shatter, and some blunted ledge
Mournfully to returning birds
Will echo our own broken words.

But which up there, and who below?
And when the night? O, if you know,
Atoms elect, make loud reply.
Fate comes double if we deny.

Matins

Where do wars go in the night?
How can strong pain disappear?
The fiend that swims unseen in us
Slips to what cave, the torturer?

Biding the hour of sweet sunrise
When we are tempted—ah, but he starts,
He stings us then, as into bliss
Of an old time we think we wake.

Of an old day before this devil,
Finned in our depths, was parasite.
So in his darkness he resumes;
And morning at our face is mocked.

Armistice

Rumors of peace, rush otherwhere if policy
Stinks in your breath, if someone's advantage blows

Still so straight and so strong, so headed for somewhere.
This is no place at all, and we are no people.
Here is the wind's end, turned to the weaker voices
Of a last victory, death words of a war.

Purposeless whisper, straggle this far if you can,
Then fail. Surrender is music here, exhaustion
Is trumpets that others will blow, standing above you
And filling the world with silver. See, we have waited
All the war years, and this one is ancient already.
Let it die with you, here where the last wind sleeps.

Not to be tricked by truces, not to be pleased
With the half brass of triumph, now we are waiting
On death words: The giants, weary, have laid themselves
    down.
Come of your own will, rumor, as sighs escape,
As humming. Nothing is lost here. Sound is reborn.
Listen. Your last is our first; is silver; is gold.

Whom the War Muffles

Stones of the street are notes for musical boys
And for their girls complaining. Manholes clank
With the running and catching up and the marching off:
Bravado. Not a youth of them but yells
Somehow the moment's meaning, blood or bells.

And age's image of them, second children
Huddled in casements, happy, their shrunk heads
Citrous with grin, tacticians of far terror:
Never an ancient there but has his day
Like a dry pebble kicked, nor canted away.

Whom the war muffles is the middle ones,
The guardians in prime. For them the peace
Longest had been laborious. What loss,

262

What premonition! Which is why they go
More noiseless in their anger, and more slow.

Bad News

Bad news of battles, now as long ago,
Is spasm in a far limb that can travel,
Swift or slow, no matter, and entrap
The home brain with woe, with springing fears
That atrophy old thought, that crack the plan
We felt by. So our fathers in us, numb,
Lose voice, and all the lines that tightened forward,
Certifying futures, loop to the nether
Fog. Where is it now, the high anchor?
Where, until we learn to send again,
Level into darkness, such a word
As no grandfather knew: as strong, as straight,
As angry, but our own? It will be strange
Even to eagles. But it must arrive.

To Arms

Woe is on them whose sons, whose fathers
Die. And double the woe when leaders
Buckle, bending to shame, to defeat,
To heaps on the ground, distorted. Woe,
Woe if no hero stands, father
To fathers; guardian of the gate.

But triple—or no, past numbering—woe
When even the gods go down, captive
And thunderless: grandsires of the blood,
Progenitors of every heart
This day that beats to death; no echo
Possible in that cold heaven.

White cities with their hundred walls,
Ports, palaces, and sunset
Fields, fallow to West; and famous
Fathers: these can fall, but never
Those. Therefore to arms, lest woe
Be utter: the last deafening wave.

Schooltime

How difficult to learn that sweet warm land
Can lie in danger, the deep sleep of laws
Be death itself should enemies rip through:
Should the mad foe, fantastic to our myth,
Come soon, before we fear him. It is cold,
Knowing; it can shake us to remember
That what we have was once not had, that time
Broods upon plunder. This was ours; and dreamed,
As we did, that a year would never end.
A bitter scent, the solstice. It is hard,
Hearing the wind as human. To defend
Everything, how monstrous; taking more
Than blood to do it, more than seventh sons,
Than weeping. It requires the going home
To history, and the will to understand:
Nothing is not watched, no acre dozes
But a wild eye is on it. Where we dance,
Death was; and will again be if too slow
The lesson. Ring us in then to our rage.

The Unknown Army

We are the civil fathers, the poor necessary
Clerks of a fair world great death besieges.
Close and far the danger; ships and houses
Equally expect ambush; the foe's line
Is not one thread, is fabric: a cold cap

264

That tightens. And the young ones have departed.
In companies destructive, daring fate
To find them, they are deepest in the net
To rend it; and they will, and the free skull,
Warm again, should praise their blood forever.
We have not gone, nor may we; except darkly
In dreams—oh, then we bitterly deploy,
We venture; and arrive at the most difficult
Crossways, where the frost is quickest formed
On heroes. Which anonymous we are,
In nightmares—oh, the cursing in those thickets
When with no moon we come; only with heated
Hatred, searching midnight for a nerve
To sever in the arm that weaves this skeleton
Cloth, this whited silence, this green country's
Shroud that in our sleep we shear away.

Observation Post

Three hours of it with Jasmin, Smith, or Barnes,
With nothing coming over, though we listen
And peer; three hours with Hallaway, as the moon
Pales at the full, in August, at sunrise;
Three hours inside a closet on Hart Hill,
A midget room that moistens at the panes
When the midsummer fog slides here from Cobble,
Castor and Pollux failing: three slow hours
In latter night, far set from Armageddon,
Safe on a knoll till sometime, till the Antipodes
Cracks, and sparks shot upward circle the world
On wings. Three creeping hours, and yet the clock
Ticks swiftly too if talk weaves over the face
Its milk web, if an old acquaintance whitens,
Suddenly, to fullness before dawn;
To absolute, to candor, and no personal
Pride. For who is anyone, and where
Is being in the vastness of this watch?

That Day

Even if wars to come sleep warm and small,
Deep seeds in action's body not yet born;
Even if horror then, sometimes the now
Looks fearfuller; is absolute forlorn;
In its own form seems final. Whence we say,
Sometimes, there is no day beyond that day,

That days of bells, of prodigal high sirens
Howling, when the harbor whistles burst
And dancers on the street take off their heads.
For the last idiot singer shall be first
On such a morning, leveler of men
With girls, and with a boy come home again.

Sometimes. And yet the germs, the little ghosts,
Still haunt us in their unmade mothers' blood.
And if we think, they grow; as time itself
Ticks in the dark, and horror in the bud
Stands giant high, a forest doomed to fall
On that day's children, armistice and all.

You Went Along

Who does not move in stream,
Who does not set full sail,
Is pitiful tomorrow,
Having outlived the gale;
Having his hollow body
Solitary and still.

Survivor, yet not hearing,
Aeolian within,
The captains of that tempest
Hum how death had been.

Their own. But someone's heart
Is throngèd with those men.

Is strung with ancient voices
That no wind can stop.
"You went along, and drank
With us the bitter drop.
And live. Be then our music,
Comrade, till you sleep."

April, 1942

How terrible their trust, the little leaves,
The odorless, uncurling into love,
The warm day round them, careless if they curl.
It is not there for them; the great clock swings
Regardless, and the circle kissing sun
Sucks its own pleasure, ruthless, noons away.

Yet now they thrust their spirals into air
As into lacy morning, into April's
Charity that hath no aftercold,
No cunning to deceive. So thin the gift,
So thoughtless. What caresses is the same
As leads me forth this fiftieth light spring,

This never to be doubted, this wide open
Wanness like a waking out of sleep:
Pure sleep, on nothing solid; for the beams
Are houseless, and the heaven I arise in
Had no hands to build it; not an angle
Shows, or mark of pressure; nothing nailed.

The leaves and I put forth a fiftieth life,
Blinking with infant pleasure at old winds
That weaken to our play; at piles of sun
That topple on us, downy; at no danger

267

Anywhere, except that bliss can die
From innocence too absolute for fear.

So ours will end; the tips that reach and trust,
My half-shut eyes in lazy April, May,
Face a far cold; the other side of time
Wrinkles, and black edges form like frost
On the known circle, turning; soon and sure
Some month will shape its mockery; then fall.

Yet that's not it. That is not why my spring
Is nipped already, even as I smile.
For them the natural death, set slow in change;
Mine murdered in the morning: a heart stopped
Even before it capers. I remember
No such May as this that men prepare.

It is the month of powder. Rage's blueprint
Mocks the soft green and scaffolds the free sky.
The dome is ribbed with rumors: a tall skeleton
Rears, insulting vacancy. Offensives
Rafter our thought, that misses one more childhood.
The pastures are all closed, and noon comes down.

To wish a May December, and war done,
With victory, and buds another year,
Is nevertheless to batten hungry Death,
Who more than flesh devours. He feeds on thinnest
Things: on freedom's fragrance over a wall;
And takes this bitterest bite out of our time.

THE MIDDLE CREATURE ❧

The Middle Creature

Man is the one most caught
Between not knowing and knowing:

Neither a beast today
Nor archangel tomorrow.

Man has most need of order
Lest he be nothing now;
So builds to the farthest future;
Yet least is lord of the years.

No more than a mole he hears
Time coming; and yet he must.
He is most fierce, believing,
Most musical in trust,

Most melancholy, honoring
The blackamoor, the change
That taps at each foundation;
That topples all the plan.

Song

To be at all, you birdlings,
On this or any bough,
Were cause enough for singing
Summer is now.

It is. But very being,
In so much cold and dark,
Is reason for your music;
That time will mark;

Saying it is for summer
As something more. As this:
When all of space, enormous,
And feathers kiss.

The Near House

Let us have deities, he said, but not as indulgence
Of a sick appetite: rare sweets in the sauce.
Temper the palate first to custom's bread,
To country wine, to fear, and a ritual faith
Repeated till it cloys not; till with knowledge
We sit again, plain brothers at the board.

Let us have gods, he said, because necessity
Clothes us; not as feathers about the brain;
No secret silk, no masking. Let them be wool
To the weather, custom's cowhide, country skin
That the sun ruddies, fearful, and tornadoes
Thicken as we kneel on sacred sand.

Let us believe, he said, in the near house,
The needful, with its rafters of raw pine
Hewn to the custom; thatched with country thunder,
And windows on the meadow side of fear.
No satin tent, no cave, no ivory windings
Burrowed away; but stoves, and an oaken door.

If Any God

If any god comes any more,
In guise, disguise, or body's glass:
Eternity's water, which the eye
Ignores as air, alas, alas;

If any god. But the One does.
Nor is He difficult to see;
Overflowing into men
Who walk and talk the common way.

Not many, though. Millenniums run
Before a heart receives Him whole.

270

And even then the least aware
Is that same substituted soul;

Who is more modest, being strange,
Than we that cultivate our good;
And hope, and measure, and compare;
And cannot fathom one clear deed.

Song

The devil in the world maintains it,
But not for charge or hire.
He drinks a little blood, but he drains it
Out of our gross desire,
That save for the surgeon's hand
Had been too fat to stand.

The devil is abroad for martyrs,
And burns them where he will.
But never does he know he barters
Live ashes for our ill,
That in his veins will die
Ere any phoenix fly.

The devil is a long time coming.
Envy is cold, and creeps.
Ours is the sudden drumming
Of anger that oversleeps;
And will again, till the day
Good grows too old and grey.

Truth Waits

Truth waits like what? Like a spider?
Like the sickle of the law? Like a sword?

Like an old maid's eye? Like a needle?
Like pox? Like a worm in a board?

Truth waits, but it has no witness;
Weaves, but the cloth is a cloud.
Past its impalpable edges
The center is napkin, is shroud.

Did you think it would open and show you?
Like a nut? Like a shell? Like a brain?
Like a tight poppy pod? Then the bursting,
And the little dry sound like rain?

Truth waits so long that we perish
Between two webs of the text.
The biggest jump we can manage,
From this one, misses the next.

Manufacture

Man, breeding, hoards his form;
The principle preserves
Of tendon and of vein,
And the convenient curves.

What then he makes is less.
The brain and hand contrive
But tangles of themselves.
The soul is more alive.

We cannot send it on.
Complexity's machine,
Though terrible and large,
Is at the center lean.

The soul, that can but be,
Is gift from such a one

As owned it all, nor lost
The little we have won.

He made it with the bones
That box it, and the mouse
Of mind that nibbles nests,
That scampers in the house.

He made them all, but most
The soul, that nothing makes.
It only is; as water
Is in seas and lakes.

Virtue

Beauty, strength, and goodness
Are such a triple gift
As would undo a giver,
Himself not three.

Not three, and yet one only;
As where the sun meets ground
Something is undivided
That numbers cause:

Roots, that from their sources
Bring up a single life;
Which waves again as many,
Branching in wind.

Comeliness and courage,
With temperance at the top:
A tree, but with this difference:
No limb is lost.

Or if it is, the others
Have withered at the stem;

That is no longer justice,
Saying I am.

Is Now

Eternity is not to be pursued.
Run, and it shortens; arrive, and it is shut:
Forward or backward, nothing but the folds
Of time; that you will tighten, fumbling them.

Eternity is only to be entered
Standing. It is everywhere and still.
Slow, and it opens: stop, and it is whole
As love about your head, that rests and sees.

Eternity is now or not at all:
Waited for, a wisp: remembered, shadows.
Eternity is solid as the sun:
As present; as familiar; as immense.

Death's Hands

Death's hands are clock hands,
They are not laid upon us.
They never leave the pale plane
Whereon they swing and warn us.

They are not jointed to extend,
Disturb a step, and stop it.
They are indifferent who goes,
Upon how rich a carpet.

Who the companions, what the pace,
No couple has recorded;
Nor even, when the tick arrived,
Have they jerked and nodded.

274

Simply that on their center set
They sail again, serenely
Wondering if one not here,
With time and them, is lonely.

The Penitent

When I did that, he faltered,
I had forgotten this:
Soberly his wave,
Including himself and us,
Seemed to encircle air,
To room an invisible house.

Whence had I stolen strength
To free this hand of its form;
Hunting alone that night,
Naked, the queer harm
Of tiger, of crooked goat,
And envy, queen of the worm?

The strength, and then the losing
Of any least passage home;
Liberty, then feeling,
Angular, the shame
Of visibility's body,
And the prevented dream.

No Such Power

Authority is instant as a light
That breaks, it is as soon as any sound
Arriving, it is needle quick, nor quiet
Past the sweet voices saying Sir, I will.
Obedience is honey that old bees,
Storing for such a moment, had kept still

275

In sweetness; so it opens cell by cell
Its summer, and announces the pure gift:
Agreement. It is sweet, the mind says,
To take truth for master; no such power
Was anywhere till now, when all is seen,
Heard, tasted, when the sharpness enters in,
The shapeliness, the terror, and sweet voices
Tame it with their murmur of I will.

Most Difficult

"The laws that if I love them set me free,
Father, are they lovable?" "No tyrant
Made them." "You are none?" "Except for power,
And more of that than any man supposes."

"More than a tyrant's?" "Yes." "Then how to love
What threatens us?" "I do not threaten, son,
I promise; and invite you to look long
At all that shows. It is a part of me."

"All the seen world?" "The least of it that stands
Is law, and does not change; I do not change."
"But there is more." "Myself." "Whom not to fear
Is punishment?" "Whom not to love is death."

"By scimitar?" "By ceasing. I remain.
I am." "And I can be?" "Consult the shown,
Believe in the unshown." "Thus tyrants speak."
"And I." "It is most difficult." "It is."

Authority's Love

Come near, my chick,
Authority's love

Is delicate too;
Is donkey, is dove;

Is no less mild
Than beads in the grass.
If you will confide,
The terror will pass.

I am shedding it now,
So you can be sure.
Come near, my downy,
My little demure,

My pleasantest thing
With the clear, small eyes:
Dew that can make
Great suns to rise,

Like me, so loving,
Like this, so warm.
Stay but a little.
Authority's harm

Is fable, is heat
That never once slew
Those that were willing;
Those that I woo.

Irony

Whether this knight was mad no fool will know.
The slipper was not found. The centuries blow
Black dust above the bones of one whose best
Man's heart there is no legend to attest.
Fine the tale that tells it: brings the prince
Clairvoyant, and the judge who will convince
Time's jury; brings the student to the stone

277

And reads it. Happy issue. But the groan
Never to be delivered: there is glory.
Nor is it dark, nor is it transitory.
Untellable, it gleams in rocky places
That the night knows, and dreams upon the faces,
Weary of words, that wisdom calls her few.
It is the oldest music, and most true.

Witness

When one to another talks,
A third gets up and walks
Round, round them or between,
Inscribing what they mean.

They do not hear him there.
But neither does any pair
Of things we know for two
Feel the fine thread come through.

One shore of the ocean thinks
Land here forever sinks;
Leviathan's west eye
Counts no companion nigh.

Never do objects learn.
Nor we. Our tongues in turn
Utter the old mistake:
Time is not yet awake.

He will be? Yet he is.
The moment was none but his.
And should we beg it again,
He will listen and write. As then.

The Elect

The blinding shield, the gun no foeman dodges,
The disappearing ring, the magnet cap,
Boots that leap a league to cut off danger,
Detective nerves that never even nap:
Heroes are helped men, tutored in a tower,
Minions of luck, and we should loathe their power.

What virtue can be loved that is invincible?
This one's breast is iron, and arrows bend
Like inchworms when they strike. That one's immortal;
Shatter his bones and see how soon they mend.
Heroes are propped things. Take away the staff,
And what are they but we: the childish half?

But none of us can be so. There is the answer.
Achilles still is magic under the skin.
The wonder is the choice. Of all its children
He was the one the world took refuge in:
Lest a spear find its heart, whose safest place
Still was a body, still was a burning face.

The flying steed, the horn that withers distance,
The helmet, the unpoisonable shirt,
Bullets from the hip, and sweet tobacco
Scenting a room with clues for one alert:
Heroes are earthlings armored against chance.
We sing their names, and death forgets to dance.

Materialist

Who is more idiot noble
Than he the burning man
Who disbelieves the fever,
And proves it not his own?

279

If heat disfigures foreheads,
It is a general fire:
So, as the atoms redden,
He dampens them the more;

Scattering into greyness,
As old as any world,
The very sparks that loved him
Before his nature quarreled.

And loves him still for madness
That makes him run and cry
Against the flame's illusion,
Lighting him to flee.

Revolution's Tether

Mankind the seventh morning,
At Saturday sunrise,
Puts home and school behind him,
And into country flies
Where even roads go under
And only hills have eyes.

Then on; and yet remembers
The turning of a street
Where master and slim pupil,
Courteous, would meet;
And where the trolley measured
Time; and rain was sweet

On house roofs. So, with pausing,
An intersection hums;
Deep in the carried person
The carried city comes;
And domiciles the truant
Thorough millenniums.

How We Shine

Why does it jog so slowly, the one rumor
No idiot doubts, no sage of us denies:
Death's hand is last? The newest breathing infant,
After so many autumns, after such toil,
Will be tucked in with him who at this moment
Clutches at sleep and has it; nor will the linen
Live: the wood, the feathers; dust is king,
Is carpenter, and builds an invisible bed.

Why is it none believes? For I do not.
The rumor limps unfed from house to house,
Fantastically poor: the last relation,
And least when he arrives. We send him on
To others, and continue at our wealth,
Our brilliance, hoarding every coin of thought
Save this one: boxes rust, and forehead bones
Powder in wind after enough of years.

How so much ignorance of what we know
If man knows anything? And does he then?
One says it is our essence that we serve,
Our nature: something timeless that our accidents
Anchor in good gravel so that sun
Can dance upon the deck and dry the sails
Eternity had mildewed. Some day heaven,
With a god mind for mirror. Some, alas,

Say nothing, it is nothing; what will hymn
Our virtue, and record our coolest strength,
Is what preserves an echo when no wave
Survives of the clapped sound; the cliffless earth
Were ivory smooth, they say, to one so tall
He held it whole, contemplative, in hand.
And that is how death holds it: nothing better
Than a poor ball he juggles up the void.

It does not matter, maybe, how we shine:
For deity, or lest Idea drowse;
Or if it must be, nothing. We do brighten
Bravely. Inward, outward, is the beam
Defined, and not a soul but has received it
Sweetly: O, how suddenly in children
Comes the tart taste, decisive, a uniqueness
Honoring each name that will be lost.

For name, taste, tune are lost: peculiar gold
We treasure, in a skeleton whose cracks
Will let all mystery whistle through and out,
Some day, though now we secretly exult,
Counting its numbers, magic to our solitude,
Potent unto seventy springs of pride.
We do not move the less because we know
That stillness: even a **rib** shall be dissolved,

A socket be a circle that no finger
Traces: mathematical to blood.
But who now sees himself as one invisible
That day? Who is determined in his love,
His duty, by a measurement of mist?
No man. Wherefore the wonder. What we know
We conquer, half in courage and half blind.
How beautiful, how blessed, both the ways.

THE DOUBLE LIFE 𝒫

The Double Life

Unnamed and named, two men in me,
Mankind and Jack, the root, the rose,
Something unseen, something awhile
Here, thorned and pungent, rash to the wind,
Then there, then where: two men in one,

Nicknamed and nameless, twine together.
Each for himself, yet one is two
When scent is servant to understanding.
Each for the other; and so the old one
Honors the young one, brief, unique.
How would the world know either was here
Except for an image doomed to go?
How could it say whence came this red
Except for the dark unheard idea?
Body and soul, particular both,
Depend in terror each on each;
So wave as one in double pride:
Myself, and he that never died.

Felix

As far as eye or tongue, as far as odor's
Fame, as far as, desperate, the breath
Can hollo, jumping hurdles of defeat,
I send it, my unkillable, my simple
Hope that no one taught me. Whence it fell
No darkest star has stated; why on me
Is secret still, and suns for all I know
Lick hidden fields to find me; but I stand
Confessed and never lose it. Even now,
As far as polar bears, as far as huts
Of tealeaves, as the Amazon's old mouth,
As tombs of rotten emperors and spicy
Saints I send it blowing, my one nameless
Joy that will come back to me, will come.

Autonomous

In jealousy of cause and pride of plan
He thinks he made himself, this happy man.
He was the decider; picked a year,

A womb to grow in, and a hemisphere;
And when he walked was master of the choice
Who fathered his first gait and tuned his voice.
Of all earth's people to its oddest ends
He summoned these few to be his natural friends;
From out the mist of women he contrived
The stepping forth of one whom then he wived;
And now that sons repeat him it is skill
Rewarded, it is accident of will.
The maple where it stands is proof of seed.
He knows it, and can measure by its need,
Among so many neighbors, a trunk's tallness;
And by its shade the aftercomer's smallness,
Dwarf to its sire. Such things, he says, must be
If soil decides. But he is not a tree;
And thinks that he was present in the dark
When skin was chosen over root and bark.

Samaritan

Lugubrious, his legs
Bore tragedy for burden;
But such a one as shepherds,
At sunset, on their shoulders,

Hopelessly, uphill,
Bring home to fire and udder;
Except he never came there
And put it down and rested.

There was no mountain fold,
No thatch for what he carried.
Lugubrious, a great plain,
Ahead of him forever,

Was lamb cote, was crib,
Was where there must be comfort;

Except he never, halting,
Abdicated kindness.

Caritas

Charity in him was like a lark
That sang as he ascended, and to us;
Was a long hindered joy that, free of itself,
Tumbled upworld, wooing our gravity.

Not the black ground he left, nor any ounce
Of his own weight was grit within the song.
Pure stream it was, and strange. For all at once,
Arriving, it awakened our old love.

And not for him. For us, whom we discovered
Pleasing as we listened down the sky.
So there is none more perfect we can name,
Knowing ourselves in honor of his joy.

Protagonist

No minion of the word,
This excellent hot man
Hied farther than he ought,
Or than a mortal can.

Maxims hissed beware,
And caution all around
Tread circles, but his will,
Past any figure bound,

Plunged; and now the dark
Refuses him its tongue;
Nor any angle known
Tells him where is hung

285

The south, the north of virtue,
Or where the limit's gloom
Is harmony by darkness,
Reordering our room.

Mutual

I envy most a man
Who says he envies me;
Who is not so contented
With change as I would be,
I think, had I his luck
Disordering degree.

For him tomorrow's distance
Dies in a waste of time
Where neither long nor short
Nor soon is, nor the chime
Of lately wedded minutes
Striking a silver rhyme.

All noise for him or nothing:
Silence, or such a buzz
As everlasting bee wings
Make, or as he does,
Roaring above the music,
Gentle, of algebras.

Of which he would be master,
Pairing the now with then
As I do, he whispers,
And so should all men.
But what I covet meanwhile
Is that chaos again.

The Reflection

Whose head is this that hangs,
Chin downward, changing self
To something less than ghost:
Nonentity in glass?

The mirror alters more
Than death does, than oblivion.
This person never was:
Sobriety possessed him

Sooner than lip, than pigment,
Sooner at least than soul.
Unless the idiot watcher
Is we. Then no one is.

So meetings are mistaken?
Something less than masks?
Identity a rumor?
Quicksilver asks.

The Diarist

What is he doing there in the dark hour,
The cold hour his bed, laid back, begrudges;
Covering the foolscap to its corners
With a slant hand reflection never smudges?

He is racing the remembrance of a day
To it far end, that sleep would sponge away.

But does he think to rescue what no man
Possesses? It was not his own to save.
One of a hundred million bleak sunrises.
One of oblivion's blanks. A bubble, a wave.

287

He does not find it so. He loves too well
What passes not to pick it from time's hell.

Fool, if he thinks one coming will comprehend.
His pearl will be a pebble, grey and small,
That men will kick before them down the path
Repeated, with none wiser after all.

He does not race with others. He is rare
And lonely. Leave him, lordamercy, there.

Shortcoming

A word corrective is a word of love
Till the voice alters and a stranger speaks;
Who can no longer see the little fault
As a dear blemish like the lily's streaks;
Who wants us blank, and afterwards will chide
Even the charnel white in which we hide.

For such a note annihilates our ease,
Whose odd unconscious colors flee the cold,
Thinking there is a warmness in quick death:
If that was all, love never will grow old.
It will not, save it learn to lose the way
As once it did in green and speckled May.

For this false winter pleases it no more
Than we ourselves find honesty in frost;
In the hurt coolness which deceives itself,
Pretending pride when dignity was lost.
The only warmth is love's, wherein defect
Blooms unaware and is uncircumspect.

Song

A twenty years of having
No one, soft, but you
Was having something better
As time unconscious grew.

As he forgot to notice,
And noon yellowed his beard,
I saw that it was never
Him we had feared.

But two, and white, behind him:
Ourselves, not knowing how.
Then, beautiful, those blushes.
But one September now.

Silver Wedding

In the middle of their life he risked it:
The rough palm, and the tongue
Possessive: You belong,
Wild heart, to master me.

It was dangerous, her wonder,
Her waiting in the dark
For change in him: for tears
Taking it back, for beggar.

But he kept king, and daybreak
Brought him more than scowls
Obedient. She had grown,
Grim girl, into a queen.

Who smiled. And it was strangely
Then he wept, for time

289

Wasted: mutual lightning
Only with grey hairs.

For Granted

My sin was not to measure,
Until your sudden tears,
How time, that fattens fondness,
Stops eyes and ears;

How much my boasted silence,
A false and bitter good,
Was faith this side the senses;
Was habitude;

Was leaving you to wonder
Whether I felt and saw;
As if, with faded letters,
Love were but law.

My sin was my assumption:
The dead end of praise;
And cause, until your weeping,
Of our desert days.

Reconciliation

Impossible the words:
Forgive me. Every hour
Of sullen silence laces
Higher the stiff tower,

Pride's monument, that never
Must tumble, or we cease to be.
Yet every minute how it grows
Topheavy, and we are not free:

Braced there to hold it so, with sidewise looks
And paleness, all our strength gone into lie:
We do not love you. No? But stand away.
There! Nothing fell. And we cry.

Old Style

Sweetly, augustly they sway, the great dancers,
Straightly advancing, then low the laced bow;
Swiftly the shoulders recover a stillness;
Dip and rise, ladies, the moment is now.

Slenderly, sweetly it slows, the high music,
Thins to a single, then mute violin;
Something more solemn is due at a doorway:
The emperor ages who soon will come in.

   There he is, ladies, decrepit in grace,
   Here he comes, courtiers, servant to you.
   Read in his wrinkles the terrible word:
   Time is doorkeeper, and nothing is new.

   None the less curtsey; redouble the file
   That he will acknowledge, limping between.
   Dip in a rhythm as if the wind's wave
   Ran over young grasses and all things were green.

Sweetly, augustly resume the loud measure,
He on the dais relaxes and stares;
Swiftly pretend he is prince, he is laughing;
Mind the bassoon, how it rides the wild mares;

How the mirth in its growling is opposite caper
To flute notes that fly, to the scream of the strings.
Yet gently. He watches. Time and the emperor
Give the best odds to obedient things.

Down World

No animal so flattens to the ground,
Hiding and sliding, as clear water will:
Its belly nowhere different from the back
Of the sloped earth it hugs, head downward still.

Spineless, it takes all shapes except the serpent's
With his neck hooped, when anger in him stares.
Water is faceless; for it leaves its features,
Spendthrift, on the very stone it wears.

Men cannot pick it up, the stubborn creeper.
Jointless it lies, head downward, sucking sand.
Yet they will try; there is no older plaything
Than gravity delayed, than banking land,

Than the filled gulch, than levelness extended
Till a wave backward laps, till boats can ride.
So the dam holds. But deep at its foundation
Heave the sunk shoulders, not to be denied.

The sodden eyelids, weary of themselves,
Dream of the crack to come, the pouring through;
Then the parched bed, abrasive, and the close
Going once again down world and true.

The Pond Ages

Where the brook turns a tile brings down four inches,
Under the poplar roots, and splashes it here
At the tip end; then it broadens, and then it quiets,
And pours out over the stone dam by that building.

292

Since the first gush descended, and the hardpan
Held it, and the new clay banks were soaked,
Earth has found out about our store of water,
Still as it is, and deckled its trim shape.

The fringes time has planted run uneven:
Sawgrass headlands, bullrush promontories
Where the frogs leap, and undermirror ferns
That tadpoles tickle, growing to be great.

And so the bottom, layered with slow silt,
Softens, and a green cloud daily gathers
Till the frost comes to clear it; but brings leaves
And sinks them: food for worms, and, God knows whence,

For the three trout a bird one noon was proof of.
See? The dead limb? We looked, and a swart kingfisher
Flashed, doubling our knowledge. Yes, we have counted
Three that can show for sticks, then off like shadows.

So the pond ages, letting its edges in
And filling with things that thicken it, that slip
Like earth's own fingers, busily over each other,
Greedily stitching solid what was free.

Gift of Kindling

Between the pond and brook
A table of fern land,
A sweet, surprising lawn
Where two trees stand:

Wolf maples, that were cause,
Deep shaders, that could bring
This miracle to pass,
This delicate wood ring

293

Whose center now is hearth;
We laid those lichened stones;
And many a summer night
We picnic on the bones

Of that old buck, the silence,
Or of that fawn, the fear;
We burn whatever creature
Was immemorial here.

Yet with the glade's forgiveness.
For not a time has been
But dry limbs, dropping,
Have said, let smoke begin.

Old Orchard

Hardly a trunk but leans,
Hardly a top but holds
One bony limb, one curving
Tusk: death's head in spring.

And there it thrusts all summer,
And there it waits in snow
For feebleness sufficient:
Snap, and the sudden plunge.

And such we burn, with praises
For purple fire: the fuel
Of kings, we say; forgetting
The king himself is there.

Or pieces of him. Slowly,
Grandly, apple dies.
Cords of him stand barren
Still among the leaves.

Tons of him, as heartwood
Still in sun and wind,
Will heat the bones of better
Choppers scarcely born.

Trimming Time

With clippers, bush hooks, and bent-handled scythes,
And six-foot sickles that a tractor pulls,
We persecute small trees. A hot hay time
Anticipated this, the August hour
When cold dew on the walls invites the upstart
Brush, the fringe of would-be cherry forest
Falling now with summer, willow shoots
That only will be sticks beneath the snow,
Laid there with starting maples and the nipped
Young master oaks we missed another year.
We persecute these infants of a wood
That never will be. Worshipers of shade,
Of great trunks up the mountain where no man
Could meadow, here we hold our open own,
Here hack and slaughter. Not a head must wave,
Not anything shall stand above these stones
Domestic, these diagonal old rows
The sun long since accepted; these clear fields,
Wedging high wilderness that we may be.

Third Growth

The little pine grove, trimmed of its ground branches,
Lets the eye through, a thread among those needles
That sew a green cloud fast to fern and rock.
In their own shade the stems, so black and small,
Are pillars of weak steel; yet nerved enough,
And tempered, to attach for soft eternity

Feathers to earth, wind music to the swell
Of soundless, of grim granite; which the drop
Of other needles, browning, will spread over,
As the grove grows, with carpet for fox feet,
With compost for silence. So the trunks,
Increasing, will be columns that hold up
A weightless, waving mountain; and no man
Will speak of stitches then. This is the time
To see it, to send vision dipping through,
And then downhill by meadows to the Hollow's
Bottom where the bone white steeple stands.
This is the century for that. Dead villages
Glisten. And the pine begins again.

Wet Year

Six of the other kind were one too few
If this, the dripping seventh, is alike
Complained of. Numbers have no magic in them,
Maiden, if you do not take this mold,
These swollen doors for benison; black days
For blessing. They were asked for, and are given.

The foolish grasses, rivaling the forest:
See how they overreach themselves, and fall
In a green swale that dew will drown tomorrow.
Look. The glade side of every sunless rock
Is heavy with small mosses, smooth or curled;
And some of them are rusting into seed.

The meadow there was sun enough to sickle—
That was before the flood—is high again
As colt's knees. Walkers in it make a music,
Heel and toe, more heady than dark ale
To an old ear remembering last summer;
Or any of the six, the sunburned years.

Not grateful when no trout dies in the brook?
You never see them, even; mud comes down,
Yes, daily. But the level of soaked earth
Sinks daily, nightly; for the sponge is filling.
An old foot loves it, under. Which I know
Is nonsense to the April in your veins.

Walking the Boundaries

We of this place who prowl its rectangles
Of pine, with their dominant oaks, their maples
That plume an old mountain, are less all alone
Than we think. Four on one side of a wall;

Or a wire, sometimes, that pierces the trunks
Where invisible staples stick in the heart;
Or nothing whatever up ancient stretches;
Only a line the memory draws:

Four of this place, presuming its limits,
Prowl in a thicker silence for something
That watches, something that hears, that presses
Hard on the wall, the wire, yet bends

No boundary: living and dead, our neighbors,
Nodding and prowling too, their confines
Never confused: identical ends
With these, the sunless, the solitary.

Bailey's Widow

Still there, as if the weathered house
Were tomb and low memorial; no shaft,
No sky thing, but a hugger of such earth
As he with horizontal craft

Knew webwise; we remember how he kneeled
And studied every silver herb afield.

Still kitchen table bound, by windows
Wiped to keep the headstones far and clear;
Still huge among her trinkets: catalogues,
Gilt cards, rag balls, and cooking gear,
She sits, the clock a goddess overhead
Less watched than watching, like the distant dead:

An old man under gravel, sidewise
Peering; and she rubs the pane to see.
Yet more that he may feel how still the cats
Prowl round her, blinking up; how three
Small dogs dispute the blessing of her lap;
And how she sometimes nods to him by nap.

Berkshire Express

Starting gardens, whichway from the tracks,
From the May train, look shivery this morning.
Yet there they spread, complacent to the cool,
And hug what they have buried: happy graves
To the hot germs within that swell in rows,
That steam in secret: embryo July.

A little further and the engine climbs,
And all outdoors is tilted. We between
Go barren as the first explorers went,
Sowing but echoes. Sound is all that sleeps
Up the cleft world; and sleeps forever, folded
In a brown skin that June turns into green.

But then no more than green. The buried rock
Hides nothing but itself where under moss
It centuries. What foison could be here?
Nothing but surface sundered into cubes

And rondures. Stubborn death it is, and beautiful,
Balancing those yielders by the sea.

THE SEVEN SLEEPERS ॐ

The Seven Sleepers

The liberal arts lie eastward of this shore.
Choppy the waves at first. Then the long swells
And the being lost. Oh, centuries of salt
Till the surf booms again, and comes more land.

Not even there, except that old men point
At passes up the mountains. Over which,
Oh, centuries of soil, with olive trees
For twisted shade, and helicons for sound.

Then eastward seas, boned with peninsulas.
Then, orient, the islands; and at last,
The cave, the seven sleepers. Who will rise
And sing to you in numbers till you know

White magic. Which remember. Do you hear?
Oh, universe of sand that you must cross,
And animal the night. But do not rest.
The centuries are stars, and stud the way.

Northern Philosopher
(Kierkegaard)

Not the world's width, but a deep vein somewhere
That disappointment lowered his mind to;
That cruelty opened, offering passage;
Sanctuary to injured sense;

Not the tall sky's excitement, spread
With provable numbers, planet and arc;
Not the known heads of men and their similar
Deeds, building to history, binding

Virtue to book and cross: not these,
Not upper light, but the sweet dark charmed him:
Tunnels he moled in, nosing the source
Of tributary, of stranger sorrows;

Rooms he was warm in, curling himself
In contemplation of scents and moistures.
Rare to the world he was. Yet many
Listened and wept. His thoughts were tears.

Northern Minstrel
(Kafka)

Having no end to sing, he sent his heroes
Nevertheless and swiftly: similar arrows
Into one dark where snow was the conclusion;
Where going on was target; piercing which,
More snow; or if a castle, the piled chambers
Tilted as they climbed them, and no top.

There was one room, he said, where sat the king,
The ladies; but his words were crooked stairs,
Were passages through dust, away from music;
Save that a cold laughter in some corners
Lied, and secret kisses, feigning fire,
Delayed them among nymphs, and ogres roared.

Having no sight, he sped them from his bow,
Nevertheless, and feathered the good dark
His forebears, singing farther, had shot through.
Then the warm goal. But not for him that heaven.

300

He did not claim conclusion, or recover
Any of all those hearts the long cold killed.

Emotion's Moralist
(*Spinoza*)

Betwixt his scorn and pity
Mankind continued host
To strangers always coming,
To travelers so lost
That even whence they started
Was legendry in mist;

Was proof, with name's announcement—
Envy, or Wrath, or Pride—
That in these bones they haunted,
Sleeping as if afraid,
Tomorrow was but the misery
Yesterday had hid.

For him they were not stragglers.
He called them, and they marched.
And if an odd one, giant,
Surprised him, he but searched
Till reason ranked and damped it,
And only we were scorched.

Latter Day
(*Tacitus*)

Historian, these hills
Mock a late race, remembering
Tall senators at dawn
Walking the dew ways.

301

Where have they gone, the guardians?
Emperor is thief, and matrons
Muddy the sweet spring, selling
Daughters for salt song.

Legions long forgotten
Rot by the marshes, dreaming
Still of their brave return:
Ah, the white city!

Historian, you envy
Him of the old days, scribe
Of the first conclave, witness
Of Jove and the moral wars.

What if he came, that chronicler—
Listen, tragedian—seeing
Gold in the rubble: one
Live soul in the cinders?

Covetous he broods,
Even now, in his low tomb.
When was such tale: The single
Saint of the forum?

TIME EDUCATES ❧

Time Educates

Time educates to tears
The very heart it teaches
Wisdom against wounds,
That courage bleaches.

Buried under braveries,
Still the spring is there.

And only now it flows;
Only now the rare

Waters of age can circle,
Inwardly, the sight
Of half a father's days
Pressed to one night;

Of candle bed; of altar;
Of him coming here
Whom tyranny kept distant,
And exile drear;

Of two stood to marry,
And nobody missing
Four that fine death
But yesterday was kissing.

But yesterday. Yet time,
Deceptive, dams the vein.
Years overflow.
Memory is rain.

Transparent

They are more fierce to conceal it,
The young ones, their love,
Than a seen animal, laboring
To be a dropped glove,
A leaf on the ground, a nothing,
Looked at from above.

They are more fearful, and go
At more shortened a pace;
Edging to windows, to doors,
Then back into place

303

As if they were no one: orphans
Of chance, of the chase,

Of the world's end, wooing a corner
Where heartbeat can die.
Yet it lives, and it outlasts the danger.
Wit, the world's eye,
Already is occupied elsewhere,
With possum and fly.

Girl with Frown

One turn of such a head,
So fiercely knowing how;
Yet fiercer to proceed,
Obeying orbit's law;

One smile from such a face,
Thoughtless, between storms;
Yet thoughtfuller to crease
Against new drawn alarms;

One notice by this child,
Queen of a dozen years,
Were rubies and brown gold
From Montezuma's jars;

Were plenty, were fivefold
Increase of happy herds;
Save that it is withheld
By right, and in our beards

We know it, the cracked elders
Who creep and duly sing
Diana's bow and Balder's:
The sempiternal young.

Not for Him

Not for him, surely,
The neat waist, the loose tucked
And negligent limbs.
Not for him, certainly,
More than the vision.

A year, and the sweet knot
Tightened. Then melted.
Nothing there now
But the smallness; and downward,
The liquefied members.

Something so suddenly,
Waywardly figured:
How can it last?
Form is most fleeting.
Art is most long.

His then the watcher's.
Others will come soon,
Bearing that shape.
Not for him, meanwhile,
More than idea.

This Boy and Girl

This boy and girl, having no secret knowledge
Of passion's plan, go easily by each other.
Both ends of the stony street receive their footfalls,
Dying duly as hallways, taking them in,
Are tacit as two notes no string performs.

Not yet. But music readies, and tomorrow
Comes the first pluck, comes the first separate trembling
Of two dark houses distance will sweetly measure,

And modesty, the mute, will redivide;
Then ecstasy, time helping, sound as one.

Until that day they go so easily homeward,
Each to a stony end, it looks to the stars
Like challenge: music dared, and fate insulted.
It is not even so. Neither has dreamed it,
Passing, neither is occupied with war.

Neither has heard necessity, like wind,
Come howling down the pavement; felt a nerve
Go twanging; wept for sweetness that will follow
As two dim porches, reconciling distance,
Dance all night, and happy cobbles hum.

Family Prime

Our golden age was then, when lamp and rug
Were one and warm, were globe against the indifferent
Million of cold things a world contains.
None there. A light shone inward, shutting out
All that was not corn yellow and love young.

Like winter bears we moved, our minds, our bodies
Jointed to fit the roundness of a room:
As sluggish, and as graceful, whether couch
Or table intercepted, or if marbles
Clicked on the floor and hunched us into play.

How long? I do not know. Before, a blank.
And after, all this oldness, them and me,
With the wind slicing in from everywhere,
And figures growing small. I may remember
Only a month of this. Or a God's hour.

Yet I remember, and my father said
He did: the moment spherical, that age

Fixes and gilds; eternity one evening
Perfect, such as maybe my own sons,
And yours, will know the taste of in their time.

Remembering Our Father

Remembering our father, said those children,
Those four in motley shadow, his death shade,
Is having one, himself a rich rememberer,
Whose mind was never present when it played.

He said it was, and lugged his laughter up
To the bright moment's mark, and let it fall;
But even then we knew; and recollection
Roars it: he was never there at all.

What he remembered then was an old world
We only saw as absence in his eyes.
But it renews itself, and it will spread
To be our landscape now if we are wise;

If we remember well, and try to see
The forest edge behind him, the rock field,
The walkers and the runners; and that lord
Of death who shaded brightness with a shield.

The Anvil

We shut our eyes to punish, lest a piece
Of the hurt boy fly hither. With no pounding
He would be lump, we say, be pig of iron,
Be puddle of poor ore; so this is just.
And yet we blink the hardest of our blows.

Had we angelic ease, eternal art,
It were a cool delight to stand and tap,

To trim, to tune him: elegant each downstroke's
Difference, oh how swift the temper then!
But we must shut our eyes, not being sure.

Not having angel art, we may but maul
And worsen, may but crack in devil's halves
This one, this ours, this ingot that we heat
And forcep. Or we may do otherwise;
May pound him perfect. Which is why we blink.

Goodbye to Children

Their laughters darken as I go;
Through double windows I detect
How they distrust the ogre train:
Its errand all at once suspect.

No need; I shall be home one night
As it is written in our books.
So they are wrong. But the strange thing
Is how to them the leaver looks.

Like something lost, their waving says,
Like something stolen, roars the steam.
Oh, these are wrong. I do deprive
Myself of more than they shall dream

Till they are big enough to count,
Till they distinguish proper gold
From what I go this day to bring;
And coming home with it, am old.

Lest He Be Jealous

Will they be there, the two
Long-legged, the almost grown

Colt sons, whose tossing heads,
Whose tall eyes dwarf the negligible train?

They will be, no volcano,
Whirlwind, intervening:
No God's act, all good,
All gracious save it would not wait an hour.

A minute. For the last
Curve lurches, and the whistle
Blathers. Let us praise
All acts, lest He be jealous of our bliss.

Let Kingdom come, let depots
Drown. Did He attend?
He did. The slowing jolt,
The water tank, the town—and there they tower.

January Chance

All afternoon before them, father and boy,
In a plush well, with winter sounding past:
In the warm cubicle between two high
Seat backs that slumber, voyaging the vast.

All afternoon to open the deep things
That long have waited, suitably unsaid.
Now one of them is older, and the other's
Art at last has audience; has head,

Has heart to take it in. It is the time.
Begin, says winter, howling through the pane.
Begin, the seat back bumps: what safer hour
Than this, within a somnolent loud train,

A prison where the corridors slide on
As the walls creak, remembering downgrade?

Begin. But with a smile the father slumps
And sleeps. And so the man is never made.

The Boy Is Late

What corner now, and do no shadows
Jackknife out of the areas? Lamps,
Bring citizens to flank him; cold,
Kill silence in that upright street.

All pounding loud, but one among them
Keeping this destination: narrowed
To this snug lock that no one hears
Receiving the safe key, the sawtoothed

Nothing that yet is all. For the sleepers
Sleep not; pillows are poison, and clock ticks
Rumor the worst. Ah, when the comfort,
The sedative sound, the boom of a door?

What avenue? Go ask the night.
Yet be here too for the sidewalk scuff,
For the sudden turn, for the entering brass.
It is a needle that stings to bliss.

Cards in Convalescence

Bright black and red
Of the four cut shapes,
Of the curlicue king
And the jackanapes,

Of the mistress queen,
Of the marching spots,

Skip to his bed,
For the evening rots

And light falls dull
On the counterpane.
Turn up the lamp there,
Over his brain;

Toss him the numbers,
Plume his eye
With ace and bower
And the blood deuce high;
Please him with danger
Delt in a trey.
So goes a long night.
So comes day.

As Birds

On such a day as birds, migration mad,
Prickle with wind excitement, and small roots
Of quills too long forgotten sting with north,
With south, with far away, this shapely man
Lost arms, lost legs; was but a bar that swung
Oddly upon no center, missing home.

A thousand miles to west, and buried well,
The mother magnet waited: horseshoe heart
To one, rectangle now, whom distance drew
Still swinging; through defiles and over plains
Still pivoting; too jerkily for peace,
Too rhythmlike for altogether lost.

Because, on such a day as birds behold
That valley and that windvane, he with a click
Was there. Figure was finished; the dear curve

Completed its old self as iron to iron
Sped kissing, and the shape that once he had
Slept, negative, across those poles of breast.

The Second Leaving

The rails that clicked him homeward
Ran from an older home,
As waves return to headlands
From the first foam.

And now they plunge to slumber,
And grizzle where they toss.
But what they left was whiter;
Was color's loss;

Was nothing, whence he blundered
Longer ago than now.
But age will not remember,
Nor death say how.

Age Is Age

Age will not let me keep my vow
Never to age, I know; or even remember
How I once picked the mythical old man
I would be if I could be.

Not mulish: that is the myth I choose:
Never to balk, insulted, when the young ones
Prop me, never to mock their sweet mistake
Of too much crutch for the cripple.

Never to bridle, never to snort,
Never to jerk away, denying the nearness

Of friendly death; who, if I think him so,
Will give me the last freedom.

Which pride would squander until one day
Death in disgust recalled it. Let me not lose it,
Boasting. And yet I shall. For age is age,
And has itself to remember.

Midland

Under the great cold lakes, under the midmost
Parallel that Lisbon too lies under—
Vesuvius and Corinth, Ararat,
Peking and Chosen, yellow and blue seas
Enormous, then the redwoods, then high Denver—
Under the wet midnorth, under cool Canada,
Swings my own West, directionless; the temperate,
The tacit, the untold. There was I born,
There fed upon the dish of dreaming land
That feeds upon itself, forever sunk
From the far rim, from crust and outer taste,
Forever lost and pleased, as circling currents
Swim to themselves, renumbering Sargasso
Centuries a wind brings round the world.
There am I still, if no thought can escape
To edges from that soft and moving center,
That home, that floating grave of what would fly
Yet did not: my own boyhood, meditating
Unto no end, eternal where I was.

Aetat 50

Will it be more of this that century day,
If day at all, if number, if I live,
Will it be this and better: what I know now

Doubled at least? I say it must, the learner
Willing. But there is chance, and damp decay,
And horrible dry eld. I know, I know;

But these things too have I, sometimes unwillingly,
Learned. Shall I rehearse them, or do all men,
Halfway between the crying and the cracking,
Honor with me the school a boyhood scorned?
No matter. It is my account, beginning
With ritual's beauty, learned at my father's grave.

No apple cheeks, no pouting, but a full
Brown figure that refuses to grow old,
Having no age; except it is not young
Nor tattered; it is all that sweeps between,
As the sea does, adding its salt to raindrops,
Then sweetening earth's crust from shore to shore.

Ritual, in repetition's colors,
Borrowing the brown, the sometimes grey,
Ritual, in repetition's language,
Borrowing that monotone, declares
How wide it is between our woeful boundaries,
The coming and the going; and how clear.

Ritual, the numberer, the namer,
Diagonals that wilderness; and where,
Passionate, lines cross that it has graven,
Upon that point a standing man is watch tower
To the whole waste; as I, when music sounded
Over my father's goodness, seen as one.

The beautiful full figure, life as lasting
All of the way, intense, across a square—
A circle, for the fierce line of the West
Bends to the East, go tirelessly enough—
The brown, the leather guardian, the grey
Unkillable tall person of our wisdom:

Him, at a death, a funeral, I witnessed
Where he looked on, careless if I mistook.
Younger, I would have; old, been too familiar
With the composite eyes. Which now I carry
Outward of mine, and pray that as I wither
The words too, commencing, will be long.

from

NEW POEMS

(1948)

THE SUN ONCE ROSE ह๛

The Sun Once Rose

The sun once rose from off a watery couch,
And soaring daylong, sank to cool again.
The eastern, western seas were limitless,
Worlds of deep dew, a double and old home
Dry light was not a friend to. But he climbed,
He curved, and he descended. So our fathers
Fabled him, gold ornament of skies.

But now he never sleeps. No dark, no wet
Receives him. Hot and high, he burns his way
Forever round the world, whose distant oceans
Parch him. He himself is cause of noon,
Monotonous. The ball he sees below
Turns the same satin side with every solstice.
Daylong is what he lives in; and would die.

Yet not for him the sweetness of such dusks
As rose an hour to meet his father, falling.
Delicate that death: a labor's end,
As dawn was end before it. Then day lived
As men do, twixt eternities so soft
That womb and grave are blessings. Or would be
If so they lived as once the sun did, soaring.

317

When Will True Love Again

When will true love again make delicate difference
In the deep place where old foundations dream;
Where stone on stone they lie; yet they can slip,
Can settle, even in sleep; earthquake adjustment,
Answering our joy. When, single again,
Will a good heart cause all the world to shiver?

Or evil; for the children of men tell
How once the stain spread on and on: to stars
That darkened, and down, down to the same old stones,
That shuddered, their vast surfaces set grinding
And groaning as the universe endured
The peril of one face that hid the fiend.

We have our labors still, and our fine loves.
We come on others, tiny in the shade,
And muzzle them. Antenna to antenna,
It is a tender meeting. But no more
Do the stones know, the faraway great fissures
That once decision's thunder shook and filled.

The Stranger's Tale

Two ages pursue each other under the sun.
Either outlasts memory; no chronicle
Tells of their alternation. Yet old songs
Sing of the wondrous difference when gods
Gather again; when men, lone in the wind,
Are suddenly revisited, and guardians
Temper all effort, sowing the earth with ease.

Then apples are eternal; beasts are friends,
And drink from the same never icy waters.
Then do no hearts dispute; each eye is ample,
Owning as much of azure as it sees,

318

As much of soil, of thicket. Where grapes hang
And melons lie, where generous birds make music,
There every foot both wanders and keeps home.

In the gold age gods are as close together
As the ripe plums that cluster; are as close
To movers in the meadow as moths come,
Kissing the daisy white. But they are huge,
These fathers, and keep faith with their soft children,
Those souls with no tomorrow, those unmeaning
Foster folk that play at being men.

Or so men say when deity, departed,
Leaves them to dig and harrow; brings the frost;
And huddles certain of them in wild cities,
Woeful yet necessary, whose hard laws
Build peace instead of music. For the tune
That sang itself is lost, and torturers
Wring harmony from rock, from gravel's word.

This is the time of man, the terrible,
The artful time, the beautiful with risk.
And none then will exchange it, though pure songs
Sing of the wondrous difference. No man then
Would save himself more easily. The time
Is his alone, to dignify or mar;
His only gold is rule, is government.

But the first age is waiting, or the last,
When men again shall be as sparrows are,
With providence for watcher, and no skill
To ruin what is round them, or to scheme
Amends. There is no peril on the path
For deity's dark foundlings. Whom we sing,
Remembering, then with sharpened gaze forget.

The Case Is New

Good monarchs have been monarchs of themselves;
The ruler was a thing that could be ruled.
But rare the case, and now that princes perish,
How will the many govern save by good?
And how then will they look both out and in,
Command and be commanded? For the case
Is new, it still is new, and no man standing
Misses in wind rumors of sour success.

For the good king was stranger, and his crown,
A sunborn jewel, dazzled the clearest eyes.
He was a soul descended, and men rose
To meet him. So they swore. That time is gone,
With all of its grim witnesses. Another
Comes; the many now must learn to rise
And overflow themselves. Yet what the yeast,
And whence, and how to keep it sweet within?

For centuries, forever, it must live,
The sweet germ within; and each must bear it,
A small seed in his heart; each be a king
Commanded, and each able to command.
There never was such task, there never trembled
Such a huge world of trouble being born.
For each separate cell must keep its smallness,
In a good heart that nothing overgrows.

The multitude is lesser than its members.
But it can swell to monster if the seeds
Within it be not sound and know their size.
Let each enlarge with the good king for limit,
The ruler and the ruled. Then the huge whole
Is leavened, and long happiness appears—
Oh, when? And by what magic will all men
Discover friend and stranger in one room?

The Long Life and the Short Life

The long life and the short life differ dimly
In the midwood where even noon is dark.
Do those about to die see both, and clearly,
Through the late hour when weakness is at work?
In the far field of sunset do they show
Like two unequal mountains, tall and low?

Too late to choose then? Is it middle still,
The wide road of that wandering? Does space
Slumber as now? Is time, the dreary ocean,
Tempestless yet: eternity awash?
Then I shall look about me in the wood,
Even by dusk, as if distinction stood.

And here it does if anywhere, I know:
Now, in the aisles of famous afternoon.
There have been thoughts that found it, under thickest
Mosses; there have been heroic men.
They led them both, the short life and the long.
Mere woodsmen, yet their wit was double strong.

They never shut their eyes against the shade.
They loved it well; and loved the outer light.
It shone in them all morning as they moved;
Unmentioned, for they would not walk apart.
Unsung, but it was what the others heard
Whenever, in still gloom, distinction stirred.

The little and the great life lie together
In a warm place eternity protects:
Midwood, among more branches than are dying.
For some of them cannot. This doom that cracks
Is timely; it is not for those that see
More difference than death, and doubly be.

Slow Learning

Intelligence all day upon us,
And every day, like snow in dark,
Inaudible, arrives unseen,
Impalpable; yet leaves its mark.

Or does it? O you dreamless skies
That flake upon us, do we change?
That shake upon us, do we show
As anything but dim and strange?

Still looking downward, as you do,
But from no zenith which were cause,
Are we so ignorant of white?
Do we break all of mirror's laws?

One face that turns, and taking you
Full on its water, on its glass:
Is it enough? And can you wait
For other centuries to pass

Till ten are there, till thousands shine,
Till all the lower world is love?
It has been long already, Light.
Or does it seem so, Sir, above?

The Sun So Old

The sun so old, the day so short—
What is it gives the heart a start
As stumbling I look up and see
This dome that was not made for me?

Why not before, when just as much
My life was poor, time's life was rich?
Why is it even truth must trim
This moment of my knowing him?

For there he sits, immense at last,
And disappears into the east;
And overstares the stiffened bow
Of one too late at learning how.

Little Places

Such power in little places:
The petal weight a coil of jelly moves,
And snails have conquered beaches.
The worm, with neither horn nor bone,
Plows acres.

Prometheus down a cold crack:
Rainstreams freezing, and the granite
Splits; as smoke of sister water
Pushes the long piston; and a copper
Hair holds worlds.

The Yes all year awaited:
Thinnest word, and yet it peoples spring
With mighty houses, lived in; No,
Enormous night; as when the bud bursts
Or does not.

Such power; with plants depending,
Thunder, and small men, and now the spark
Whereby a town is merry.
The end, that neither feels nor sees,
Thanks nothing.

When the New Growth No More Is Green

When the new growth no more is green,
And every summer's foliage fails,
The horny stem, the original,
Stands boastfully for all its ills.

When the sweet edges of doubt go,
Those gentle borders shy to the word,
How arrogantly spirit speaks;
How happy that the sound is hard.

But at the center even then
The dozy wood prepares to die;
And something honeycombs the bones
Of him that swears green truth away,

The curled, the tentative, that lives
Amid extremities of leaf,
And is more firm in any wind
Than he, original and stiff.

Death Indeed

So close death flew that when I walked away,
Still trembling, still stopped about the heart,
I walked as two men, and the livelier
Was he that had been stopped for good—yet came on
Standing, and revisits now all places
With someone lesser, with myself, the seen one.
Nobody notices. Which makes me wonder,
Had the wingbeat been final, whether death,
And death indeed, is not the walking on,
Just this way, of the selfsame legs and shoulders
And the fool's face of yesterday; yet lighted,
And with each weakness gone. For him I see
Is perfect in decision; him I hide

Is errorless, is angel. And I ponder,
After so many deaths, how full the world
Must be of his companions; for till then,
That day, I heard no rustle; and now, even,
Nothing I do reveals him. It is death
Indeed that will unfasten him, my friend
Whom no one else can see; and someday no one.

Question

Do certainties, like persons being doubted,
Suffer? Solid persons, by their lovers
Doubted? There is difference: substantial
Flesh, that can survive the darkening in;
The core is gone, but color still in streaks
Says outwardly that something, someone is.
Are certainties so dogged against death,
Even unwillingly? Oh, did they ever
Hang there, did they ever in their turn
Be anyway, and only with our love
Be happy? Then be mocked with a bright form
That wore no visible wound accusing faith?
Do certainties, like persons, have both soul
And body? Or someday is our oblivion
Enemy to all? A sudden sun
That shrivels what was nothing but thought shade?
Not even nerved, like night? Not even mold?
Do certainties, like lovers being doubted,
Suffer? Solid lovers, that die twice?

Dirge

Time, with its terrible old hunger,
Devours our bodies one by one.
Still it is famished; looks for more;
And finding it, feeds on and on.

Whole pastures perish, the green custom withers
That nourished our once feeling souls.
Change cannot die, but change forgets;
Landscape can lose all its hills.

Our fathers buried more than flesh
When they lay down in their tall tombs.
So we grow sleepy with the slow
Death of bright meaning in these rooms.

Tools tarnish, and mansions settle,
Absurd, in swamps that pride had paved.
Justice sits on, but where they stood,
Those orators, salt water waves.

The private peace that all might have,
Or most, or some, where is it now?
The teeth have taken the last wall;
Moonlight is naked on your brow.

Statesman

Courage. If such a crowd,
More than you ever saw,
Seems wilderness—mankind's
Great plains of residue—

Remember as you go,
Taking yourself entire,
That two are there: the waste,
And he that would explore.

You also can be strange:
One man, and yet so much.
The goodness in you, whole,
Might garden them to speech.

That barrenness but seems.
One word has been enough,
Ere this, to plow and plant
And harvest it. Be off.

Let There Be Law

Wherever earth is home for men,
Beyond what mountains, by what seas,
Let honor and pride live; but now
Let there be law, transcending these.

Let there be law through all the world,
Whose children love their ancient lands.
May that love grow, but in the shade
Of justice's most mighty hands.

Let those be guardians of our strength,
Lest in long anarchy it cease.
May something deathless now be born.
Let law be father of our peace.

Song

Spring of the world again,
Oh, is there such a time:
Eternity of April,
Past hills, past green?

There will be grass again,
There will be buds, be lambs;
Here. But what of the outer
Spaces fate lives in?

Good of the heart again:
Can there be such a spring?

327

You everlasting winter,
Does it come on?

THE CLOSE CLAN ह‍ॐ

The Close Clan

Even from themselves they are a secret,
The like ones that dwell so far asunder:
So far, and yet the same; for gold is gold
In any earth, and thunder repeats thunder.

They are the scattered children of what pair,
What patient pair so long ago extinguished?
But the flesh lives, in certain ones that wind
And dust and simple being have distinguished.

Whatever these, and howsoever born,
They are the ones with perfect-lidded eyes,
Quieter than time, that yet can burn,
Can burn in rage and wonder and sunrise.

They are the ones that least of all the people
Know their own fewness, or the loving fear
Such lineage commands—that ancient couple,
And these their growth in grace's afteryear.

In them the world lives chiefly, as gold shines,
As thunder runs in mountains, and hearts beat.
They are the ones who comprehend the darkness,
And carry it all day, and sweeten it.

These Things

We could not love these things in others.
We should not love these things at all.

In him, though, they become themselves
As death does in vermilion fall.

We should not be so happy, seeing,
We should not feel so warm, under
The pinched green, and then the great,
The hectic bloom, disease's wonder.

We should not, yet the end of shade
Surpasses June; as he is more
God's likeness than a hundred good ones
Prismless at the clear core.

The rainbow of his hottest pride
Sits in red gold at the extremes.
Selfishness in him is painted
Soul. It flushes our white dreams.

Merriment in him, and anger—
Forgetful, then remembering us—
Are the autumnal teachers; are
Man in his blaze, miraculous.

Old Hundred

The blacksmith did not hobble here
To the small church, on the hard hill,
In summer, to be told of stars;
He came with meek and tempered will;
He came, this hoarest of bent men,
To hear Old Hundred sung again.

But the young voice above the Book
Praised Him who built the heaven's fires;
And the old listener grew still;
No congregations and no choirs
Were in the grave with him at last;
Nothing but him and the sweet vast,

Nothing but those he soon must lose
If death was losing; and death was.
He saw them, wonderful and old,
But with no power in them to pause
As they sailed on, as they sailed on,
Over his unmoving mound.

Little Servant

Little servant with the softer voice
Than hands among these hallways, be more loud
In laughing when the master sits at home.
With the same strength that makes the silver shine,
Shout in the dark rooms; be unafraid
Of coming and of going; tell quick tales
To windows, slam the doors, and on the stair,
Little servant, sing—sing in the proud way
Of wrens upon the ridges. For as much
You cause a house to be, as much you owe
The sky the pretty skill of your soft voice,
That only need be happier to fly here,
Fly there among the hallways—even to him,
The master in his gloom, who thinks he wants
All quiet, and queer shadows. But as much
As you and the shrill wrens he wishes heaven
For cover; and would have it if your song,
Little servant, lifted the whole roof.

Lady of Where She Lived

The round old lady with the little eyes—
Lady of where she lived, of the split shingle
Walls, and the warped door that let four cat feet,
Cat feet in—the white old one, she perished
Even as planned. For where she lived she was lady,
And the lamp knew it that she tilted over:

Tilted, and it poured obedient flame
Due upward till the cupboard papers caught.
There must have been more oil in secret places,
For the first valley warning was the last;
The windows were too bright, then not at all
In the one peak of red, the pyramid
She built, this queer old queen, to shrivel under.
The cat feet, cat feet fled among the highway
Asters, and they never felt again
For the gone door she must have heard them pressing
Till the warp freed them. They are wild now,
As she is, but they were not sacrified.
She ended it alone. And lives alone
In the one place of which she could be lady,
The wild place of weeds; and of these clockworks,
Melted at the hour, the little minute,
He the lean one left her years ago.

When Rubies Were

They told this tale of her, that dying
She suffered robbers in the grave;
For ruby rings; that well were gone,
Since she awoke and time went on.

And time went on, and beauty bloomed
As if reborn in her twice bright;
For there was that about her gaze
Which glitters even to these days.

Even to these days come down,
Her beauty proves the story true;
As mystery is known to shine
In the found cask, the buried wine.

The buried wine our sun again
Sees into as the princes drink:

331

So must it once have been with her;
And so it was, when rubies were.

Bulletin

Did he seem happy? Well, he was serious;
Smiled, and was serious. But I saw
More than I used to in the difference,
More than I thought was possible there.

In him, in us, in anybody,
More than I thought could lie between
Quick kindness—you remember that—
And oh, so slow, the crooked shadow.

Yet it was difference I could measure.
He did not mix them. How he seemed?
Well, he is serious past saying.
And more of the old smile is smile.

Socratic

He suffered every fool alive,
But not as Lord and children.
He did not bless them, or predict
More light in them than could be.
They guttered, and he knew they would
Forever; yet he found them good.

We fled them, or we slept away
Long hours of them, of droning;
Of smoky wicks that were as smiles
Flattering confusion.
Familiar, but he liked it so;
And that was how he learned to know.

For he that stood, and shows the stain,
Is wiser still than we are.
The lamps we bear are brassy bright,
But he himself is lantern.
As they are. And if he is best,
He only claims him stubbornest.

Even than Water

He pushed him in and he held him down
Till no more struggle, and no more sound.

How many years had he hated that back
The crayfish fondled, and turtles perhaps?

Around it once met two white arms
With no more mercy in them than worms;

No more mercy upon him, standing—
Oh, right here; and again it was blinding,

Again it was dark, and he could not see
How too much silence soon would be;

How no more struggle, and no more sound
Would save her for him in dry ground;

Would give her to him, but quieter then
Even than water that sleeps with men.

The Fine Plan

The dust has long been settled that she rode,
A goddess in a buggy, with straight back
And blue ambitious gaze. For she was born

In a wild moment, and at twenty was taken
For better, worse, by husband and by pride.

And one of them is gone, but the other lives
As she does, thin in bed, remembering dust
And the hot horses; and when they were home,
The sons she would assess. For she could measure
By no rule but her own, that rode with her,

Superior to clouds; where now is clearness,
And weeds that have forgotten how she sped.
And strangers in that house. For the sons have scattered.
Only one gaunt lady will remember
What they were to have been, or what she was.

Here now she lies, with one of those she wedded
In the wild hour she fiercely lives again.
Here now she lies, and rages and refuses
All sixty years since that one; all poor time,
All persons, all that tempered the fine plan.

Odysseus

The broad-shouldered lord of rocky Ithaca,
Conqueror of brine, Athene's darling,
Listener to song and silent weeper
At his own name, Odysseus, loved himself
As the gods do, nor was it blasphemy.
The earth was in him, aching to be loved.

What man so happy, finding a sweet spring
Where nymphs hid and olive trees were old?
But it was blood to blood, as when his wrath
Sang swallow, and his bed postponed the dawn.
The pride of his own heart was strength's announcement;
Being in him boasted it was good.

The homecomer, shouting over waves
To the one world, his island, that it stand,
Even then was there; for all the globe
Rejoiced in him. Insulter of its giants,
Tamer of its sorcerers, he swam
Forgiven—greatness in him, and home ground.

Achilles

He that was deer was lion:
Fleet-footed, yet so huge
That Hector found him terrible
Nine years—and now,
Here where the fig tree stopped them,
Found no refuge.

He that was mother hearted—
Thetis, under the sea—
Robbed every mortal woman's
Tall son; and chilled,
Beside the bath that waited,
Andromache.

He that was wrath was pity,
Seeing another sire
In Priam when he trembled;
And his own doom
To be white bones in honey,
After hot fire.

HOMAGE TO SIX ҉

To Homer

Master of ocean stream, those men you made
Were weaker than its waves, its bitter waves

With their deep smell of caverns never sounded.
Out of dry land you made them, out of dust,
Of bronze; and likened them to bees and lions,
And the lean cranes that flew. Smaller than gods,
Feebler than sun and thunder, less than hills
You reared them, and you set them far away,
Little in strength, from their dear native land.
Yet who so strong? For miracle is in them
Still; still their throats produce a music
Angry and long ago; their armor walks
As waves do, never resting; and their wills
Keep liberty no fate would comprehend.
Submissive to decree, they still are crowned,
Princes of themselves, and rule all verse
As one ruled then from Ida. What so strange,
Master of man's littleness, as this,
That still you most augment him? Still you give
Those governed ones the glory. Sovereign men
Through centuries since have been their subjects still;
And wondered at you too, lord of the sea waves.

Dante Alighieri

As if a cabinet became alive,
And the recesses in it, the small curios,
Burned with an equal being, the huge world
Let him come in; made itself little and patient;
Lasted in shape and singing till his eye,
His delicate ear, solved secrets and moved on.
He wound his way in miniature, beholding
All that can be in corners, all that can shine
In curves a candle, intense and sudden, shows.
But it went far and deep, that shelving place,
Till light itself, a penitent, broke sweetly
And swelled; and swelled again, beyond the mountain
Whose top was tawny spring; swelled, and in bursting
Circles blinded his thought. So he fell down

And down. Yet not to nowhere, for the cabinet
Kept him. As the brain holds every object,
Ticketed, in caverns, so this world
This man who most enlarged it; who with mouse steps
Measured its last echo, singing little,
Singing long of all that may be and that is.

To Chaucer

Those waves of understanding that arrived
Were the least ones. You let the long swells go
In their own darkness on around the world
Till they piled high and broke in afterwoe.

For you the choppy ones the sun had wrinkled.
They had come far too, and they still come on.
But in you then they rested. You gave forth
The sound they seek, of old men young at dawn;

Of men that have forgotten nothing woeful,
Yet at their waking smile. The world is fool
Forever, and its tears are not to cease.
But neither is this birdsong, high and cool,

This answer, like your own, to those least waves
That come with sunwarmth dappled on their crests:
The ones unseen except by old late men
And silly larks, up early in their nests.

To Shakespeare

Mankind had been so rank a field,
And you so knowing in its blossoms,
You were not lost, sir, but you came
Never home to other harvest.

Not lost, and yet no head appears,
No shoulders even, where you stood,
The tallest, surely, of those growths,
Overlooking them in wind.

Looking, moving, yet your feet
Have left no path. We cannot follow.
How many leagues to where you paused?
Was this the stile, sir, where you started?

You did not stumble back again
With your own sheaves to show and bind.
We shall not know you, sir, except
We go in after you and stand,

And overlook the waving souls
As once you did, in sun, in tempest,
Never turning or explaining,
Never singing of yourself, sir.

Thomas Hardy, Poet

With older eyes than any Roman had
In a stone hole, or Briton under barrow,
Steadily he gazed; and bleakest worlds
Grew warm—illicitly grew warm and moved;
For hope in him was backward, and love narrow.

Belief in him but squinted; God had died
Of palsy, and mankind, alone with feeling,
Was a poor skinless thing. Yet maids and squires,
Ghosts, organists, and gypsies, and small clerks
Mused in his tales, and oxen kept on kneeling.

It was a late hour and cold when he looked out:
The last man that remembered country singing.
And first to call it pitiful. Those folk

338

Outstayed themselves, he said. Yet as he listened,
Wanly, what sweet bell tongues took to swinging!

Emily Dickinson

Between her window and the maple tree
How many lines crisscrossed; yet none could see.

None but herself, for every object there
When she looked out was woven of tough air;

Was center to a web whose anchor pins
Were far as where Aldebaran begins.

Diameters of silk so intersected
That pit and pole and windowpane connected,

And a seen worm conducted her by rods
Of filament to Satan's house, to God's;

Where the fine nerve, inquiring, did not stay
For the long anthem, for the raven's lay.

The quicker bobolink meanwhile was home
And did as well the honors of this dome,

Immense and small, wherein her suffering plucked
String after string, that joy too could instruct.

TOO LONG AGO ࣸ

Too Long Ago

Those beautiful, young, breaking eyes:
Regard them and go on; they are not

339

Letting that forth which middle oldness
Ever again will understand.

One day when you are in the ground
They also will have hardened over:
Their beautiful young fear escaped,
Their fondness loose in the still world.

As yours is now, and let it be.
It cannot answer what they ask.
It is too everywhere and thin
For the new soul that seeks an image,

For the sweet beast that only now
Wakes out of it: the mother dark
Too long ago by you forgotten,
Too far away this latter evening.

Proud Song

Let not the mover know,
Unmoved, the deep effect,
The spark that sometimes leaps,
The minnow in the flesh:
Sudden, the very self
Discovering to grow.

As if a father found,
One day, the infant plan
Cross charactered: a strange
Bird print upon an arm;
So let the first of all
In puzzlement be bound.

Whence are we? Let him search,
Unsure, in shaded time.
Let memory in him

340

Be startled by the mint,
Stepped on, of hidden mind
Outscenting the tall birch.

They Hurt Us Most

They hurt us most by loving us
And showing us they do.
Simplicity is sweetest then,
Yet harshest, tearing through.

The paper ring that might conceal
The pig, the tiger face—
When it is gone, and one of ours
Is there in his first grace,

The rent is here, not where the doubt
Across a circle stretched.
The sound is in the suddenness,
The pauperdom enriched.

The Soaked Ones

Where is that couple of slow boys,
Those downpour-lovers in drooped hats
Who on a day like this one went
And were to meadows as muskrats:

Disappearing in drowned hay
Before they shoved into a wood
That shook its great drops on their shoulders—
Overplus to what was good,

To what was falling everywhere
On those two lovers of wet death:

341

Of daring all that rain could do,
Entering, to put out breath?

For that was what their pride brought home,
Those dripping stampers up the stair;
Unwrapping the same spark they bore
Among arch-enemies of air.

Where is that brace of sober breasts,
Warm then before a second cause?
What dry logs now are laid for them
In what far land where Noah was?

The Ancient Couple on Lu Mountain

Into the pool of silence our tears made,
Our secret tears when lord son went away—
How straight his back among the willows was!—
Into this lake of time whereon our house
Is a small hidden island, nevertheless
Sound falls: a single dropping of sweet words,
With every moon, into this upland sea
That no crane visits, for the shores are lost.

Lord son is faithful. With each full of the moon
A letter comes here from the capital:
Comes dripping, dripping its clear characters
Like raindrops, one by one, into soft water.
No silence then. Yet afterward! yet now,
When the moon wanes; when memory grows weaker
Of the few musical, pure drops. How deep this pool is
Only the dark cranes know that never come.

He's Coming

He's coming. He just called. Said he was coming,
Maybe, right away. O southern river,
Kiss that trestle sweetly,
Rub that upright gently,
And keep no train from home.

He's coming. Said all papers would be signed
By Sunday. O you honeysuckle timber,
Wrap those tulips, redbuds,
Hold those oaks from falling
Down on the right of way.

He's coming. Said expect him. There! what music
Rails already make, and pounded switches:
Wheels inside the south wind.
Where? O you the south wind,
Keep soft and strong today.

The Great Wrath

It was cold, it was slow anger,
Gathered against the grain;
It was the consenting of soft valleys,
After all, to be volcano land.
It was the difficult decision,
Sailing, to murder murder.

And this was done. Historian,
Remember the fair time before.
Set down the peacefulness of that plantation.
Law was the bravest word among those towns
Whence, bitterly, brute wings
Took off to strangle strength.

It was a cold, a slow music,
Played with a grim skill,
Remote, in dragon places.
And it beat on to silence; rested only
When the raw noise it reared itself against
Was gone with the slayer, slain.

The Great Return

Someday ten million Ithacas will have them;
They will come steaming home, come banking home
Past the big cloud the god of our suspense
Built high above sweet springs and shingled houses.
Someday, someday, the oceans and the air,
Man-loud, will bear them hither in slow swarms—
Slow, but a host will gather, and long shores
Live with familiar feet, and inland acres
Shudder beneath fond weight, and cars and cattle
Caper again; the factories, the highways,
Fields, and old hedges musical with rain crows,
Parlors, and potato-scented kitchens,
Be as ten million nests for homing men.
Who as they nod and settle will remember
Others that never flew—the jungle holds them,
And the exploded abbey, the shrill street
Where snipers are no more; nor comrades either.
Sweet is the land that death too once desired,
Sweet the acknowledged waters, the roof ridges
That faded in a far dream or did not—
Not now, except for these who are the world's
Forever as they halfway too come home.

After the Great Victory

After the great victory a lonesome man
Unwounded went listening for what had stopped.

Not the guns merely, or spent fragmentation
Pattering on helmets: enough for a headache;
Remembering, he rubbed it. Not merely
Mired rations, and men with grey mouths
Thirstily swearing, not officers in first fear
Whispering impossible orders; the colonel
Shot half away and crying—old crow he was,
Cawing in blood on the ground, old black
Magnificent crow, tuning Italian forests.
Not Fortresses, riveting more sky,
Not mortars in the ravine, nor the calamitous
Heavies, rip and boom of a last judgment.
These, yes, but he could not hear them if he tried.
The other—was it living? Did it ever
Live? The seventh sense he had then
Was full of it, he knew. But nowhere now.
Or did he listen wisely? Was the world
Hiding its heart? He listened, lonesome warrior,
And went crippled; not from fire but from no fire,
No echo out of the seventh cavern, cold
And inward evermore, a single secret
Dead with the colonel, crying—old crow
That shared it with him then, as danger shook
Both faces; but the shot one looked away,
And his last curse was music in the wood.

Nowhere, Nowhither

More than the remaining distance
Daunted him. That took but legs,
But counting druggedly the towns and miles,
And the slow tiles
That drained this dreary country into ditches
Where muskrats paddled. He, homecomer here,
Equally was searching the soft bank—
But time, not water; and he shrank
From the bleared vision
Of all their memories run so together,

With name and face now every color,
That the tired man who spoke
Would be but smoke,
But haze out of a history. Himself
Saw that way too from weariness: no wife
In the first warmth, no children clear of limb
Waiting in one place for him.
Nowhere, nowhither. But he straggled on,
Remembering old tales of brave return
And hoping some were true; and walking faster
As one suddenly seemed so—of the grown son
And the greyhound who ran to meet their master,
And the sweet mistress of the lighted hall
So still beyond; but loud in stall
His horses neighing,
And high in wind above it all,
Elms swaying.

HOT HEAVEN ࣰࣸ

Hot Heaven

Cool night, cool night out of Canada,
Scatter bright fires over Cornwall.
There! Vega through the frosty trees
Burns all the hotter, and the Northern Cross
Flames in the Milky Way as ice flames,
Streaming with smoke of snow. Aquila
Tempers its wedge; and Corona,
Queen of horizon, kindles her last caverns.
Sagittarius is more on fire
For the cold waves he shoots through, for the chilblains
Bluing his fingers. Scorpio, late sunk,
Leaves, nevertheless, its double
Barb blazing. Fiercely, fiercely
Over Cornwall, cool night out of Canada,
Scatter these intensest embers.

346

Glitter with them. Let all hectic,
Hectic have hot heaven,
Frosty night.

The News of Snow

The news of snow full driven at the face,
Or settling, settling, not to be denied,
Comes on and on, as if the world had waited
Only till now to show its other side:
Then all at once, for whispers in the air
Say walls have turned and white is everywhere.

And it comes on. For not the cold, the blowing,
Not the shy rustle where the leaves were shed,
But always, always the arrival hither
Of what was yonder once, of what was dead:
This is the outer, this the ancient thing
That shrugs and comes, as if a shroud could sing.

As if the ash were all, the hoary cloak
Worlds wear to show that time is done with them;
As if immensity, that murdered earth,
Now cast its mold, its powdery diadem;
So the lost atoms, ending themselves here,
Whisper in white at so much nothing near.

False Summer

In the dead middle of the longest winter
There was an hour like this one, hot and still.
I can remember coming home by footpaths
Whitened as these, but not with daisy frill.

I can remember how the sun hung suddenly
Idle as I entered by the gate;

And flies from nowhere buzzed; and steadily, steadily
The eave troughs dripped, as if disconsolate.

But not so; that false summer was accepted
With the same happiness this true one hears.
Warmth rose, and water fell, and small musicians
Tumbled among the ghosts of the grass's spears.

If it was brief, so is the longest hay month,
When the sun dozes, dreaming that change is lost.
Time finds it with his terrible thin fingers,
That dice all day with honey and hoarfrost.

Coming Home Carelessly

Coming home carelessly,
Nine thoughts away,
The tenth took it in—So!
The dog days are over.

Sultriness never
Survived such a green
Last evening as lay,
Mint strip on the hills,

And sliced the long summer,
And sheared the heat's end.
But I came alone; so
Eleven is yours.

Looking Yonder

Ice on a hundred highways
Keeps seven cities home;
Yet keeps some there at windows,
Prisoners of room;

Keeps me, as morning glitters,
And the street steams with breath,
As blind to what is round me
As though this were death.

But it is looking yonder,
And what lives thus is warm
With something more than crystals
Comforting its form.

One small slope of mountain
May know when I come over
By how I name the meadows,
The moss ones, the clover;

By how I see through whiteness
To the least rock and mouse
Where ledge runs into woodland,
Opposite that house,

That house with sleepy buildings
Haloing its head;
I count the folded ladders,
The wood in its cold bed,

The kerosene, the hanging
Saws; and even by day
The stall with its hot lantern,
Lengthening wild hay.

The Mountain

The mountain he is more than there,
Than lying there northeasterly;
Than being where he is at all,
Eating horizon hungrily.

The mountain he is quieter
Than quickest glances tell to us;
A sudden look is what he likes,
Yet there he sleeps, mysterious.

The mountain can be live, be dead;
His weight absents itself, returns;
The mountain he is masterly;
Concerns in him are unconcerns.

Camp Night

A little water will put out the fire.
But wait. A little wood will keep it breathing.
It is a heart we started with ten sticks
That now are nothing, like a hundred others
Shrunk to this hectic person whose last life
Would drain the whole cool forest if it could.
Another handful, then, though it is late.
So much in little, such a hungry principle:
We are not lightly to extinguish that.
Quiet a little longer, while it hisses
And settles, keeping secret the sore word
That soon enough its embers will forget.
Our own existence, partly. A wild piece
Of me and you we presently must drown.

Having Won

Dawn comes difficultly;
Strains, disinherited blood,
To ooze back through all distance;
Forces tough tissues, till with tiredness
Slowly they thin;
But sullenly, as if the red might fail:

Defeated morning, while one sleepy bird
Knows only that it sounded; a slim note
Kindling no others; and it grips again
The twig, night's tendon, tautening the deep.
But then companions brighten. Far and near,
Minute first flakes are shed, first glimpses spring
Of the new body, paling into strength
As now whole clusters fly,
Whirling and filling newborn everywhere
Translucently with music. The mad red
Grows milder, having won, and with this chorus
Whitens to silence. The full day has come,
The visionless, the deepless, to be seen through by all eyes
Of objects, and all animals and men.

The Chickadee

The chickadee has three short songs
To love the world with, spring and fall;
And winter,
For he loves it all.

And two of them are cherry sweet,
But one is diligent persimmon;
Children
Love the last, and women.

And it is cheerful at the door,
In snow, when nothing else will sing.
But woodsmen
Hear a different thing.

In ragged pines, in melting March,
Or in September's softer prime,
Two sounds,
Or three, in saddest time:

Most plaintive, as the happy heart
Can be, pretending. So they say,
Those men
Alone, and look away.

The Sparrow

Is there no All,
The sparrow in his small
Domed head asked darkly of himself?

Is there no One,
The sparrow in his dun
Wing coat said, hopping up the bush?

I have heard it—No—
But who in all this woe
Of winter watches each of us that flies?

Someone stands
And claps great hands
And smiles upon our smartness—someone does,

Or why such pride
In certain that have died,
As if a witness went with them to ground?

Is there no Him?
Why then these trim,
True bodies, all asunder, all the same?

There is—for see me now,
The sparrow said, and flew
Straight down, and flicked a grit of yellow up.

A Hundred Minnows

A hundred minnows, little-finger length,
Own the slim pond. In sets they make
Maneuver: all one way
Change-minded, yet of one mind where clear water
Clouds with their speed an instant;
All one speed, one purpose, as they veer
And suddenly close-circle; and some leap—
There! at an unseen fly,
There! at nothing at all.
Brown minnows, darkening daily
Since the thin time, the spring,
Since nothingness gave birth to such small bones,
Beat the soft water, fill
The wet world; as one,
Occupy movement, owning all August,
Proud minnows.

Tall Jack

The big bay stands in the rain with his blinders
Spattering drops and making him blink.
Tall Jack waits in the field for someone's
Step on the grass—not mine, I think.

The rain is only beginning, and so
He will be there still when I come and stand;
He will be indifferent and warm
Under the mane where I run my hand;

He will lower his great long head a little,
He will peer from his blinders round at me;
But not for this has he drooped in patience
With rainstreams darkening down each knee.

Not for this one who comes friendly,
And yet is alien as he strokes

353

Nose, flank, and shoulder—not for him
The rump in the cold rain steadily smokes,

Shifting its shape as the grey hind hooves
In turn lift upward, looking for dry.
Big Jack waits, and the hitch rope drips,
Drips, that the right one must untie.

Those Wings

"Giddup, giddup, you old forgotten
Hobbledyhorse, you goggle-eye!"
But the plowboy never saw that field
Where the young ravens used to fly.

"What's in your rotten bones today
That makes you clump and stumble so?"
The shadows of those morning wings
Beside these feet went poor and slow,

These foal's feet with their mother's racing
Down to the wood's edge where the spring
Bubbled forever—but "Giddup,
Giddup!" is all a boy can sing

Who never was told of the curly neck
And the tossed head that teased the mare;
Or the black shadows of the black
Evening wings outdistanced there;

Or the quaint mind that dew could feed
Between sweet intervals of grass;
Thinking then and thinking now:
Days of summer never pass.

Under Cover

Put it away in that building; rust and dust
And rats are there, and spiders, and dry rot;
But the roof is good, and so those two great robbers,
Rain and sun, will go and hunt elsewhere;
And so gravedigger time—old naked time
That moves without a shadow—he'll creep on
To things no hand has hidden. Lay it away,
For that is what men do. Time, sun, and rain
Would have all earth as one—look how they soak
And wither, and sink hugest objects in.
Even dark buildings; but forget, forget.
Think only of the open, and how smooth
Time keeps it with his tools of wet and dry.
Even stout rooftrees; but repair them now.
The difference between late death and soon
Is inches, time will mumble; yet men know
How golden is that space, how not to be spared.

Moonrise Limited

The low, the large, the umber moon
That suddenly we saw was sailing,
Sailing level with the train,
Sailing leftward and unlawful,
East as we were, east to ocean;
And its tender side cut steeples,
And it sliced at trees and cables
As it raced—a rearward madness,
Renegade to west and over,
Runaway from arch's calm.
Low and dizzy it went with us,
Out of the window south ahead;
Pressing with us till we shuddered,
Laughing, and pulled down the shade.

355

It Was and It Was

It was and it was; that day, that day,
Born double, was time's twin headed calf,
A monster if we ever saw one—yet
The four sweet eyes made all of us laugh.

Yet two of them had their terrible brown,
Dusk in the middle of innocent blue;
Their terrible black, for it was no color
At all our deep hilarity knew.

Under each face that squinted in wind
And reddened in so exciting a sun,
Behind each forehead the gravest delight
Lived for a day, and only that one.

Never again have I at least
And never I think have they, have they,
Smiled to the center: serious gods
Watching the whole world darken away.

Waterfall hours, with a hidden roar.
Noise at the heart that broke and broke.
Never again I think will eternity
Make and murder at one stroke.

The Little Cities

The little cities of New Orleans
Where the dead lie—
Tilted, flowering tombs inside four walls
Quiet and high—

The little streets, the temples in low rows
Where sisters sleep,
Where fathers of old families, old bones,
Old letters, weep:

No sweeter wind blows anywhere today
Than through these tufted
Crannies in the crumbled brick, these shelves
By slow truth shifted.

For here the rumor of ten thousand deaths
Is gentle, is soft;
Is January smiling; though all woe
Winters aloft.

GODS AWHILE ॐ

Gods Awhile

The burning cheeks of lovers, the stopped breath—
But then it comes again, and whispers death
So sweetly they will have no other hour
Than this their secret one—the mortal power
Of lovers is to waste all alien time
And wither every sound except this rhyme
Inside them, of the blood that doubly beats
And deafly; until even that retreats:
The last sense gone, as there they lie
Untouchable, and in their blisses die.

There is no death like this one of well lovers,
No woe like this that wonderfully hovers
Over good warmth and guesses when to fall,
Blanketing like night the world and all.
Like night, but it is day. No death, no woe
Save as they live again and call it so:
Again close clinging, and despising time
That does not strike with them, that does not climb
And break its waves forever on the shore
Of two in one, immortal here once more.

Unless

With lovers there is language
For everything but this:
The creeping cat of a desire
That springs, and will not miss
Unless the other one awhile
Too weary is—unless.

Neither lover learns, alas,
Unwritten, the cool sign:
No jungle now, no stealthy
Sweet fur, and whine
Of longing; only peace,
Peace be mine and thine.

So when by grace appearing
The leopards leap as one,
Each finds the other stranger
For what in dark is done;
Yet dreams then of no other world,
Secretless, like sun.

Down from the Waist They Are Centaurs

The cool fall, a little out
Then flowing down; the clean curve—
It might be woodland water, but it is
Dry fire: the burning secret of all men,
The precious danger seen and yet not seen,
Confessed when unconfessed.

Women do not know the might
They move in, cannot stand apart,
Stricken, and behold this sudden thing:
The wilderness they wade become aloud,
Alive; the ancient animal they drag
Breathing its full power.

Yet slyly, for the eyes of men,
Blasted, give their tongues a blindness,
Maddened, seem to close. The instantaneous
Look is all there is: bonfire of fancy,
Dampened in a moment by forgetting;
Or else—and then the blaze.

Relapse

The atoms of an old jealousy, rejoicing,
Gathered in him again. Oh, but they fell
Far upward to refind him. Once he had watched,
Once he had wondered proudly at his power
As down he seemed to shed them like shook sand:
Grit that had left him, master. Long, long ways
They plunged, they disappeared; and he was well
With smoothness, and his charity could smile.
He thought strength had done it. Then they poured,
Oh, upward; the deep void had topmost doors
That opened as the fall became a fountain.
Strength, but it was not his; nor ever had been;
The clear time between was hollow lie.
He heard them here, rejoicing in reunion:
Shape again, and function; a whole heart
To forage in; he felt them at their feeding.
So grace in him drained drearily away:
The freedom, the self love, that now as sand
Thirsted in space's desert, the down gulf
Whence atoms had ascended. And still came.

Who Finds His Love

Who finds his love a whore at heart
Was mad to find it—why go there?
Why look? Why feel? For from the start
It must have been so everywhere.

It must have been that she would turn
When she did turn. But when was that?
Who played the ape? He will not learn;
There is no name for him or it.

There is no history of whore.
It heaves out of another time.
It is another horror—more
Than wildest madness will redeem.

For he is lost that now has looked,
And looking, found; and finding, felt.
Eternity's evil is unhooked
From the white wall, and slips its hilt,

And plunges through so thin and far
He cannot say what let the blood.
The horror now is not the scar,
But how this stillness shakes his bed.

The Bitterest Things

The bitterest things are sweets misunderstood,
Or worse, refused in fury: the struck face
Of Desdemona, doubted; the searched word
More innocent than milk, but by this madness
Curdled; such a forearm as Diana
Shed once like a shadow over pain
Chopped into lecher's meat, the eye despising
What is most whole, most his, the heart distributing
Minced gifts to others; jealous generosity
Letting the benefactor's own best blood.
The bitterest is the purest; but mistaken,
Most poisonous. To her, and then to him.
For he is last to know what lavish gold
He vinagered, what water, brackish now,
Is spiderless no more; and that he drinks it.

Consider, Man

Guilty lover of that queen,
That spider lady whose torn web
Spangles with such pretty tears,
Consider, man, the cost to her
Whose luxury is suffering.

Consider if you had not come
And strung with her those dusky strands
In the dark corner where confusion weeps:
Consider, man, the cost to one
Whose whole sweet wealth is suffering.

She will not say so, guilty drone
Who helped her weave the pattern out;
She charges you with ruin done;
But every rent is riches there;
Consider, man, the suffering.

Consider well the dreary cost
Of not a sigh in all that silk;
In all that dancing no sweet death;
Her majesty considers, man,
What she must owe you, suffering.

Recovery

The lump of sore silence
In two throats at once
(The slenderer, sweet-filling,
Outsuffered its mate),

The lump, the unspeakable,
Lay for too long
Not to go slowly;
But then it was gone;

And now it seemed sudden,
As if the world sang
Six hundred sunrises
Together in ring;

Together like minutes,
Slumbrous in time,
Till gong! till the chorus,
Awful in cry,

Of stars understanding
The multiple dark:
Joy in two persons,
Secret, at work.

Sleep, Sleep

Sleep, sleep, slug in the sun,
Be limp forever, like warm grass.
Be lost to shape, be legs and arms,
Be body separate, be sweet soul
That melts and spreads like innocent spring
When time undoes it. Be green song
That sighs unto itself and dozes;
Dries, and into summer brown
Relaxes. So be young and dead,
Beloved, be as nothing there,
There in the sun while I keep watch,
There with the grass while I remember.
Sleep, sleep, beloved of worlds
That will be jealous, will awake you.
Sleep, until they stand and ask
Who this was by you all the while.
Forget me now, though, sleep and sleep,
Slug of my heart, O nothing of mine.

The Mistress

Nothing, no one comes to see
Honorable him and me.

Has either of us turned to snow?
Gossip ended long ago.

Was I cheap for him or dear?
Nothing, nothing passes here.

But one of us did not mistake.
I lie and say it, wide awake;

And do not think his doubt has come
Even to that simple sum.

It is not backward that he counts
The happiness my lips pronounce.

Having never to decide
Is how he loves me still, his bride.

WORDS FOR MUSIC MORE OR LESS ❧

Then Both Shall Be

When icicles around the earth
Are played upon by one long wind,
And crickets winter in warm grass,
Then I shall be as once I was.

When midnight mushrooms march away
And owls are motherly to mice,
And there is only one great star,
Then you will be as once you were.

When rocks remember being fire
And time to come ticks on the wall,
And truth is mirror of each man,
Then both shall be as both have been.

And Not My Wounds

Tell him I was beautiful,
Tell him I walked well;
Tell him I was columbine,
Brown daisy, and harebell.

He talked of these things that I was,
And called the world to see,
Like one who had created them,
Then manufactured me.

Tell him I am stars by night,
And stillness by noonday.
For he must know, that left me here,
Nothing has gone away;

Nothing is dead or different—
Tell him, and make sure.
For he must understand that I
And not my wounds endure.

Will He Come Back?

Will he come back, O will he, will he,
Dandelion and yellow daisy?
　　He will come back to you, tall daughter,
　　When loving him is easy.

Will he come back to me, O will he,
Horses, horses, wild in the meadow?

He will come back with ice in August,
And sunshine in shadow.

Will he come back, O will he, will he,
Minnows, minnows, deep in the pond?
    He will come back when air is water,
    And the high sky is sand.

Will he come back to me, O will he,
Midnight moth on the windowpane?
    He will come back when I, when I do—
    Whisk! and I try again.

Will he come back, O will he, will he,
Heart in my body, weakly crying?
    He will come back when you can no longer
    Hear what I am saying.

Soft, Soft, Soft

Soft, soft, soft
Is her gazing when I leave her and am gone;
When I leave her;
Soft is her coming, coming where I am,
By sunlight or by moonlight, halfway around the world.

Soft is my truelove's
Looking when she listens, listens to my name;
Just listens;
Soft is how she ever is, coming, staying,
By sleepy night, by sleepy noon, my fair love.

Strong, strong, strong
Is her softness that will never, never change;
Never change;
As water to be water, as air being air,
Firm, firm, firm is the purpose of my love.

But never, never hard
Is the looking of my love, lonesome love,
When I come;
Soft is the waiting, the waiting of her eyes
Halfway around the water world and sweet dry land.

One Red Rose

My love she is a rose that lives
When nothing else does any longer.
Winter deepens and worlds die,
But one red rose meanwhile is stronger.

My love is that one, and I live
Because she does, in wind and rain
That are as warm as when we first
Were slips of summer to be slain.

Yet this my rose, outliving frost,
Is fresher now than any new one.
She alone, of all that smile,
Is red and loving, is the true one.

Where She Is Now

Where she is now, with people,
Do passages and rooms,
Do table edges know it,
The sweetness of her clothes?

Does wood she touches tremble
That such a person moves,
Remembering me always?
For this she sweetly does;

And swings me with her, modest,
A thought upon her thighs,

A lover there, and lazy,
Till both of us come home.

Then who but I, unwrapping,
Will know it all the night:
This looseness to the center,
And sweetness every part?

Sometimes I Believe

She loves me or she loves me not,
I am a fool, a wise man.
Sometimes I believe I know;
Then she is wild, is woman.

Some days she is worldly kind,
As to the millionth beggar.
I think it is for me she feels,
Then find I was but neighbor.

Some days when I least am looking
Love comes to my shoulder.
Sits and sings; but she has sent
Nothing, she says, from her.

There she lies, in sleepy shade,
And all her blood, I fancy,
Blesses the sharp thought of one
Who like a thief will enter.

So shall I slip and with outrage
Be winner of that warmness?
Sometimes I believe I see
She loves no one, this woman.

Burden of Ornament

My darling with the single daisy,
Porcelain, pinned in her hair,
On other afternoons will glitter
With earrings, silver, or a fair
Gold brooch; that supper changes
Into an apron, crimson, there.

My darling in these dolorous days
Does all the work of courting birds;
Or in far places, long ago,
Of Scythian men, who to be lords
Went forth in feathers; or of gods
Whom still a band of glory girds.

My darling with sweet-william nosegay,
Artful, under slope of breast,
Or giant buckle, set loquacious
Over that littleness, her waist,
My darling bears the ancient burden
Smiling; nor doth dream of rest.

The Bridegroom's Chantey

When I was farther away than a ship
Would show—two beautiful eyes in a tower—
The wind here was the same dry wind
That kissed my sails a certain hour.

When I was longer away than a clock,
Remembering, could tell in the room,
Those birds there, with their beautiful backs,
Were the same three that sat on my boom.

When I came lonely into port,
The hill of ocean all behind,

What made my pillow that night so soft
Except these beautiful stars that shined?

When I am again with you, with you—
Beautiful lips that open so free—
Why do you think you must deny
You sent the whole world after me?

Song of the Two Vagrants

Alone I came to cool Manhattan,
On a fine day in friendless fall;
And would have left it but for someone,
Someone I don't blame at all.

Neither for goodness that I stayed with—
Oh, the short time when nights were long—
Nor the quick change in her that banished,
Banished me: it was not wrong.

Yet who so lonely on the road now?
Again I wander, and years die;
And maybe where she lives is marble,
And someone's luck it is to lie—

Oh, that's the reason time goes slowly,
Wandering with me far to west;
Remembering those sweet long evenings,
And the low voice that gave us rest;

And the gold hair that once in hallways
Burned in the darkness, being kissed.
Oh, time and I have turned from many,
But she was the one, the one we missed.

Unto Death

He made her love him, oh, he did,
He did, and it was unto death;
Except that government of sighs
Imperfect is, and of this breath
We do not notice, in or out,
So wantonly it wandereth.

He could not ask her why it was,
So faithfully she tended him.
She did, and it was unto death;
Except for certain sudden dim
Midsummer dusks when a ghost walked
Between them, luminous and slim.

Dunce's Song

The wind that comes, the wind that goes,
Never tells me what it knows.
The wind is witness of all things—
Of water's birth, of Saturn's rings,
Of sin's undoing, of love's laws,
And revolutions without cause—
But still my face is famine lean;
The wind that sees cannot be seen.
If I could turn a sudden head,
Sidewise perhaps, as the wind sped
And its dark edges rippled by,
I might grow wise enough to die.
But here I stand and only know:
Wind come, wind go.

Beggar's Beatitude

In wanderment I came to where—
In ragged woe did I arrive—

Suddenly I stumbled, for
The corners of the world were five.

Direction lost its way among
Wild grasses where the pavement stopped.
And I fell down as in a web,
A flowery web whence sparrows hopped

And sang that in my laziment
I had come home to stars at last;
For that was how this pasture spread,
Soft as midnight, and more vast.

Direction was no tyrant there;
The sparrows, though in darkness, sang;
Yet morning moved among the stars,
And glory in me rang and rang

As round and round the world's five corners
Spun—and yet no sound was made—
As if all light took me for cause,
In spanglement forever laid.

Bay-Window Ballad

The old man in the window,
With his hair all combed,
The old man in the window
Will drive no more.

He watches down the valley,
In his collar and clean cuffs,
He watches down the valley
As the teams come up.

There, by the big rock,
Seventy Junes ago,

There, by the big rock,
He tipped his load.

How the old one scolded,
The old one who is gone;
But that old, old one
Never was young;

Never at this window,
With his face all washed,
Never at this window
Tapped the glass.

Tap! and the great roans
Answer with their feet;
Tap! and a grandson
Whirls his hat.

What's Wrong?

Said the engineer to the fireman,
"What's happened? He didn't come out."
Said the fireman, pulling the bell cord,
"That's for old Jiminy Trout.

"Didn't you hear? His daughter—
Beautiful, some say—
Found him dead as a cricket
On the doorstone yesterday.

"Found him after we passed here—
Remember how he waved?
As always; but it took him
Most of the strength he had saved.

"The rest of it he sat down with,
And saw us around the curve.

That's for you, old Jiminy,
But it isn't what you deserve.

"It ought to be slow and heavy,
A toller, and doleful long."
The engineer leaned over:
"What did you say? What's wrong?"

Until, Until

How much the place pleased him
He never would tell,
Any more than the clapper,
Deserting the bell,
Will swing to no purpose
In vacancy's well.

They played on each other,
He and that ground;
It was not for a stranger
He struck the icebound,
The butterfly meadows
To alternate sound.

It was not for immensity's
Ear that he sang
As deep the lane listened
And rough the wood rang;
Then silence, as sometimes
The whole bronze will hang,

And the swinger within it,
Sleepily still,
Is strong to no purpose,
Is iron without will,
Until the wind wakens—
Until, until.

The Wind Has Changed

South wind, suddenly
Cool among the curtains,
Cunning as the dark is
To pour indoors;

South wind, thrusting,
Thrusting into corners,
Without any keenness
Your sweet force comes.

South wind, gentlest
Of night's old changes,
South wind, softest
For all your power,

South wind, south wind,
Loosen every heart here,
Sweeten every forehead,
With memory of rain.

The Sad Child's Song

Heavy, Heavy, hangs in my head.
Not over, over, not superfine.
In here, in my head, hangs Heavy, Heavy,
And nobody knows.
Dead down he hangs,
Nor sweats, nor swings;
Pure weight, pure lump, is Heavy in here,
Here in my head where nobody sees.
Not over, over, not lucky and fine,
Not something for others, laughing, to say
Is mine if I want it, mine, is mine.
What shall the owner do to redeem it?
I can do nothing with Heavy in here,

Here in my head; and nobody helps.
Dead weight he hangs,
Pure lump, nor swings.
Heavy, Heavy, is all I have.
Heavy, oh Heavy, is mine to keep.

The Glad Child's Song

Where are we now,
Says thistle ball,
And so say I, and so say I.

Me and my body
Went off together,
But who cares where, but who cares where?

Nobody guesses
That here we are yet,
With people around, with people around.

What do they notice,
My body or me?
And which of us cares, and which of us cares?

One of us changed,
Yes, but he did,
Into a dancer, into a dancer,

And whirls the other one,
Oh, so lightly,
Oh, so lightly, oh, so lightly,

Around and around,
And neither will ever,
And neither will ever
Be tired any more, be tired any more.

How Shall We Know Them?

How shall we know him,
The man he will be?
Not by this walking
So far and lonely.

How shall we know her
When ladytime comes?
Not by this husky
Song that she hums.

This pretty believing
That two are but one—
How shall we know them
When April is done?

Summer and winter,
The dry and the cold—
How shall we know them
When each is old?

We shall not know them,
Having been wrong.
True love walks in him
Lonely and long.

We shall not know them,
Having this doubt.
True love forever
Sleeps in her throat.

LULLABIES ૨ॴ

Chipmunk, Chipmunk

Chipmunk, chipmunk, little and small,
Roll your stripes into a ball.

376

White horse, white horse, winter is warm
With a shaggy coat for wind and storm.

Owl, owl in the hemlock tree,
Hoot till morning for all of me.

Robber, robber, snug in your den,
Pick the bones of our old hen.

Lighthouse, lighthouse, tall by the shore,
Shine on the shipwreck no more.

Maple, maple over this roof,
What do you listen to, far off?

Train, train around Great Hill,
Whistle again and then be still.

Down Dip the Branches

Down dip the branches,
The long leafy branches,
Down dip the branches
To bring old robin in.

Underneath the haytops,
The warm windy haytops,
Underneath the haytops
The mice are creeping home.

Soon it will be sunset,
Red and yellow sunset,
Soon it will be sunset,
With everything indoors.

Apples for supper.
Sing, sing for supper.

377

After, after supper,
Sing awhile in bed.

Mouse in the meadow,
The green sleepy meadow,
Mouse in the meadow,
Fold your little paws.

Robin in the branches,
The dark sleepy branches,
Old robin in the branches,
Shut, shut, shut your eyes.

Where Did He Run To?

Where did he run to,
That old rooster?
Fox, fox,
How fast did he run?

Where is the mule gone,
That old rope-tail?
Manger, manger,
Where is the mule?

Where are the kittens
The old black cat had?
Blinker, Blinker,
Where are the kittens?

Where does the dog sleep,
That old shepherd?
Lambs on the mountain,
Where is your dog?

Where is the big boy
That swung on the gatepost?

Bedclothes, bedclothes,
Where is the boy?

Old Ben Golliday

Old Ben Golliday
Jumped off the wagon box,
And trotted with his horses,
Clop, clop, clop.

Old Ben Golliday
Was angry with his little wife,
And didn't see her bonnet strings
Fly, fly, fly.

Didn't look around
At the thank-you-mam, thank-you-mam,
Didn't see her somersault
High, high, high.

Old Ben Golliday
Trotted to the barn door,
And went in with his horses
To sleep, sleep, sleep.

Old Ben Golliday,
Dozing in the manger there,
Don't you know your little wife
Sits in the sky?

Old Ben Golliday,
Who will get your dinner now,
Who will sew your buttons on?
My, my, my!

Sleep, Grandmother

Sleep, grandmother, sleep.
The rocking chair is ready to go,
And harness bells are hung in a row
As once you heard them
In soft snow.

Sleep, grandmother, sleep.
Your sons are little and silly again;
Your daughters are five and seven and ten;
And he that is gone
Was not gone then.

Sleep, grandmother, sleep.
The sleigh comes out of the winter woods
And carries you all in boots and hoods
To town for candy
And white dress goods.

Sleep, grandmother, sleep.
The rocking chair is old as the floor,
But there he nods, at the noisy door,
For you to be dancing
One dance more.

He Cut One Finger

He cut one finger
And the other finger bled.
He cut off his head;
But he didn't have another,
So he's dead.

He shut one eye
And the other eye was gone.
He put his glasses on;

380

But he couldn't see to see,
So he's done.

The dwarf ate the giant
To become a giant too.
He grew and he grew,
But he couldn't hold him all,
So he's through.

The cot became a bed
And the bed became a boat.
But the boat couldn't float,
Being heavy; and the lights
Went out.

SPRING BIRTH

AND OTHER POEMS (1953)

THE BIRD DESIRE ह्रे

I Went, I Saw

I went, I saw, but will not tell,
But cannot tell, what things were there.
They are not here; but even so,
There is this difference of air.

Excitement then, like spicy smoke,
Invisible, yet followed me.
It curled among the corridors,
It burned above the hills, the sea.

No person's eyes that looked in mine,
No woman's, but a pepper scent
Filled room and street and blowing field;
And nosegay children came and went;

And animals, so pure of coat
They glistened in that sleeker sun—
But where this was I will not tell,
Nor things I did there—no, not one.

Because You Go with Me

All women are beautiful,
All men are brave,
Because you go with me
This side the grave;
Because the same shadows
That I see and fear
Shorten before you
And disappear.

All women are beautiful
Because you are one;
All the world's courage—
But I have none—
All the day's splendor
Springs out of you.
Even I, knowing it,
Am carefree too.

Even I, dangling
The sun at my side,
Sometimes can wonder
If those shadows lied
That said they were longer
Because of my doubt;
So deep, my darling,
You burn it out.

My Poor Love

Keep up your humming, west wind, and your silly
Songs, you birds; and all you trees, half bent
With sound, keep whispering to the grass, the ground.

Keep noisy, world; yet leave one little crack
For silence to slip through you, one thin cleft,
One hollow vein that my poor love can follow.

My poor love, it cannot cry—not loud
It cannot, nor so sweet as those small sparrows,
Piping, nor so warm as her eyes, weeping.

There she waits—oh, I know where—and truly
Listens—O my love, she truly leans
And listens; for my silence here she listens.

Let it go then, wind and thunder, let it
Pass between you, songbirds, let it pierce you,
Trees, like words upon the wing—oh, these.

She Lives with Me

She lives with me and is my careless love;
All of my faults are funny in her heart.
All of her faults—but she has buried those;
I cannot find them with my fondest art.

I watch and pry, and have a name for one,
Should it be ever proven and confessed:
There is no dark religion in her love;
I am not God, but a forgiven guest.

My faults are foibles, like my very strength;
My deepest virtue she indulges too.
I am not terrible to see and hear;
My work is play that curious children do.

She lives with me and is my laughing love,
Nor would I have it different in her mind.
Her single sin—but it is never so,
Nor could I wish it any sweeter kind.

Let Me Not See

Let me not see the one I love,
The bright one, that so blinded me;
The sweet one, that like sudden roses
Filled all evening easterly.
Let me not have those senses back
That sleep in her, and only lack
Knowledge of their captivity.

They think they are awake in me
And working, as they did of old.
And still they do with her away;
Then everything is clear and cold;
Is single, and I hear its name.
Oh, let it never be the same
With her whom clouds of love enfold.

She comes, but not herself is there.
She moves, but in a mist I make.
Oh, let me never burn away
All this between us, for love's sake.
Let my desire be even such
As darkens most what then I touch—
Sudden midnight, and fireflake.

The Liquid Heart

What if it is happening now;
Even now: the slow drain,
The drying, drying, drying up—
Oh, what if even now the gods
Go elsewhere in the joyful night?

They lay with me, and when I rose
They would not leave my happy side—
Unhappy too, but oh, how sweet

My bitterness was then, how full.
They lived with me and were my love.

Together we made worlds and worlds,
By night, by day, and none was calm,
And none, save at the center, clear.
Not one but was our changeling child
Whom only I must then subdue.

Yet now that I am master thus,
Where do those tall companions range?
I know, I know. The liquid heart
They lie with there—were it my own,
I would not for this world be wise.

The Bird Desire

I took my gun,
I walked a mile,
And shot and killed
The bird desire.

Still it flew.
I shot again.
It fell to ground.
Desire was dead.

What then is this
That dips so near,
And on not two
But twenty wings?

No, a hundred.
Thousands now.
Where shall I hide?
Should I be proud?

I gave a mortal
Thing this life.
I made a god.
He multiplies.

Goddess of the Gown

The close world of thighs that silk and cotton
And the smooth wool conceal—how would it be,
O custom, if your curtain fell away
One day,
O custom, and it worked as waves work,
Openly, on, on, and on,
To the eye's limit, to the thinking end?

That wilderness of soft and moving monsters,
Those riders of the plain—how would it be,
O mythical sweet art, if you resigned,
And the slow mind,
O mythical sweet seamstress, quickened;
If sleepiness in dogs and men
Gave way to round and rolling wonder?

The forests of them then the sun perfumed!
Or, spicily in rooms, the overflowing—
O hider of all that, would you return?
We burn,
O cunning cover, as it is, in dream.
Could we do more—could we as much—
Goddess, if no silk assisted?

Hector Dead

Andromache, when Hector fell,
Cried out upon her fate, not his.
He lost but this one thing, the world;
She gained its million miseries.

388

Without him it was no more round
And perfect, as pure death can be.
A field of wry-shaped fragments wailed,
Each one of them sharp-voiced as she.

A wilderness of woes it was
By which she measured, that long day,
The quietness in his great throat
That once held every dog away.

Home Eagerly

Home eagerly to give the gift,
The single thing bought on this day
In the whole world for that lone one.

That one who pays by keeping there
The room you come to, and herself
Is lone receiver, cord and box.

Which now unwrapping, nevertheless
Remember. It was giving more
To stay and open this white door.

As Time Goes On

As time goes on, and tells us less
And less what we have language for,
Still we converse; that vacuum
Is something still we must abhor.

As mind lives on, and feeds itself
With self, yet cannot name the taste,
Still we conceive; there is a world
Inside us that we may not waste.

As joy survives despite despair,
And yet despair declines to die,
Still we consent; it is our lot
To love without good reason why.

IN THAT FAR LAND ક્ષ

Only for Me

When I was twelve in that far land,
And was in love with summer nights,
And was in love with Linda Jane,
Whose very name was dancing lights
About my dark, my country bed,
Once I dreamed that she was dead.

And woke; and not one window star,
As I looked out, but wept for me.
I looked again, and my own tears,
Like magic lanterns, made me see
The very eyes of Linda Jane
Weeping everywhere like rain.

Then the sunrise, cool and red,
And then the new day, white and hot.
And after that the growing up
And the forgetting—oh, but not
The selfless woe of one that died.
Only for me, for me she cried.

Neighborhood Enough

The mind at last fills up with men
Whom infant thought found wonderful:
The next-door men that made the world
So curious, so multiple.

Then down the street the stranger ones,
And on and on to millions more;
But these alone were universe,
Were firmament and fiery shore.

The talk of them was news enough,
And when they died, was history.
The simple purpose of the sun
Was that they were and still should be.

And still they are, without their names,
Next door to memory grown old;
When further stars are faint to see,
And all between is dark and cold.

The little world is warm again,
Is numerous, and windows blink;
And men within, obscure as mice,
Make neighborhood enough, we think.

Homer, Sidney, Philo

Homer, Sidney, Philo,
Strung along the Wabash:
Beads in the black land.
Corn grows, but no change
In these little towns.

After forty springtimes
Nothing to look out at.
Seven miles, eight miles—
Strangers in the blue express
Yawn and despise them.

So would I, certainly,
Except that I remember
Homer Park on hot days.

We took the interurban.
We kissed in the shade.

Sidney was our junction;
Six trains a week there.
We rode the dusty local—
Opening all windows—
Then to Detroit.

Philo we drove through,
Cold nights, with horses.
Once there was a dim lamp
Showing, and my father
Stopped for oyster stew.

After forty autumns,
Only I am different.
Here they are as always;
They cannot remember
Themselves as I do.

Spring Birth

The lord of increase, traveling with me,
Said: "Look! There are more than you will see,
Yet look!" And laughed, and pointed at the small
Pigs bouncing as they ran, and at the tall
Bewildered foals, their four legs wildly braced
Lest the ground heave again; while kittens chased
White butterflies, and calves, all ears and head,
Butted and sucked as their great mothers fed.
The lord of increase grinned. "A few of mine,
With foster-help. But listen!" And the whine
Of mayflies filled my ears, and far away,
In wilderness, eggs opened unto day,
And little serpents—were they noiseless?—slid
Through the warm sand. Bare birds above them hid,

Faint-peeping, and a hornet lifted wing
For the first time in nature—not to sting,
But trying the blue air. "All these, and more.
Now close your eyelids." And the forest floor
Padded with feet of foxes, old and young,
As ugly owlets blinked, and beetles clung
To ridges of last winter's bark. "More yet?"
But I believed him, lord of all beget.

Edge of Town: Indiana

Windy spring wakes color up.
See? The green blood returns, and stains
Hedges and hills; and wanton meadows
Wave at the windows of great trains.

Not here, though; the black engine halts
By houses that keep winter time.
This weatherboarding will not bloom,
Whatever happens in May prime.

Whatever comes by upper air—
See? The high trees: their secret flowers!—
These dun verandahs will not flush
With excess joy like ours, like ours.

Like ours. Except the last one there—
Look! The clean curtains, red and white.
And who is this young woman bending
In the green breeze, and pulling tight

The string he plants by? Straight the rows,
Straight the backs of two that stand,
Suddenly, and smile at us,
Leaving them to their sweet land.

The Merry Trainman

Apologetic, the old person in the black hat
Fumbles to descend, saying: "Once I could do this faster."
"Can't fool me," fellow in the blue cap answers. "Dancing,
Dancing—you was up all night—I know it—dancing!
Shame on all such girls. Where's Henry?" And the grandchild
Jumps from the top step of the vestibule—clear down—
And clings. "Old-timer! Well! Hello! And how is crops?"
They both go comforted. He tilts his dusty cap.
"Indianapolis local! Last chance this morning
To visit the state capital and bring back home
Some silver souvenirs. What's that? Three quarters of a half hour
Late? Not by the sun"—he squints—"but what if so?
Who hurries, and who worries? Up with you, Tom Carson.
Smoking car on the right. But I don't recommend it.
Board! All aboard!" And the coach, creaking among cornfields,
Bears on the summer rails his chosen people, smiling.
Seat by sleepy seat he ministers, this Mercury,
This clown of the blue cloth, while overhead the high planes
Hum, with kings in them, or queens for all he cares.

Path Out of Town

No way is straight, so this one wanders
As the first mind did, and the feet,
Obedient, that bending wove,
In the still grass, thought's little street.

And no one since but absently
Winds likewise; not the lover's will,
Not the thief's haste, but history
Determines how we take the hill.

Or is it more, and natural:
Necessity in every curve?
The old man coming with his basket—
He will not hesitate to swerve

As the ground swings, upholding him
For the last time perhaps he fears.
The blind wife, bearing lunch to field,
Touches her dog's attentive ears

And sings, for now the way is sure,
The serpent way some first one found:
Commendable to man and girl;
Commodious for wind and hound.

To Be on Trains

To be on trains, perfection of alone:
The one among the many that the blue cap
Counts not, sitting in the roar
Of such a startled stillness as the whistle—
Where?—unmakes and makes as whirlwinds do
Necessity of sound. To be this one
Yet no one that the blue cap, bending, sees.
To be nowhere but here, and yet not, yet not
Anywhere by night, by day—which is it,
Brother in the green seat opposite, sister
Ahead there, swimming under time's
Thick water, under firmaments of—oh,
To be and not be numbered—let it go
Oh, anywhere, this absolute alone.

Civilization

Before the eaves stop dripping, there they are,
Those martins. They come out of doors and sit.
They shake off showery drops. They almost hold
A hand out, testing the sun's intention.
One of them, in shirtsleeves, reconsiders
Darkness; but his neighbor treads the porch,
Looks right and left for enemies, looks up;

Looks down; and—what no man could do—dives,
Dives, and comes back up with a bent twig
That disappears with him as dead grass does
A busy minute later; when more birds,
On the north side, near where the thunder was,
Issue and sit, reflective; then decide
And fly, and fill the air all afternoon
With comings and with goings; and between,
The looking down. They say this little city
On the high pole is theirs, and that they built it.
Better for them than the poor hollow trees
Their first parents fashioned—all those tops
That tossed, and bark that rotted; and the squirrel teeth
That chattered. None of these but can remember,
Gazing east, the wilderness that was.

In Douglas County

In Douglas County winds do blow—
No doubt of it—all night, all day.
And did long since. My grandchild cheek
Itself remembers, in dry May,

How the first men here, setting forth,
Took their own faces for a guide.
Where the wind struck, on eye or temple—
That was southwest, and would abide.

So off they journeyed—green the waste,
And sometimes flowery, but no trees;
No tell-tale tops to mark the land:
Compasses for throats and knees.

Nothing but this that must not shift;
Southwest was here where the forehead stung.
One man was lost. But I believe
The whole high world that morning swung.

What Fury

What fury in the white sky
Showing over Shepherd's woods!
Look! Is it a kingbird
Or purple martin pouncing so?
There! He almost had the duck hawk
Down. But then he let him go.

Courage? Would you call it that?
Spirit, in a speck as wild
As windy leaf, as falling flake?
Now the updraft—see him rise
And give it to him hard again—
Always aiming at the eyes.

Wrath? Or is it even felt?
Rage at least would have a reason.
Where in such a little brain—
But it is finished. There he went.
He was only playing blazes
In blue air. A spark, and spent.

Single Majesty

Behold him, that great solitary
Tree in the forgotten field.
Fences, falling, left him long ago
To lord it, and he does,
That archer,
That great reacher oak,
That master of this meadow, bent
By nothing but strong wind.
No fellow crowds him,
Nothing but the sun on all sides
Shapes him—oh, so full
That crown, as if no other lord

397

Lived anywhere, no grass
But waited for this shadow,
No birds were
But his.
Behold him and forget him if you can,
That king
Of this lost meadow.

The Only World

The meadow hedge hides meadowlarks
Whose voices rise as rise the roses,
Breaking at the top in bloom
Of sound and scent while daytime dozes;

Dozes over wind and dust;
Dozes over tractor roar—
Behemoth of the middle world
Murders music more and more.

Yet here by hedge the hidden throat,
The buried thorn decline the death;
Sending bubbles up and up
Of sweetly broken heart and breath

Till every leaf is overlaid,
Till every drop of air is drowned,
And sleepy daytime dreams again
Of its own scent, of its own sound.

This is the only world that was;
That will be when Behemoth dies;
That is at all, the meadowlarks
And roses murmur as they rise.

Culture of Corn

The great machines that mouse these fields
In May, between the long, dark showers—
How they do master and despise
The stick, the hoe that once were ours.

Even the coulter, tearing sod,
Even the horses, our huge slaves—
The red machines remember nothing.
Man and beast are in their graves,

And only metal that moves itself
Goes back and forth here, biting in.
Yet truth to say, the softened fields,
Supine, are willing that it win.

They lie there, those great breeding queens,
Brown at the breast and cool of womb,
And wait for seed; nor ever sigh
Because no two feet, four feet come.

Granary

The tall new crib is woven steel:
A humming cylinder in wind—
This wind—that once on weathered boards
Stopped dead. It made no music then,
Nor knows perhaps it whispers now
Among the meshes of such walls.

So high it is, so huge and old,
It may not hear what things it does,
It may not care if wood or wire,
If buildings, if October trees,
Stand out of earth a little way,
Opposing it a little while.

Come closer. Listen, and look up.
The whole sky—does it seem to sound?
But let your memory climb too,
And spread and spread till this be gone.
What did we say? Did something sing?
Does corn still blossom? Are there men?

The Uncle I Was Named For

I

The uncle I was named for
Is not there now, four muddy miles
Northwest of Wapanucka, Oklahoma.
But I remember 1939.
"Ask anyone in town how to get out here."
I had the letter, and I asked
At the first filling station.
"Mark Butz? Believe I seen him."
"Where?" "Oh, down a ways."
And so I started, but was stopped almost at once
By a fat person in loose overalls.
"Are you Mark Butz's nephew?"
I didn't need to tell him. "He's in town,
He's looking for you." "Where?"
"Why, could be anywhere. Might try the drugstore."
I hardly got the screen door open. "You
Mark Butz's nephew?" "Yes." "Well, he's been here
All day." "Been where?" "Oh, down a piece.
Been looking for you." "Has he?" I disturbed
The flies again, and started on.
The whole town turned and looked at me,
And waited—oh, they knew—until I came
To the hot awning and the five old men,
And one of them stood up,
The tall one, that my mother named me for.
He's not there now, or anywhere;

Nor has to be, as long as I
Keep on this earth
And can remember.

II

He went ahead with our own boys,
In an old bronco car that jumped the ruts
Or splashed in them, and laughed
At the worse way I picked as we pursued him;
Then suddenly turned in, uphill a little,
To the squat, square, cement-block house
He had replaced his cabin with,
The log one he lived in as a bachelor.
And that was not so long ago; he married late,
At fifty, and he let the cabin stand
For lumber, or for firewood, off one corner
Of the new porch Aunt Cora waved from.
No log was left now
Of the disorderly old room he had inhabited
Forever, by our legend. A relation
Coming, he would take his shotgun down
And stand in the door and shoot one of his wild
Chickens, and boil it tender in the fireplace.
But that was then. Aunt Cora
Waved, and this was now, and he
Was proud of being different. "Well, get out."
And so we did, for supper in a varnished
Kitchen, under a droplight.
"Your Uncle Mark," she said, "was a hard man
To marry. I had to be a widow first. He wouldn't
Ask me in those other days. In these—
Well, I asked him." And his blue eyes
Were pleased. He was my mother's
Brother, with the same blue eyes; and so we talked
Of her, and Illinois; but not of the time
His father, my grandfather, a little and old
And angry man, disgraced him—sent him off,
I never heard what for. He walked a mile,

401

Then there was Grandma Butz, come through the oak woods
By a short cut. She cried and gave him money.
He didn't know I knew.
"Well, now!" he said, "how long can you be with us?
You didn't really mean it—just one night.
After thirty years, not just one night!"
But so it was. I think he never slept when we did.
I looked out once, and he was reading,
With silver glasses, upright on a cot, still in
His underwear. He wasn't tired,
As we were. Or was excited. Or had sworn
He wouldn't miss our first peep in the morning.
He had of course to wake us up, for pancakes.
"I'll go with you and put you on the good road—
Yes, I will!" insisting. So the boys
Climbed in with him again. Aunt Cora waved
Her apron, and we went; and stopped
When he did, maybe ten slow miles away,
Where the concrete began. Then he got out
And looked at us. "Good-by."
"Good-by." He still could be there,
Looking. He knew it was the last time.
He found it hard to die, Aunt Cora wrote.

No Word, No Wind

I

What god was there
When the slow buggy, appearing and disappearing,
Slipped in and out of moon and maple shadows, down
Those least of earth's depressions, up those low,
Those prairie rises? Eighteen miles
From town to sleepy town, and not a lamp
In any passing window—oh, so slowly
Passing, as the mare's feet
Shuffled, and the delicate wheels
Answered, invisible in windless

402

Dust. No weather then,
No breath of any god, no loud intelligence
Looking. Nothing blown out of the north,
No word.
What understanding, nevertheless, what hidden listener
Brooded? For the whole of that great place
Consented—I remember it—
Consented, and we nodded in the narrow
Seat, and safely crawled up hills
That were no hills, down grades that were but folded
Ground, with gentle pockets of cool air
Where the night sighed, considering itself.
No rain, no sun, no sting of snow,
No sound of rivers, sluggish, far away among their sycamores
In bottom land, forgotten.
And no wind.
What god, if nothing breathed? I might go back there,
Maybe, and find out. But that same night
Is not there now;
Never again, I think, will such a stillness
Be, and not be spoken to.
No word, no wind—I swear it,
Not one sign
That the world knew we went that way at all.

II

Whereas in whirling March—oh, I remember—
Or the dog days,
Or knee deep in the Christmas drifts
That crusted later—all white ice
Both ways a thousand miles to where the mountains were,
And are, that leave that valley to itself,
Lonesome, and vast, and unreportable—
Or mournfully, in fall,
When the pale corn, suffering the southwest
Trade winds, rustled by night, by day, as if a dead sea
Whispered, pitying the labor
Of its own waves, interminable, intentless—

403

Then what mind presided? Father
Or mother of all those men,
Those midland children, what lost mind
Like theirs looked down and listened,
Sharing it with them, that great place
To which they both consented? Someone did,
And does. Or are they several, enormous, many-
Minded, with no single
Voice that yet can sing, that yet can say,
As some day it may do, what meaning lies
In the long vacancy between those silent mountains?
So far, not a thoughtful
People; so far, not an articulate
Deity, unless that world of weather
Itself is god, is goddess, trying
Their patience whom alternately it blasts
And lulls to slumber
On hot nights
When grain but not idea grows. I might go back there,
Maybe, and look sharp; and shall,
Some day, and listen. There is no other
Sky that I would rather, after these distant
Years, see face to face.

He Loves Me

That God should love me is more wonderful
Than that I so imperfectly love him.
My reason is mortality, and dim
Senses; his—oh, insupportable—
Is that he sees me. Even when I pull
Dark thoughts about my head, each vein and limb
Delights him, though remembrance in him, grim
With my worst crimes, should prove me horrible.

And he has terrors that he can release.
But when he looks he loves me; which is why
I wonder; and my wonder must increase
Till more of it shall slay me. Yet I live,
I live; and he has never ceased to give
This glance at me that sweetens the whole sky.

Leaves

Past even wondrous flowers—past white and red,
Past the streaked poison petal, strange of name,
Past cups and hanging bells, past wild or tame
Sun-yellow, past bright blue that goes to bed—
Past all of these with whom delight has wed
Since the first dawn moved any to exclaim,
Earth's kingdom loves its leaves, that are the same
Green ever as forever they are fed.

The king himself loves leaves; see how he thrusts
His hoary head among them—heart-shaped things
He fills and fills; for all their veins are his.
See how his breath sleeps in these delicate wings
That never fly away as summer dusts
And dews find out the only world that is.

Between Sunset and Dark

What is it then that beautifies the fields
Between sunset and dark; or soon before,
When the last light and the long shadows pour
So rich a stream, which overflows and builds
Great banks of blossom? Is it death that gilds
Those groves, and that cut grass, outliving more
Than daytime does, than green? Where is the shore
Of all our world, when thus the center yields?

Why is it then that anyone must know?
Enough that now, midway of noon and night,
Suddenly this is. Suddenly cool light,
Caressing its sweet self, turns into dream
These very stones that not so long ago
Were only what tomorrow they will seem.

The Oldest World

The genius of these hills I see in sleep
Chose wisely for himself. They are his rest
From rocks and trees. They roll both east and west,
Barren of all but the smooth shape they keep
As steadily they climb, leaving the deep
Long valley where I lie and count them, lest
One fold of them be gone. They are the best,
The oldest world, before men lived to weep.

The genius of these slopes was jealous then,
And is this night, I know, of stones and groves;
Of wind and tears; of anything upthrust
Or thrashing. Long ago and now again
He herds them, tall and lone. Look how he roves,
Guarding this little earth and my cool dust.

406

Aftermidsummer

Aftermidsummer, like afternoon,
Suddenly sound-poor, laments the birds
That not so long since, with soprano words,
Shrilled in the trees. And will again, and soon;
They only rest for a hot hour. Their tune,
Up-tumbling, will awake the drowsy herds
In the smooth fields below, as daylight girds
Against the coming sunset and the moon.

The harvest moon, and fall. It is not dark
But cold that comes. Midwinter is the cause,
Far off, that every bird clings to the bark
And listens, letting time tick warm away
As if it were not, and the year, the day,
More perfect for this music in the pause.

A Deer Is Feeding

A deer is feeding in the orchard grass:
A doe; with young ears, maybe, watching her
From the pine thicket southward; not to stir
Until she starts; and then the two will pass,
On amber ankles, delicate as glass,
Among great stones and trees, by dust and burr
Unbothered; or by me—oh, foreigner
Forever, and most terrible, alas.

See how she looks and fears me, all her skin
Atremble. But her eyes—I know them best,
From some that I saw dying once. Within,
How dark, without, how moist. What agony,
What dew of old despair, that even we
Who love them cannot ever burn to rest.

The Keeper and the Kept

The dog indoors, the cat upon the stair,
Four-footed, are at home; and they were so
When other men were here, and the white snow
That fell was not recorded, save as air
Remembers. Wolf and lion, lynx and bear,
And the cold-blooded serpent that must go
Unseen among the rocks, will never know
Of the small beasts that comfort thus our lair.

And satisfy themselves. For wall and rug;
And, past the fender, that unnatural fire,
That sun by night; and milk and meat not dug,
Not wild, but warm in dishes, they accept
As theirs and ours—the keeper and the kept,
And both of us contented with the hire.

Like Raining in a River

Like raining in a river; like the dove,
The mourning dove, when day already dies;
Like dawn at noon were there a sun to rise—
But oh, there is, and she is my own love—
Like dreams in dreams her bounty is, above
All asking, and all wanting, were I wise;
But I am not, and so it multiplies—
My happiness, that nothing will remove.

It is the child of such a sweet excess
In her that loves me, it can never end.
See how she tries, by giving, to be less,
Yet grows; and so my love does, that is friend
To trees and stars, those great ones who confess
All night how far love's limits do extend.

Sullen Love

My grievance that so mounted and so mocked
The very sounds it rose on—where in space,
Between what stars, confirmed in their cold grace,
Does it lie now and sleep, with planets rocked
And great suns soothed and warmed? My wild words locked
So long the truth of love in, and my face
So guilty grew, remembering, no near place
Could be their host. But heaven is not shocked.

I still can listen, if I shut my eyes
And shame me, to the falsehood I put forth.
And part believed; the fabricator tries
His best in sullen love to prove the worst.
Faint, though, and far. That anger now is nursed
Only by constellations east and north.

The Mean of Love

"Does he love you?" She hesitated long,
Then listed all the signs of yes and no.
He kept her in his house; but sudden snow
Blew sometimes, and the windows opened wrong.
"Do you love him?" The question was a song
Itself, and she was ravished. Sweet and low
She heard it—leaned and heard it, breathing so,
The very silence answered pure and strong.

How could he be uncertain? There she stood,
A fugitive this hour from those extremes—
Of fire in him, of ice—and called it good,
The difference. How can men throw gold away?
Yet it was not for me to think and say.
The mean of love is never what it seems.

My World's Body

"Identify the logs in the fireplace, burning?
They are not logs at all, if one remembers—
I do—where they lived, and made December's
Picture on blank snow; but the sun, returning,
Thickened the leaves above them, and discerning
Birds built in that darkness. These are members
Still of my world's body." "Even as embers?"
"Even as dust and ashes, even as learning—"

"Oh! Don't say it. Death?" "Why not, my dear?
This blaze came suddenly, by our own act,
But they know now." "Don't say it!" "Then you fear
Before your time. Have we been carried in?
Has any match been lighted? And a thin
Smoke started? Patience, dear, until the fact."

The Misanthrope

For he so loathed the world, this nameless man,
That he said nothing. Something was too much,
Was tribute, was a taste of him, a touch,
A wooing it to change. So as it ran
He watched it, like one pleased with any plan
It had in its great head—that he would clutch
And crush could this be secret, and not such
A glory as never was since time began.

The world, unguessing, went upon its way
Toward its own end, that no one still has seen.
On his deep grave the shadows fall as green
As anywhere since hate and love were born;
Since noiseless night, since musical noonday;
And death down under, fingering his horn.

410

Remembered Gaiety

Remembered gaiety hurts mind and heart
As present pain is impotent to do.
The moment's loss, courageously lived through,
Can die; but not those sudden days that start
And breathe again, immortally apart
From earlier, from after. They are few,
And chance's children; yet their smiles renew
More sadness than death does with all his art.

The people in this picture think to stand
On this same rock forever; he that waves,
And she that simpers—underneath what sun
Do they lie now, forgetting? Wind and sand
That blow here since— O, tell me why time saves,
Merciless, one moment, only one?

Who We Are

It never is ourselves that we hear talking.
Just under, or way over—thus it blows,
That wind of words, and not a listener knows
Of the small animal between, sleepwalking,
Who slips from sight and sound, and from all stalking
Strangers. Down and down their circles close,
Then hover nothing; they are cuckoos, crows,
And jackdaws to this dove they would be hawking.

Or so we tell ourselves, not speaking plain,
Not honoring Time the hunter. Late or soon
He finds us; piece by piece, and heart by brain,
He picks us out of darkness. Who we are
We say at last, like any stone or star,
Or fellow man, or face of the full moon.

411

If Luck Has Senses

If luck has senses and perceives us here,
And punishes our boasting, is it eyes—
Sharp lidded, laughing, since we think us wise?—
Or feelers in the dark that bring her near,
Then break us? Or a single ass's ear,
Suspicious? Or a sting to paralyze
This pride in us that vainly, vainly tries
The very edge of danger falling sheer?

For something in her knows. We tap the wood,
We tell her not to come, yet even now
She listens. Or she looks. Or the thin hood
That hides her trembles quick, as if with breath.
Or is she woman? Short of sudden death,
Luck will not answer who, or when, or how.

Nature's Grace

So natural his grace, men called it more.
They said it was God's own, descended thus
On this light walker who so dazzled us,
Sometimes, we turned away and shut the door.
Yet never sharply. Envy was not sore,
Beholding him, nor were they perilous,
Those eyes, so inward fair, so courteous,
We dreamed of angel times gone long before.

These were the latter days, when men forgot
How spendthrift nature is. With empty space
She plays, rebuilding heaven and old hell
Most cunningly, most like. Yet not so well
That her own maker is deceived; yet not
So wisely that he names it his, the grace.

412

None But Death

How was it when he knew that none but Death
Had come for none but him? He of all men,
He must have been the most unready. Then,
There was this stranger. Oh, it takes our breath,
Thinking of his that stopped. The preacher saith,
Prepare. But how was he to die again
Who never once had dreamed it—even when
This burden grew that every man downlayeth?

He bore the dark sky lightly. He looked out
As if from under happy leaves, in showers.
But a wild storm—he carried that about
Daylong upon his head; nor laughed at those
Like us who could not. Now the beaten rose
Lies flat. The heavens fell. Weep, all you flowers.

Equal to Equal

Courtesy was born among the stars.
They were the first to sing as love looked down
On morning's chaos, heaving. Still the frown
Of fear on every face, and rumored wars
Of thunder between worlds. So love in tears
Sat looking. But creation did not drown
Like death in its own silence—oh, that sound
At silver sunrise, east among the stars.

Nor were the dark ones modest. Great and small,
They sang alike, each one of them more proud
For knowing each was master, and could call,
Equal to equal, across heaven's waste.
And yet it was no desert if they faced
Due inwardly and smiled, and sometimes bowed.

413

Cold Change

Nothing is more implacable than change—
Cold change, the heart's hard enemy—except
His will that one time made it. Then he slept.
And sleeping still, beyond the farthest range
Of fashion, there he lies, and is more strange
Even than time that breaks us. He has kept
No tally of our losses, nor has wept
At the worst woes our folly could arrange.

For we ourselves play doom, and dare the years
Never to alter. Or we think and shift
As if we too were gods, and turn the gears
Of the great engine that he built; and lift
Our fortunes—oh, a little. But our fears
Fall with us, in eternity's downdrift.

What Beast Is This

What beast is this, not bellowing, not stung
With blood, that moves upon us to devour?
For it is near—the never ending hour
Of our own death, that all the saints have sung.
But where is the great animal? Among
What rushes does he build his ruinous bower?
Why is he not louder? So much power,
And hidden! All that fury, and no tongue!

Be still. How do you know the beast is strange?
Look in your neighbor's eyes. He may be there.
Look in your own. Nothing so much can change
As man. The very foulest was most fair
In Eden. Then be still and let him range,
That shadow monster met upon the stair.

414

Humanity Unlimited?

Humanity unlimited? Oh, ring
Fire bells; unleash the bloodhounds, and the tall
Mastiffs; and start building, somewhere, wall
On wall that daws and eagles on the wing
But no proud man can pass. Do anything,
My masters, to confine us one and all—
You, too—within the pasture and the hall
And the grey church where sadness used to sing.

It sang that we were prisoners of ourselves,
And jailers—oh, the echo doubled back
And crushed us. There was not a lighted crack
That let the worst, the best of us go through.
Yet it was sweeter. Mice upon the shelves
Of our great cupboard envied us; and you.

Yes, I Know

Political our life is—yes, I know.
The common good is golden, and the deed
Most manly is to love it, and to lead
Those other ones that hesitate to go—
Look at them. Their souls are pale as snow
With ignorance and fear. See how they feed
On darkness, and the root of such a weed
As wisdom might make blossom. Yes, I know.

Then why am I this season sunk so far
In my own shadow? Now am I the same
As others; nor do I remember still
That sun we saw together. Dangers are,
And deaths, and wide disasters. But my will—
Oh, woe—feeds on itself and stubborn shame.

415

The Time of Martyrs

The time of martyrs may be come again;
Yet as of old, no single heart is foul.
Security, blindfolded, wears the cowl;
Stupidity sits here and judges men.
The best are most despised, as they were then;
As long ago they did, the worst ones howl
Loudest of fair intentions—wolf and owl
And dark hyena, guarding our great den.

The time of martyrs may be come and gone,
And we too late discover what is lost.
The beaten dog most happily will fawn;
December's flower forgives October's frost.
The time of martyrs—is it aging on,
With no spring meadows waiting to be crossed?

The Deepest Dream

The deepest dream is of mad governors.
Down, down we feel it, till the very crust
Of the world cracks, and where there was no dust,
Atoms of ruin rise. Confusion stirs,
And fear; and all our thoughts—dark scavengers—
Feed on the center's refuse. Hope is thrust
Like wind away, and love sinks into lust
For merest safety, meanest of levelers.

And then we wake. Or do we? Sleep endures
More than the morning can, when shadows lie
Sharper than mountains, and the cleft is real
Between us and our kings. What sun assures
Our courage, and what evening by and by
Descends to rest us, and perhaps to heal?

416

The War God

The war god is not guilty any more.
Time was he winced, meeting our angry eyes.
And even then prevailed, yet knew it wise
Not to seem proud, sending sweet peace before
As sister, goddess, queen. But with a roar
Now he blasphemes her, and his bluster flies
Like desert wind, and fills the dirty skies.
He says that peace is his dishonest whore.

And who of us but laughs, though bitterly
We wonder at the change in us, and charge
Now him, now fate, with fathering such blood?
War's moment, lengthened to eternity—
What else is our religion? What so large,
So terrible? We worship it, the Flood.

Too Many Fears

God is not gone? Fear rules us as before?
But of too many things, the prophet said;
And counted them by tapping his lean head
Whose eyes so long had pondered, keeping score.
Those dreams that burrow nightly, and that bore
Still deeper all the day—as in the dark
Some worms, insatiable, are never fed—
Too many! and he sighed. But you have more.

Nor is one fear the father of the rest.
God is not gone? Then why are these so wild?
Why are they unnamed, why unconfessed?
Oh, none of them is dutiful, is child,
Is messenger to him whose terrible breast
Still broods; and still with mercy could be mild.

Again, That Laughter

Censorious, the old remember days
When punishment fell instantly on fools;
And knaves were not; or if they were, the rules,
Read to them on gallows, in the gaze
And audience of others, showed them ways
They should have gone. But now the ghosts and ghouls
Outnumber upright men, and mercy pules
Excuses at the center of its maze.

So croak the old ones, and the young ones smile
And say it is their weakness. Were they well,
And the blood bounded in them, they would pile
Pity on pity too, and take the shame
On their own shoulders. (Listen. There it came
Again, that laughter. Do they hear in hell?)

Born Brothers

Equality is absolute or no.
Nothing between can stand. We are the sons
Of the same sire, or madness breaks and runs
Through the rude world. Ridiculous our woe
If single pity does not love it. So
Our separate fathers love us. No man shuns
His poorest child's embrace. We are the sons
Of such, or ground and sky are soon to go.

Nor do born brothers judge, as good or ill,
Their being. Each consents and is the same,
Or suddenly sweet winds turn into flame
And floods are on us—fire, earth, water, air
All hideously parted, as his will
Withdraws, no longer fatherly and there.

The Prism

When Adam fell, and Eve, and the gates closed
Forever, with a clang that lightning now
Repeats, and thunder mourns, perfection dozed;
And dozes still, save that a happy brow
Sometimes in wind remembers, and somehow
Adam is not dead; the scarlet-rosed,
The green angelic garden he reposed
And climbed in sings again from every bough.

But all men since are gone. The patriarchs,
The heroes—even they were broken beams
Of the first morning light, that fell on larks
And lived: no single splinter of it lost,
As piecemeal in our minds the truth is tossed
On waves of darkness here, and dawn but seems.

There Was an Island

Did the gods ever, manifest in form,
Come to men's houses at the hour of meat,
And sit, and taste? And did small children greet
Their greatness, bringing coals to keep them warm?
They had come far, though instantly, through storm
And upper darkness. Did they rest their feet,
And did the housewife smile, and serve them sweet
Clear honey from the hive, the summer swarm?

There was an island, misty in the sea,
Where thus they wandered—not in stranger's guise,
Not beggarly, not human, but as he
Their chiefest lord once made them; and his eyes
Always were on them, lest they cease to be.
(Odysseus, tell us truly. Were they lies?)

419

And Now by Dark

The big and little stars that burn by night—
There is one time they should not, yet they do;
And all the more fiercely then, as if Great Who,
Great What so high above us loved this blight
Of dryness here, these streams sunk out of sight
And the green pastures withering—men, too,
And beasts, lamenting springs where coolness grew
By grace of thunderheads both black and white.

Now nothing but hot days and dying trees;
And now by dark, as we come out of doors,
These pitiless huge gazers—even these,
That once could hide, and did, in overcast
And whirlwind. But the time for that is past,
Old Scorpion sings, and licks his glittering sores.

After Long Drought

After long drought, commotion in the sky;
After dead silence, thunder. Then it comes,
The rain. It slashes leaves, and doubly drums
On tin and shingle; beats and bends awry
The flower heads; puddles dust, and with a sigh
Like love sinks into grasses, where it hums
As bees did once, among chrysanthemums
And asters when the summer thought to die.

The whole world dreamed of this, and has it now.
Nor was the waking easy. The dull root
Is jealous of its death; the sleepy brow
Smiles in its slumber; and a heart can fear
The very flood it longed for, roaring near.
The spirit best remembers being mute.

420

And Did the Animals?

And did the animals in Noah's ark—
That was of oleander wood, with cabins
Cunningly bitumined in and out—
Did all those animals lie quietly?
For months and weeks and days, until the dove
Came home, and they were dry on Ararat,
Did every bird, with head beneath its wing,
Did every beast, with forepaws folded in,
Did every reptile, coiled upon itself,
Lie sleeping as no man did, patiently?
A man might think this tempest would not end,
Nor timbers cease to creak, nor the light come.
These did not know it rained, these did not know
Their kind survived in them if it survived.
A thinking man might doubt it, and in misery
Listen. Did they listen? But to what?
They did not know of time, they did not count
The waves. Then did they cry out in their dreams?
Or did they even dream, those specimen souls?

The Rainbow

"Though every man be evil in his mind
From the first breath of thought, I now do promise
Never again to wish all flesh destroyed,
Either by flood or fire." So Noah heard,
And wondered. Even the animals, God said,
Were safe beneath His rainbow—all poor things
With blood in them to come and go forever
As day and night did, and as winter, summer.
To live and die. Poor things, and yet His own.
So Noah wondered; and so all men since

421

Have said: Is it not strange, His disappointment?
For knowing all, He still knew not the deep ways
This creature most like Him was bound to go;
Or if not bound, did go, has gone, and will
Till the round earth itself no more is dreamed.
Is it not wonderful, men say, that even
He of the vast vision, even He
That brooded above the firmament, and fished
Each form out of the void, the desolation,
The darkness and the wind—oh, even He
Anticipated nothing. Not a soul,
They cry, but must amaze Him; so much more,
So other than His plan; all these recesses
Singing in the heart; all these volutions
Of the still motley serpent in the skull.
So all men since the rainbow, looking inward,
Have wondered at themselves; and flattered thus
The very flesh He wanted to destroy
Yet did not; for He pitied the poor thing.

The Prophet Enoch

Who were the sons of heaven that looked down
One day and saw earth's women and desired them?
Samyaza was their captain; Asael,
Urakabarameel, Yomyael,
Saraknyal, Zavebe, and Armers
Were prefects; all in all, two hundred angels
Fell that day so deep beyond redemption,
Only the darkest desert now contains
Their bones, that still are burning as they burned
That day they saw our women, and deployed
From Armon, wooing sweet flesh in the lowlands
Where men were, and their wives, and winsome daughters
Not meant for incorruptible delight.
In both it was corruption; neither earth
Nor heaven knew this thing until that day,

When curtained beds, and mosses in the fields,
And river banks and caverns by the ocean,
Shadowy with love, conceived in shame
A progeny of giants, who devoured
Earth's animals and fruits, and would have eaten
Man himself, had not the deluge come
That cleansed us. Angel to angel, dust to dust—
Love then was true once more, as still it is,
On earth as it is in heaven. For no woman,
Wife to a man, pollutes him. And no star,
Wed to another there, wanders mistaken.
Or so the prophet Enoch says and sings.

Abraham and Isaac

A solitary ram that day was grazing,
That day of all days, in Moriah grass.
Thin grass, and thoughtless ram. It did not need
To think, that silly sheep with the curled horns
Held ever downward, moving on and on
As if by its own choice—for instance now,
When it came near an old man with a knife
Uplifted. Shining knife, about to fall
On a stretched boy, silent among faggots.
Silent boy, eyes open, facing up.
All of Moriah, silent. The ram moved
Again—its ultimate free act, for brushwood
Caught the curled horns. It butted, but was caught.
And the old man listened. Not to this,
But listened. Then he looked, and his hand trembled,
Suddenly, with joy. The ram was here
By no thought of its own, nor was its last act
Free. It had been destined for this day,
And lived it as it should, head ever downward,
Moving on and on, even to where
This brushwood was, that rattled. But the old man,
Listening, had not heard so near a sound.

It was God's voice that said to him, Let be.
Only that soon he looked; and sacrificed,
Instead of his one lamb, this chosen sheep.

Rebekah

Abraham's old slave, come to the well
At Nahor, seeking water for his camels
And a good wife for Isaac, found Rebekah—
Perfect in simplicity, found one
Clear girl he could thank God for, and adorn
With rings and bracelets, and at sunrise take
Forever home to be the wife of Isaac.
Whom she deceived. Rebekah in her womb
Felt twins at war, and knew that she must favor
One above the other when both lived.
She favored Jacob; and if Isaac more
Loved Esau, with the hairy hands and neck
That smelled of dewy fields, and of wild animals
And grain, being her husband he was helpless.
For the same girl it was, grown old with him,
Who tricked him now by sending Jacob in
For the blind man's unalterable blessing.
The skin of kids betrayed him, so that Esau's
Sons, by Ishmael's daughter, and by ruder
Breeds, were never children of God's line.
But Jacob walked with angels, and his son
Was Joseph. So Rebekah the deceiver
Had the same mind that Abraham's old slave
Found once as clear as water. And it was.
Even that day she knew—or did she then?—
That she was God's own virgin, born at Nahor
To visit on these men this mortal hurt.
But guilty Jacob slept and dreamed of angels.

Dinah

For Dinah ravished, all of Shechem's city
Paid with all its blood. Shechem's, too,
It chiefest prince, who longed for Dinah so—
To keep her, whom he ravished—he could smell
No craft in Dinah's brothers till they smote
And smote, and every house, red with the horror,
Died; even Shechem's, where in silence
Dinah sat. But her they rescued. And
She wept. Was it for joy? Or walking slow,
Did Dinah weep for justice—all the blood
Of all that lover's people drying now
In sunless rooms behind her? Did she turn
And look, and was it well that Shechem's face
No longer hoped for kindness in these eyes?
For afterward-consent? Shechem's hands—
Did Dinah shudder? Nothing tells of this,
Or anything she thought that bloody day
Her brothers bore her home, and she could hear
The captive herds about her—all the sheep,
Bewildered, and the beaten asses braying.

Joseph Wept

"The old man of whom you spoke—your father—
Is he yet living? Is he well?" Red-eyed,
The sons of Leah nodded. "And your youngest
Brother, of whom you told me—is this he?"
For Benjamin stood there, clear-lidded, beautiful,
The son of his own mother Rachel. And four more,
That maids had bred. But Benjamin alone
Was cause that Joseph went into his room
And shut the door and wept. The twelve of them—
All here, with Jacob far away in Canaan,
Starving. All together at this end
Of bitter time. For ten of them had hated

425

Joseph, their bright brother. Only Benjamin,
Whose blessed birth had been the death of Rachel,
Only he had not. Therefore these tears.
And yet the ten that sold him into Egypt,
The ten his dreams offended—they were cause,
And older. For he thought: I was the bright one;
I dreamed and told my dreams. I did not hide
My light in loving clouds; I did not shame
To shine full in their faces. Was it God's
Cunning and deep purpose so to cleave us
That now and here, in Egypt, a thin remnant
Of Israel might live? Nevertheless
I boasted, and despised them; thought me different,
And better. And I was. But am no more.
The dozen is made one. God's miracle
Is that we all are met—they in their garments,
Bowing, and I in mine, a gorgeous stranger,
Lofty, and their lord. Now I must go,
Must speak to them: "I am your brother Joseph;
Our father—is he well?" Then all shall weep—
I know it. Can I do this? Can I still
Not weep myself? Yet why should I not weep?
Why should there be that difference then, when none
Is here now in my heart? So half in fear
He bathed his face and opened the gold door
Between them, and sat down with them to eat.

Joseph and Jacob

In a swift chariot, with horses jingling
The red gold of their bridle ornaments,
Joseph drove deep into the land of Goshen,
Then stopped. This might be Jacob, his old father,
Coming. And it was. The patient wagons,
The sheep, the cattle, herded by good hands,
The asses' pointed ears, and all those people—
Fifty, sixty, seventy—it was Israel

426

Coming. And he walked ahead to meet them,
Looking right and left for the old man
His father, who had thought him dead. "My son!
Now that I have seen you, I can die."
Here then he was, descended from the forward
Wagon. And he limped. Come all the way
From Canaan, in the desert dust, he limped—
A small old man, the socket of whose thigh
Still hurt him. And they fell upon each other,
Weeping: Joseph, vice-king of all Egypt,
In linen robes, with gold about his neck
And a great signet ring, and sons at home
By Asenath, the daughter of the priest
Of On, by whom he almost had forgotten
Israel and its woes—Joseph mingled
His tears with those of Jacob, who one night,
So long ago that only a hip remembered,
Wrestled in the dark with God's tall angel,
And won. But when the day broke over Penuel,
He limped; and ever had while Joseph dreamed
In Egypt, that rich dying land, and prospered
By famine. Now from Canaan these had come,
These many sons of Jacob, with their wives
And children. Sixty-six, the whole of Israel,
Exiled. They were desolate and poor,
But young; and they would multiply; and Joseph,
Savior of them all, would be forgotten.
Brilliant in his linen and his gold,
And welcoming their caravan with tears
And smiles, even he would be forgotten.
For he was not of them, this prince of Nile
Whom God Himself one day would scarce remember.

How Moses Saw God

"No man can look upon my face and live.
My glory you may see, but not myself."

The people at the bottom of the mountain,
Nor Aaron, nor the elders, heard Jehovah
Say it, topmost there on Sinai,
Beyond the cloud whose darkness hid the truth
As thunder hatches lightning. And already
Trumpets had sounded, and already fire,
Seeming to consume itself, had smoldered,
Smoldered, then had vanished. But the mind
Of Moses heard, and his ears trembled. "Man—
I know your name—retire into that cleft
Of rock while this my glory passes by.
My hand will hold you there. Be not afraid.
It shall be more impossible to look
Than, having looked, to live. Be not afraid."
So He that was no other than He was
Passed by, and did not turn again. And Moses,
Gazing as into sunset, saw God's back;
And bowed; and fasted all of forty days
And forty nights in wonder; then went down
To his own people, waiting. Who in fear
Avoided him. For now his very skin,
As if it had been tested in a furnace,
Glowed; and they avoided him, until
He veiled himself. As thunder wraps hot lightning,
So Moses hid the truth of what he saw
On Sinai that day. No other man
Has seen as much; and even he but saw
God's back, as at the setting of all suns
That ever yet have risen or will rise.

Jephthah's Daughter

Jephthah, son of a harlot, had one daughter,
Born in the land of Tob, where he with brigands
Raided the flocks and herds. But Gilead's sons,
His brothers, who had banished him, were sorry,
And sent for him to come and save them now.

"And if the Ammonites go down before me,
Then will I be your chief?" They swore it, Yes,
And armed him; and he vowed, if he were victor,
That the first living creature whom at Mizpeh
He met by his own door should die for God.
He triumphed, and rode home; and lo, this daughter
Ran to him—with tambourines and dancing
Ran to him; and wondered why he wept,
And why he tores his clothes. "My only child"—
So then she knew, and knelt. But when no blow
Descended—none was ready, in his weakness—
She cried to him: "For two months let me live.
Alone among the mountains let me wander
With my few maidens, mourning my estate."
For not one man had known her, and no man
But Jephthah would be desolate that day,
Two full moons hence, when the keen knife must fall.
If he consented gladly, did he rest then?
Did Jephthah rest? The thing was still to do.
A thousand hours, each one of them more terrible
Than this one that was over—yet not over—
How could he pass them? How did Jephthah, chieftain,
Son of a harlot, pass them? No one hears;
Or whether on the mountains she regretted,
Too, that gift of time—all those sunrises,
Powerless to prepare her for the dark arms
Of the one husband she would have at last;
And had at last; and lies with him eternally,
Mourning her bright maidenhood below.

The Ark of the Covenant

An empty box, the sons of Baal said;
Nothing inside except the mumbling words
Of one no man remembered; he had lived
On mountains long ago, and he had lighted
Israel out of Egypt; but where now,

And who, and why should any stout foe fear him?
So they abducted the acacia chest
That Moses built and overlaid with gold
Inside and out; even the rings and poles
He overlaid with gold; and placed inside it
Nothing but parchment texts of the decrees
He heard on Sinai once, and well remembered.
Nothing but those. Yet bloody death was in them
For the stout sons of Baal: plagues and tempests,
And Dagon falling down, and slaughtered thousands
Crying upon the silence; for no sword
But silence, silence killed them. So the Philistines,
Secretly, by night, sent home the terrible
Box; and the bearers listened; but no sound
Came out of it, no mumbling. It was the silence,
Silence, that had killed them. "Thou shalt have
No other gods before me." Even this
No bearer heard; for the deep sleep of faith
Was on the world that night; and if a dream
Disturbed it, Israel too shook in her bed,
Foreseeing all the shame, all the forgetting.

Last of the Judges

"Then you may have your king." And the proud people
Shouted. But they had not listened close.
They had not heard the whirlwind in his throat,
Whispering God's wrath; for now as always,
Samuel, their pure judge, was but a horn
Through which the past and future blew, and truth,
Welcome or unwelcome, hummed in the airways.
It hummed there now, and doomed them, but they laughed
And shouted. Even now, his head and shoulders
Higher than the highest, Saul was wandering
In search of lost she-asses; and became
Their king; and blundered daily; till his death
Was their death too, though David's time, succeeding,

And Solomon's, seemed blissful. But it blew,
That whirlwind, even then, and only struck
As the long sun of Israel went down
On Jeroboam raging, and the white bones
Of Jezebel, that no wild dog would eat,
Manuring the dead fields that still would mourn,
In utter darkness, hideous captivity,
While prophets groaned, and some few souls remembered
How the proud people once had wanted kings;
Thrice warned, had wanted kings; and here they had them;
And the hoarse words of Samuel, and the lost love
Of God were but as desert lamentations
In a cold corner of the night as far
Away and long ago as Abraham.

Michal

Michal, that she-wife whom David had
For his first comforter, from Saul her father—
But then in fury Saul withdrew the gift—
Michal was another man's awhile;
Was Paltiel's; till David, king himself,
Remembered, and he sent for her by Abner.
Instantly she started—with what words
And what good-bys to Paltiel we know not,
Or whether with embraces. Yet we know
This husband followed, weeping all the way
And watching—all the bleak way to Bahurim
Watching David's wife who was his own,
His own. And yet no longer. So the dust
Was bitter that he breathed; till at Bahurim
Abner, looking down, said "Go, return";
And Paltiel returned. But Michal went
Straight on, the bitter wind sweet in her nostrils,
To where the king was whom another day,
When both of them were older, she would scorn
For dancing in an apron, by the ark

Of God. And he would hate her till she died.
And she would bear no children, either his
Or Paltiel's, until she groaned and died.

Abigail

She met him in a wild pass of the mountains—
David, whom she called her lord, and said:
"I bring you bread and wine, I bring you raisins.
Sheep I bring, and corn, and cakes of figs.
Accept all these, my lord; I am your servant;
I save you from blood-guilt. For you are bound
Where Nabal is, my husband, who insulted
Certain of your soldiers. Do not kill him.
Nabal's very name, my lord, is Fool.
Then do not kill him. When my lord is king,
What pity if a fool's blood blights his conscience.
I am your servant, saving you." He looked,
Beautiful himself, upon her beauty,
And said: "So shall it be. Blessed are you
That kept me from revenge. I would have killed him,
Surely. Go in peace." And David left her.
Then was it with his beauty in her heart
That she went straight to Nabal, who was drunk,
And told him of the danger there had been,
So that his spirit sank in him, like stone,
And in ten days he died? For she was ready
At Carmel when those messengers came in
With word that David wanted her for wife.
She mounted up at once and rode to him,
And married him forever, and forgot—
Or did you, Abigail, that first one's fall?

Bathsheba

When Bathsheba, grown old, one day had audience
With David who was dying—she must speak

432

For Solomon, their son, against the danger
Of Adonijah's coming to be king—
Abishag was there. But Bathsheba
Looked elsewhere; only warned of Adonijah,
Then went as she had come. Did she remember,
Did Bathsheba remember, worlds ago,
Being Uriah's wife whom David saw
On the hot roof, in sun and shadow bathing?
The shadows were against the one great eye
That burned there, and the little ones of men—
On which reflecting, she grew warm with shame;
And turned; and someone told her David saw.
The great eye now was his; the sun went out
In worlds of heat that builded unto heaven—
Save that it was not heaven. For Uriah
Died in war, by David's word, and God
Was not well pleased. And yet they lived,
Those lovers; were the king, the queen; and Solomon
Lived next, whom Adonijah on this day
Threatened to unthrone. So Bathsheba
Spoke only of their son; not of the beautiful
Abishag who stood beside the bed,
And every night lay in it, on the bosom
Of the cold king, whom fleeces could not comfort,
Nor silks, nor the far fire. Only this maiden,
Beautiful as blood, sustained his heart
As once Uriah's wife did, worlds away
And wars ago. So David listened, shivering,
Till Bathsheba retired, and dark came down,
And Abishag lay curled inside his long cloak
Like a warm worm in leaves. While Bathsheba,
Alone, with no eye on her, God's or man's,
Sat wondering at this moonlight in the room,
And yet no moon. Was it his mind, remembering,
And following, and feeling her poor warmth?

433

Sarah of Ecbatana

Tobias, son of Tobit, felt desire
For Sarah, the sad daughter of Raguel,
Before he ever saw her. Could this be?
She was of his people, far away,
And destined for him, Azariah said;
And beautiful, and sensible; but sad
Because of seven bridegrooms she had lost
On seven wedding nights—a demon's work,
Not hers, although the maids accused her so.
The angel Azariah said: "Go up
To her, Tobias, and possess her without fear;
For she is yours, and was from the beginning;
Pray with her, then draw the curtains close,
And sleep all night; I tell you it is well."
And so Tobias, with obedient heart,
Was full of love for Sarah long before
He ever saw Ecbatana, her city.
She was of his people; and was beautiful,
And sensible; and wanted to be dead
Because she did not know the very boy
Was coming who could save her, and whose bride
In truth, not lust, she was from the beginning.
So Azariah said, whose other name
Was Raphael; and obedient Tobias
Eagerly walked with him all the way.

The Word

The people whom He chose to hear His word
Had the one mind that could remember it.
And with what heat they did, until captivity
Cooled them. Or it seemed to. For their voice,
Grown inward now, repeated not to deserts
Nor the wind ears of aliens what they knew
Of further things unfolded, of the hidden

434

Person who was coming—always coming,
And they alone knew why. Yet knew not when.
For the one people He could trust with truth
Had then this terrible, this inward duty
Forever to deny it. He must fail
Who came. Or seem to fail. Oh, the dark word
That in their long captivity they warmed,
Lest truth itself grow cold and die—oh, word,
Oh, wonder, it is still by their surviving
Saved; and by their silence, that keeps warm
And dark the word that too much sun would kill.

SOUL AND CIRCUMSTANCE ꝫ

Praise Him, Praise Her

Praise him, praise her, praise all
Soft steppers, all slow smilers,
All sweet sleepers under
The stars. For they praise them.

By foot, by face, by lying
In bed so lightly, these
Praise them, and therefore Him:
He made them sing together.

And still He does; they know it;
They listen, and they move
Like dancers, and all night
They smile in their sweet sleep.

So far it is down hither—
Praise them, His poor children
Who think they do so little
For such immense reward.

Praise Doubt

Praise the good angel doubt,
Guardian of us that walk
On the deep waters of this world.

Praise him. He never rests,
However weary the way
Over these dark, salt, dangerous meadows.

Do not look down, he says;
Beware with me and the sun
Of faith's innumerable caverns.

Monsters can be there.
You will have plenty of time.
Too soon descending, you are devoured.

Praise him. He believes
In the long day we are given.
Praise him. He dances upon the whitecaps.

Never Another

Praise Him who makes us happy
When not another would;
There is so little reason
In our so little good.

Praise Him who waits all morning,
All afternoon, all night,
All year until this moment
Of that arriving light;

Praise Him who sends it dancing,
Praise Him who lets us see,
And move with it, and listen,
And sing, soberly.

Praise Him who when we lose it,
And twilight thickens sound,
Remembers where we slumber;
Marks this nether ground;

And waits upon our waking
As never another would;
Praise Him who is the reason,
Praise Him, the only good.

The God of Galaxies

The god of galaxies has more to govern
Than the first men imagined, when one mountain
Trumpeted his anger, and one rainbow,
Red in the east, restored them to his love.
One earth it was, with big and lesser torches,
And stars by night for candles. And he spoke
To single persons, sitting in their tents.

Now streams of worlds, now powdery great whirlwinds
Of universes far enough away
To seem but fog-wisps in a bank of night
So measureless the mind can sicken, trying—
Now seas of darkness, shoreless, on and on
Encircled by themselves, yet washing farther
Than the last triple sun, revolving, shows.

The god of galaxies—how shall we praise him?
For so we must, or wither. Yet what word
Of words? And where to send it, on which night
Of winter stars, of summer, or by autumn
In the first evening of the Pleiades?
The god of galaxies, of burning gases,
May have forgotten Leo and the Bull.

But God remembers, and is everywhere.
He even is the void, where nothing shines.

He is the absence of his own reflection
In the deep gulf; he is the dusky cinder
Of pure fire in its prime; he is the place
Prepared for hugest planets: black idea,
Brooding between fierce poles he keeps apart.

Those altitudes and oceans, though, with islands
Drifting, blown immense as by a wind,
And yet no wind; and not one blazing coast
Where thought could live, could listen—oh, what word
Of words? Let us consider it in terror,
And say it without voice. Praise universes
Numberless. Praise all of them. Praise Him.

Dialogue in December

In so much dark no light is little.
    But can light be at the end of the year?
Only listen. It will come.
    And put out dying? And put out fear?
Yes, but listen. Good heart, listen.
    I do, I do—I see, I hear.

That star is enough in this much night.
    It glitters. But a child has cried.
He is the first one in the world.
    Even the old world, that died?
Even the new—he is all the living.
    And all the dead—are they satisfied?

Listen and look. Is there any weeping?
    Only for comfort, only for joy.
Only for love. But the child that was crying—
    He is a beautiful, strange boy.
He is little and weak, this lord of the world.
    But oh, too strong, too strong to destroy.

What We Wanted

Good old rain god, somewhere now
He sits and sends it, what we wanted.
He was dozing, with his hat off,
But it drips again and soaks him;
Droops around him, beard and shoulder·
Hangs there heavy, like his greatcoat,
All the skirts of which run rivers.

Good old sender, there he sits
Supposing this is all we wanted.
And it is, upon the shingles,
And it is, among the hay roots;
Not a horny tree but thanks him.
So he blinks and is complacent:
He has wetted all his children.

Good old ancient, doze again.
There was something else we wanted.
There is still this desert inward,
These hot thorns that hurt each other.
You have nothing for that ailment,
It was not in the beginning,
There is no way rain can reach it.

Good old giver, nevertheless,
Thank you, thank you. It was wanted.
We receive it as the daisies,
We declare it with the puddles—
Listen, listen, on the windows!
Long enough, and who remembers?
Yet we do. It is our weakness.

The Six Swans of Grimm

Their tongue-bound sister, terrified,
Thought only of the starting flame—

Not yet; the faggots were still cold;
But round her now a crackling came—
Not really; it was in her mind,
With panic and supposèd shame.

And yet the king, and yet the crowd,
Heard something too, and looked aloft.
A wedge of wings it was that made
This roaring in the air so soft,
This whirr, as pure white feathers fell
On tower and mead and fence and croft.

"My brothers!" For the six were there,
Standing in coats that proved them men.
"My brothers!" But they did not know
How wonderful it was again
For the sweet words to fly away
Like wind and smoke, like raven and wren.

Soul and Circumstance

Wait not, my soul, on circumstance;
It does not wait for you.
It nibbles at you now, and will
Devour you; I say true.

For I have seen its hungry face
Be satisfied with one
That stood like you, uncertain here,
Thinking himself alone.

And so he was; but circumstance
Was not the friend he lacked.
He had not yet the bitter taste
And strength of his own act.

Insipid sweet, he still denied
Himself and his great kind.

And so I saw him eaten through
And spit away like rind.

The Problem of Good

Ponder as you may, philosopher,
This excellent spirit,
You will not reach the origin
Of so much merit.
The white secret rose
Blooms without cause;
And dying, leaves nothing here for mind to inherit.

The black one, if you will, sir,
Connect with coal;
The red one with river clay;
The brown with wool.
Imperfection sits
Impatiently, and waits
To see itself in intellect, that loves it after all.

Stare into it long, philosopher,
This blinding goodness.
There will be no reflection in it
Of your rudeness.
The white, white rose
Is older than its cause,
Like the great sun, that never thinks upon its gladness.

Nothing Returns

Evil abominates the good
Because the good does not explain.
There was no reason Ruth could give
Except to speak her love again;
And then to prove it with a deed
As soon as Naomi had need.

441

Cold Iago, though, went mad,
Seeing simplicity in power;
Judas could not bear at last
Perfection's music hour by hour;
And struck, but with a senseless kiss
That made the very god we miss.

Evil is sooner understood,
Yet not for this, that still is strange:
It looks upon its opposite
And hates it without hope of change;
Evil abominates and burns;
But all is waste. Nothing returns.

Beauty Is

Beauty is not had,
Beauty is not made.
Beauty hates narrow;
Is wind-wide.

Beauty is not studied,
Beauty is not sold.
Beauty is no king's,
No church's child.

Beauty is not delicate,
Beauty is not dear.
Beauty will break out
Anywhere.

Anywhere beauty is,
All men smile;
Except its prophets;
And they fall.

442

The Good Workman

From there to here, from then till now—
What patience brought him all the way?
What knowing how to wait? And yet
He was not idle any day.

Each thing he did was done for best,
But then tomorrow, glancing down,
He shook his head; and with our smiles
Mingled his own secret frown.

Not that the way was endless; here,
Master of all but death, he lies.
The wonder is the patience—how
He lived with time, and took each rise

As water does, that waits for waves
However close it feels the shore;
As love does, that considers long:
Most is last, and child of more.

To Him That Hath

Those are helped who need no help.
To him that hath it shall be given.
So we see it is on earth,
And so we hear it is in heaven.

And is it true for saints as well:
To them that know it shall be told?
He that was loved is loved again?
He that was lonely—still cold?

And is it terrible at last?
"What else?" the falling pebble sings.
"What juster than this gravity,
That saves me all that waste of wings?

"What mercy is it would permit
My wandering away from here?
From there"—and into center sank
As morning meteors disappear.

If They Spoke

The animals will never know;
Could not find out; would scarcely care
That all their names are in our books,
And all their images drawn bare.

What names? They have not heard the sound.
Nor in their silence thought the thing.
They are not notified they live;
Nor ask who set them wandering.

Simply they are. And so with us;
And they would say it if they spoke;
And we might listen; and the world
Be uncreated at one stroke.

The Animals Slept On

The answer came by dream.
"They do not know of death.
So they can sleep and sleep,
And never count their breath;
They do not live by number,
The very name of death."

The animals slept on.
They did not know I heard.
"And therefore every conscience
Of every beast and bird
Is free as air, as water,
Of what the wind has heard."

The animals lay still;
They did not know I dreamed;
And let the world turn with them
Entirely as it seemed;
And sleeping was but waking,
And waking was but dreamed.

WHEN THE WORLD ENDS ૨⚭

The Mirror

Nothing could this man dismay.
He held a mirror in his hand:
A small one, but it looked away
As time does over sleeping land.

It showed him worse things coming yet;
So all our present, by compare,
Was only bitter, was Tibet,
To those ice absolutes of air.

He saw the poles beyond whose white
Two tireless eyes gazed here at him;
And had been gazing since the night
Before creation's interim;

And still would gaze when time again
Slept in eternity's slow arms;
That hushed the seas, and muffled men
Against great waves and wars' alarms.

Yet no man now. Each is his own.
He smiled; he pocketed the glass.
Serenity in him alone
Lives on and on, alas, alas.

Breathing Was Hard Enough

Breathing was hard enough,
Poor body,
With my child mind that altered hour by hour,
Startled by mouse fears, dreaming
Intimately, self-pleased,
Of ghosts that did not matter.

Breathing was harder still,
Tough body,
But you did not complain when gathering storms
Struck at us both, and proved,
Palpably, in man's day,
My terror was full grown.

Breathe in and out with me
Now, body—
Now—breathe in and out, as by a machine
Built to keep two alive—
It may, those doctors tell us—
Oh, in this worst of worlds.

Breathe on as if the best,
Tired body,
But waited, for the time of man is long;
But waited, like the deathless
Air, and like my mind,
That will survive this song.

The Same Stones

The same stones, one upon the other, stand.
Walls, familiar, do not fall.
The people, going, never cease to go.
There is no body-change at all.

446

No liquefaction. Yet what deadly eye,
Cold as the future, and as thin,
Has been here, looking? Not a thing but shows
Where one of those sharp rays went in.

Shot through, the inaccessible
Center is no longer dark, no longer
Soft, concealing
Firm seed, secret of the form to come:
Familiar form, like its own father's once,
Yet singular, yet strange;
Yet looked for, and—delivered—oh,
Most loved.
The arrows of what deadly cold,
What needle gazer,
Through and through have pierced it? What
Distinction now of out, of in?
All, all translucent—oh, this universe of glass
The keen ray threaded and exposed at heart:
All breakable,
All brittle,
All ready for the last
Change coming—when?

The same stones, one above the other, rest.
The people still stream up and down.
No alteration in the wind and rain.
No prophecy that earth will drown.

No image melting. Yet what thinnest god
Lives in the crevices and laughs?
Thief in the vein—what principle exults,
Dreaming of deep things' epitaphs?

That woman there, that man,
That dozing doorway, and that cobbled street,
That flagpole—none suspects,
Yet each of them already

447

Changes; each
Is riddled by a million splinter lines
Of chill light inward. Glass,
All glass.
The ancient shape without the ancient center—
Nothing will go but that.
And that—already
It is gone, with its soft seed
Of darkness, its firm secret
Of the surprising, the familiar form
That ever, ever was to come
And now will not come,
Ever.
It lies there still but is transfixed, is air;
Hides, visible,
As water does in water,
Ice in ice.

The same stones, next to one another, sleep.
Nothing is different by day.
Nightly the same men listen to this wind.
Every substantial thing will stay.

Will last its while, but with what missing part,
What core that crystal death preserves?
Already frost is white upon the vein;
And shines among the inmost nerves.

The World Waits

The world waits, holding its breath so quietly,
Death's rattle sounds like prophet's bones.
No desert raven ever was so raucous;
No other end threatened so many thrones.

Of big and little kings, of poor maids' men,
Of farmers in the field, of mice in burrow—

No sovereignty now, no subject sand;
No world, for there will be no more tomorrow.

So possibility, with half its voice,
Suspends the whole of this most panic time.
The held breath hears nothing but the croak
Of glories that were proper in our prime.

The song nobody sings—what did it say?
Goodness is difficult, and yet can be?
Death is certain? But the terrible raven
Says that, says that, too, unstoppably.

Was there no different thing bright angels knew?
Still was it thus when gods walked here as men?
Always the world has waited? O, white bird
Of morning, tell the dark truth more sweetly then.

Orion: October

As firelogs hiss, Orion gleams
Recumbent in the eastern cold;
And did when not a roof was here,
Nor any brain to think him old.

We go outdoors in fall and stare
At each of his great seven stars,
And number all the sunken ships
It witnessed, all the risen wars.

But he was there when not an eye
Looked into his, when not an earth.
No direction yet was named
When that deep universe had birth.

Nor cold nor hot. How white he is,
How ancienter than frost or fire.

We go back in. We shut him out.
Oblivion's sons forget the sire.

How Deep to Go

How deep to go, how dark,
O you that made all things in number,
How deep, how dark shall my desire descend?
And is there any happy coming
Home from that cold end?

There have been those that dived,
O you that made all things in weight,
Until solidity, that locks things in,
Suspending mind and body both—
Where did that death begin?

Why should it not be good,
O you that made all things in measure,
Not to sink deeper than the nether side
Of this we see, this film of world
Spread now so fine, so wide?

How near, and yet how changed,
O you whose glass stands always full,
How bright might this reality then be,
By undermirror watched; how warm,
And how quicksilver free.

Soon and Soon

As through the unthinking body waves of wellness
Once more run (mysterious their start;
Where was it? What the spring whose agitation,
Gentle at first, then overwhelmed the heart?

Then sent these racing outward: little seas
That break in joy at blood's extremities?);

As happiness, that thinks not but is thought,
Returns and tells us we are sound again,
So that we can forget, as spirit does,
The channels of permission; thus—yet when,
Yet where and why?—the sick world on some day
Will mend and smile, and put its self away;

Will neither feel its body nor its mind,
Nor the deep cause to which the soul consents;
Nor, intricate, the history; for oblivion,
Here at last, still hushes all events.
So, in the world's great nature, be it now.
Or soon and soon. (Say not a word of how.)

When the World Ends

When the world ends it is too much to hope,
And yet I do, that neither knife nor rope,
Nor sudden flame, nor worse than sudden freeze,
Is executioner. No less than these
Implacable, what if gold autumn came
And stayed till it was weary—spread the same
Cool hectic over waters and wild boughs
That now arrives for but a week's carouse;
Then winter? What if such a wonder fall
Kept on as if it were the end, the all?
What if it were, and centuries of red
So flushed each field and roof and river bed
That death itself lay down, and nothing died
Till all things did, beneath a shower as wide
As oceans of together-dropping leaves?
What if it were, and still no late reprieves
Canceled the utter end? I do not keep
That hope; and yet I dream of this slow sleep,

451

This indolent, this all but evermore
October such as never came before.

DEATH WENT AWAY ࿇

Death Went Away

The little fox, demanding to be seen
In the cut field that fall, was not so little
To the first eyes he found, the middle-old ones,
The still ones over the wall, that saw in secret
Faraway death—huge death, the silent sender
Of neat four-footed omens saying Now,
Or pretty soon, make ready; this is the last
Surprise; nothing more comes out of the woods
In your time, ailing fellow. So they stared,
Those eyes, as every day the cricket hunter—
Or was it mice he pounced on—paused and looked;
Rippled his tail and pounced; then looked again.
He wanted to be seen. He came for that.
Quizzical, he pricked his ears and waited
On the smooth rise, and smiled his tapering smile—
All wizened fates in one, triangular—
That said: Come on, the dark long since was ready.
He did this every day that rainless fall.
And if the boy there, and the girl, clapped hands,
And the full-skirted wife ran twice to watch,
It was not thus at all for the tired father
Who turned and counted, then was off again
To the bleak woods, to the big hemlock clearing
Where the arms hung that cracked the useless bones,
That put the last light out.
                                    But the light, living,
Put the omen out. So he remembers,
Smilingly, this man, and sees in secret
Faraway foxes, well in their winter holes.

452

Midway the Race

Black time that blinds me—
Steals my peace—
Oh, could we stop
Midway the race.
But while I sigh,
He simply is.

And yet no end
Save night on night.
I know this well—
Oh, could I wait,
Oh, could I watch,
Remembering that.

Oh, to stand still,
With him the thief
So manacled
That I might laugh,
Then push him down,
Cliff after cliff,

Till, feather-falling
And wing-light,
We floated both
In the immense white,
In the vast Now
(Not yet, not yet).

As Time Makes Love

One quick breath, and home resumes.
One wide eye, then staring stops.
The traveller, caressed and fed,
Is no more new than time that drops,

That drops here as it always did,
Like love, on his own coffin lid.

Where has he been? What siren sang?
They ask it, but their ears are sealed.
Already they are listening,
As if far off, to honey spilled,
Drop after drop. Slow and alone,
Familiar love makes monotone.

And would forever, save that sweets
Can tire of dropping in one place.
All these must wither, as he must,
And lie with stone across the face;
Never listening again
As time makes love to other men.

Memorandum

Things on my desk to be remembered.
Tomorrow, and next Monday. Next May.
Next world, almost. Yet certainly
Not that. No need of letters to myself
About not being here. Not yet.

I do remember, though, some friends
Who now are nowhere. And their pages, blown
By an illiterate wind, nobody
Reads. They certainly do not. They come,
They go, regardless, disengaged.

So I have written this white slip.
Where shall I put it? Bottommost, perhaps.
Topmost, though, is better still.
It notifies the looker, and the smooth wood
He leans on: both of you, remember.

Time Didn't Love Me

Was the hound lonely that you and I saw there,
Trotting in the dusk? Do you think he was?
Where he had been, and whither he was going,
Neither of us knew, and I laughed; it is strange—
He did not hear me, and so I remember:
A long while ago, but I see him in the great field,
Trotting toward the river and those ancient trees.
Every night he did this? Probably, for water.
But that isn't it. He was serious, I say.
Like the last man on earth, he was serious;
Or any man now; like you; like me.
Time is so slow about whispering that it loves us—
Only at youth's end, shadow of the end.
We are not old; but time is, and tells us
Long before we die, in the middle of the field—
Where that hound was, trotting toward the river.
He knew, too. He didn't hear me laughing.
I was ungrown then; I was unlonely;
Time didn't love me. It loves you.

Another Pride

The father of the family, stoop-shouldered,
Has now another pride:
Not to mind much if his unspeakable authority
By smiles has died.

By laughter, even; he has learned to listen;
Secretly he basks
In the warm sun that wantons with his terrors,
Which time unmasks.

Which grey age has killed in him; he knows it,
And sometimes he sighs,

Wondering if this indifference be wisdom,
Or strength that dies.

The father of the family, forgiving,
Is himself forgiven;
But not for any sin, he thinks, wandering
That second heaven.

The Plague

"Little boy, what ails me, that you walk
So fearfully and far around?
You stare at this white hair
As at a ghost come out of ground.
I am not dead," the old man said;
And smiled, and frowned.

"Oh no, but it is catching, what you have."
He watched him from the windward side.
"I run like anyone;
I keep the distance good and wide."
So you ought, the old man thought,
And inly sighed.

Outly, though, he laughed and looked away.
"Little doctor, this disease—
You know it is but snow
And frosty blood and wits afreeze.
Yet not for you"—he searched him through—
"Save by degrees."

Envy the Old

Envy the young who have no words at all,
And the old, for they have had them. Now by wall
In sunshine, or by candle at the dance,

Or corner-warm, stillness is circumstance
Conclusive: there they sit, and no one says
They should be heedful of bright sentences.
Their silence, innocent of insult, tries
For how much truth? Who knows? It may be wise
Or sleepy, may be amorous of death
Or heavy with remembrance—the slow breath
Of sluggards at the goal. Who blames them here
For blinking? They are privileged to peer
Past us, past Him, past anyone at all,
And speak no word, those sitters by the wall.

Courage in Sons

Courage in sons, with wisdom's hesitation
Lest the good thing be lost, lest the far thing
That flutters be not seen, or seen too soon,
By dark, and so forgotten; justice, too,
Rejoicing (man's old music, heard again
Though every elder died); and even temperance,
Captain—by whose voice were these demanded,
Miracle past all? Not by the careful
Father's; or if so, not thence the cause.
Hope could not force it; asking might have marred,
O Providence, this prime result, this dream
Of none but generous gods. To whom, quietly,
Thanks for temperance, justice, wisdom, courage;
And to the generous sons that did receive them.

Startled, I Remember

Immensely the low sun
Paints all our city—shines
Prodigal on water towers;
Sweetens deep windows.

457

There it is, suddenly,
The soul of it: New York
Gold in the late day,
Dying and smiling,

Startled, I remember
Him that most loved this.
Where is he now, then?
Didn't I hear—

Oh, but the least—yes,
Certainly I felt it;
Mind and body turning, turning,
Trying to see.

Only as his would—
Once again, once again—
Oh, but he must sleep, though.
Let the night be.

In Memoriam

Look, till all of his years,
Foreshortened in your gaze,
Become, as under glass,
A few intensest days.

See? The courageous head—
The brown one—the white—
It flickers like a single
Star in densest night.

Listen. But no sound.
Not even glancing here.
The fever in him flashes:
The love against the fear.

Anxiety in this man
Yet could not kill the heart,
That now is burning coal,
And his immensest part.

The panic, the distress—
Oh, brothers, do not cry.
His love alone is climbing
The fences of the sky.

Epitaph

Let this be true, that I have loved
All men and things both here and gone;
But most the men whose love surpassed
My love, and so lives on and on.

MORNING WORSHIP
AND OTHER POEMS (1960)

ALL SEASONS &

Morning Worship

I wake and hear it raining.
Were I dead, what would I give
Lazily to lie here,
Like this, and live?

Or better yet: birdsong,
Brightening and spreading—
How far would I come then
To be at the world's wedding?

Now that I lie, though,
Listening, living,
(Oh, but not forever,
Oh, end arriving)

How shall I praise them:
All the sweet beings
Eternally that outlive
Me and my dying?

Mountains, I mean; wind, water, air;
Grass, and huge trees; clouds, flowers,
And thunder, and night.

461

Turtles, I mean, and toads; hawks, herons, owls;
Graveyards, and towns, and trout; roads, gardens,
Red berries, and deer.

Lightning, I mean, and eagles; fences; snow;
Sunrise, and ferns; waterfalls, serpents,
Green islands, and sleep.

Horses, I mean; butterflies, whales;
Mosses, and stars; and gravelly
Rivers, and fruit.

Oceans, I mean; black valleys; corn;
Brambles, and cliffs; rock, dirt, dust, ice;
And warnings of flood.

How shall I name them?
And in what order?
Each would be first.
Omission is murder.

Maidens, I mean, and apples; needles; leaves;
Worms, and planets, and clover; whirlwinds; dew;
Bulls; geese—

Stop. Lie still.
You will never be done.
Leave them all there,
Old lover. Live on.

All Seasons

All months, all days, all hours,
All sister seconds even, oh, all seasons
Beautify the world and bless
The walkers on it.

Some of whom they drown,
And some make die of thirst; they burn, they freeze,
They kill us every minute; yet
We must adore them.

Supposing them gone out:
Time's candles. Then no joy or darkness either.
No bitter, sweet; beginning, end.
Oh, mercy on us.

Get Up, I Say

Get up, I say, and see them,
The green streaks of morning:
Long and low, with white gold
Alternating, adorning—

Get up, I say; and sometimes,
Just as they are striking,
Obedient I do—ah, those
Lances, so to my liking,

That reach here so straightly,
Unswerving, swinging,
And pierce me—ah, little birds,
Almost to singing.

After the Wind and Rain

After the wind and rain
How softly the surviving
Subjects of old Sun
Sing hymns to his great age.

He was December's too.
He was before the Flood.

These were not dreamed of then,
But that same father now

Sends hither, one time more,
Sleepy, the sweet love
They sing, and by their singing
Rebuild beyond the world.

Undersong

1

In wonderment I walk to music pouring
Out of so dark a source it makes no sound:
Not waterfalls, not wind, not eagles soaring
On wings that whistle insult to the ground;
Not insect whine at which the flower rejoices;
Not instruments, not voices;
Not, taciturn, those numbers where they wheel
While the fixed stars, creation's counterpoises,
Sing in deep throats a song of commonweal
More ancient than mankind, than beast or bird
Coeval with the Word:
No, none of these is what I overhear
In wonderment, in walking every day.
A harmony more hidden, as midway
Of the whole world it hums, and yet more near,
More secret in my ear,
Keeps coming to me, coming, and I know
As long as I go forth it shall be so.

2

Each day I walk in is made slyly one
By symmetries whose names I never seek.
For if I did, and found them, and were done
With listening, with looking, and could speak

Love's language with the subtlety they do,
It might no more be true.
For it is music's language, meant to please
No mind except its own, and if I too
Attempted it the melody would cease;
As birds do in the forest if a foot
Too suddenly is put
On pathways saved for silence, or for such
Plumed echoes as are proper to the place.
The music is not mine in any case;
I only let it come, by sight, by touch,
As often as by hearing; though the ghost
Of sound is innermost;
And mightiest, as if the great one there
Had burst his heart and scattered it in air.

3

Down it falls, that wild unfigured tune
Which nevertheless reorders all my earth.
I walk, and every acre is bestrewn
With witnesses of morning in slow birth,
And of the sky's contentment that things be
Just as they are to see.
Different were deadly, something sings
In a low voice as of a leafy tree
Preoccupied with shade, and two sure wings
That aim at it to enter by and by
When the half-day shall die,
And perfect sunlight shall hang due above
Like a dark lantern swinging. Something says,
Barely aloud, in less than sentences:
Just as they are, together in their love,
The whirlwind, the dove,
The contraries. Listen. That rough chord:
It is his breathing, it is our overlord.

4

In times of tempest when disorder seems
Order itself, the very rule of motion,
And moaning as they bend, the trees and streams,
In horror at their own perverse devotion
To chaos come alive, strain not to shatter
Form, and the first matter
Of which all possibility was made;
But then the roar increases, and winds batter
Winds above the world as fields are flayed
And savage grasses, blowing, strip the bones
Even of sunk stones;
In times of tumult when the lines should snap
That lead like silk from note to kissing note,
And the sweet song should strangle in the throat,
There it still is, miles above thunderclap,
As audible as when on halcyon days
It mastered the same ways;
Compounded of all tones, including these
Of stricken ground and hideous green seas.

5

And if there be those who would mock me, saying:
Music? None is here save in your head;
Noises, yes, delectable, dismaying,
But not in measure, as if more were said
Than owls and larks will tell you, or mad crows,
Or the wind-ravished rose,
Or human chatter, changeless year by year;
Then soberly I say to such as those:
The sound is one, and is not sinister.
It is an honest music through and through.
And so the chatter, too,
And so the silences that wait sometimes
Like a tired giant thinking, so they all
Return and go, then come again and fall,

Evenly, unevenly, as rhymes
Rival the pure chimes
Of never-ending truth, that for so long
Has sung to such as me this undersong.

DUNCE SONGS 🖎

Dunce Songs

1

Where is the bell, the horn,
I hear as I go by,
Go by the invisible wall
That holds up half the sky,
The sky whose other half
Falls down like gold wheat chaff
And sprinkles all the air,
And powders my dull hair?
So people cry and cry:
Who wears that glittery crown,
That crown? And I say I.
Oh, what a falling down
As I go by, go by.

2

If rain rose,
And leaves fell upward—
Oh, me, oh, them
Sky-high together.

That is my house.
Here I am homesick.
Bright, oh, bright,
Forever, ever.

Raindrops, leaves
Round me like mica.
Snow whirls
In a ball of water.

Give it a shake.
That's me in the middle.
White, oh, white—
See now? I am laughing.

3

Some day,
When the great clock
Of dawn strikes, and keeps on striking—
What's gone wrong, the president will shout, why doesn't
    somebody,
Somebody stop it?—

That day,
When the music starts
That no man ever heard before—
Bong, bong, the bells up there, whish, whish,
The windy singing—

That time
Will be my time:
No minutes, years, no coming, going—
Night, poor night, laid out in white—oh, my soul,
The death of darkness—

Whee, whee,
The waking birds.
(Yet I do pity them a little—
Come close, I'm whispering—yes, I too will miss their brave
Songs at sunset.)

4

Then I'll be four-footed,
And modest with fur.
All over, all under,
Seemly and still.

Then I'll be patient:
A part of the ground.
I will go slowly,
And lowly—oh, sweet,

Then I'll be one of them
He that made all
Looks after the longest,
And tenderest loves.

Then I'll be quiet—
You can be quick—
And lie down all summer,
All winter, and sleep.

5

I have no enemy.
If I did,
I would wait for him, in the black dark, and thwack him—
Ha! on the head.

Or else I would grow
A green worm in my heart
And feed it all day till the strength of its poison
Was death to the world.

Yes, but I have none.
All are my lovers—
Harry, and Jack, and even the great ones,
That cause the long wars,

469

All are my little
Sweet friends that I wait for,
In the warm sun, and stroke them, stroke them—
Ha, my poor head!

6

Her hand in my hand,
Soft as the south wind,
Soft as a colt's nose,
Soft as forgetting;

Her cheek to my cheek,
Red as the cranberry,
Red as a mitten,
Red as remembering—

Here we go round like raindrops,
Raindrops,
Here we go round
So snug together,

Oh, but I wonder,
Oh, but I know,
Who comforts like raisins,
Who kisses like snow.

7

If I had a wife
I would love her as kings
Loved queens in the old days, or as princes
Maidens,
Met in the dew, by a stile, of a morning—
"How do you do, my pretty?"
And all of that.

If I had a wife
I would come home sometimes

Dressed like a stranger, and when she stared,
"Lady,"
I'd say, and woo her in wonder—
"How can there be such shining?"
And all of that.

If I had a wife
I would never be done
With remembering how it is now when, oh,
I am lonesome,
And no one is here but my dog and my cat—
"Well, old boys! Hungry?"
And all of that.

8

Pepper and salt
And summer savory—
Those are for luckier tables and tongues
Than my old woman
And I have.

The sun and the wind,
Those are our seasoning;
With maybe nine drops of rain on a Thursday—
Yes, my old woman's
A smart one.

She holds up her bonnet
Just when He is looking—
Oh, the love in His eyes, oh, the millions of tears.
Even my old woman
Is weeping.

9

Love me little, love me long,
Then we neither can be wrong:
You in giving, I in taking;

There is not a heart breaking
But remembers one touch,
Or maybe seven, of too much.

Love me more than halfway, though.
Let me think, then let me know.
And I promise you the same:
A little wild, a little tame;
Lest it ever seem long:
Tick, tock, ding, dong.

THE LOVE SONGS OF OBERON ૐ

Proem

Titania is queen
Of fairyland and me;
But woman first of all,
And mistress, and girl.
Listen to me then.
I am as other men.

Titania's Eyes

There are no eyes as black as night
Except Titania's by the sea;
Or in the forest, or this room—
Oh, anywhere they look at me
They burn the rest of darkness out
As absolute consumes degree.

More black than black, Titania's eyes,
As if a candle dimmed the sun;
As if a tear outwet the waves,
Or certain stars resisted dawn.
Blazing black, Titania's eyes;
And I am the consumèd one.

For in the darkness of this room,
And in my own dark where I lie,
Remembering ocean or the woods,
With sweet Titania standing by,
Suddenly, more near than near,
She darkens darkness, and I die.

My Love Comes Walking

My love comes walking,
And these flowers
That never saw her till this day
Look up; but then
Bend down straightway.

My love sees nothing
Here but me,
Who never trembled thus before;
And glances down
Lest I do more.

My love is laughing;
Those wild things
Were never tame until I too,
Down-dropping, kissed
Her silvery shoe.

Lute Song

So soft her voice, so drooped her head,
I did not then suspect the power
She had to be rememberèd.

For nothing dies of that first hour
When there she walked, and all her gaze
Flowed down as to a sister flower.

473

Not then to me, nor through these days
That wander since and hold their breath:
Never to me, who yet do praise

This strength in her, more strict than death,
That where I go it followeth,
That where I go it followeth.

How Can It Be?

She is woman, she is wife,
Yet is a maiden to the life:
Mine, or yours, or anyone's
Who shall be first and rudest—runs
And throws her down among the flowers,
Aha! as sudden thunder showers
Can blast a blossom. There she lies,
Half-buried, weeping; yet will rise
And be as ignorant again
As if there were no husbandmen.
God of storms, how can it be
That nothing wracks her? Who are we,
That she survives us? What am I,
Who will not live to see her die
When all the world ends—oh, the woe
Of springtime that must watch her go!

Slowly, Slowly

The lover loves the eyes that close,
And closing, shut the world to shame;
Then parted lips; then helpless blood;
Then breast and breast, the two, the same,
The all in one, awaiting there
Himself, the other—hears his name—

474

And answers; but he loves the most
What now he neither hears nor sees,
Yet has at last—oh, wonder then—
Down there—his very own—the knees
That slowly, slowly melt his bones
As summer sun drowns honey bees.

Dressed, Undressed

Dressed, undressed: the difference leaps
Millenniums, past even time
Millenniums, for where it lands
Is then, is there, is everywhere,
Oh, dizziness, is everywhen,
Is furlongs east of Eden, miles
From nowhere if nowhere is now,
Is now, is all this blushing blood,
This blinding modesty made free
Of there, of then, of self and shame
And nowhen. Now, oh, only now,
And here, oh, only here, take off,
Take off, Titania, everything,
Take off the least thing that can cling,
The least, the last thing—there, oh, there,
Titania—nothing, nothing left
But you, but me, in one lone world
Of millions that were here till now,
Till now, Titania, now, till now.

This Way, That Way

Titania, be still
And let me love you as I will;
This way, that way—yes, and more:
To ten;

But then,
Why not a score?

Titania, look up
And let me; nightlong now look up
And let me, and keep softest count;
Till number
Slumber,
And day mount.

Titania, sleep there
And let me lie as light as air
At last upon you; till the sun,
Our friend,
Descend,
And you say one.

Titania, say two,
And love whatever I shall do
Until the darkest of our days;
Till light
Be night
Always, always.

Love to Come

Titania is weary,
Not with love over, but with love to come,
My love, her love, one love together,
Drowning as in a dream, but that's to come,
Titania, expectant of this honey hour,
Deliciously—I see it—is love weary.

Her eyelids tell me,
And the slow way, as if in heavy water,
Indifferent to deepest death,
She comes where I am, comes, and passes me,

Drowning as in a dream, but I can reach
And save her, die with her one death together.

Titania knows well
How weariness bewitches me, her lover—
Similitudes of sleep,
How all of them become her in this honey
Hour when nothing more of love seems possible,
Then is, then is, and so we dream we drown.

Titania's Own Love Song

Day, be long aborning.
Stir not in the womb.
Let this one night be childless—
O, sweet bridegroom,
O, lover dark by me,
Whisper: do you agree?

Your hyacinth loves sun;
My columbine weeps tears
Lest morrow never wake.
It must. But oh, the years,
Sweet lover, we shall spend
Before evening's end.

Night, be no mother now,
Bring forth no bird nor flower;
Be mistress of old Time
With whom he wastes an hour.
My king is young—yet see,
Ah, how we agree.

Lovers Must Wonder

These little birds that feed all day so fiercely,
All week, all winter, keeping their hearts hot—
Gems in feathers—why such a length of labor?
Is it for love in June, or have they forgot?
Was something less intended by their maker:
That they maintain mere fire? Oh, no? Then what?

When mistresses all morning move in coolness,
Speaking and doing: daughters of mankind;
Was it for this the mother of their being
Put, without difference, tongue in them and mind?
Lovers must wonder. How does such clear seeing
Measure night's minutes, animal, blood-blind?

Love Lives On

Child-bearing Bess, bedraggled proof
That love lives on in this poor world,
Is no temptation; she can pass,
And no man dreams of her as curled—
Golden caterpillar—on his bed,
With crushed white pillows about her head.

Yet love lives on; she is the sign,
And one man sees it. Where is he?
In what damp corner does he wait—
Earth's worm—till both again shall be
All that they were when Bess went by
And he was bedazzled as by sky?

478

Desire Like This

So long had he withheld his hands,
She found him slow to learn:
The way a breast, a thigh, can yield;
The way snow can burn.

You thought me once a goddess, boy,
And so I am, she said;
Desire like this is not of earth:
More, and we both were dead.

Oh, no, he cried; but even then,
Like one brand ablaze,
They broke and fell, and each went out
As stars extinguish days.

I Have Come Home Again

I have come home again;
Not from so very far;
But love computes absence
As, star beyond star,
Worlds turn to nothing,
And chaos is there.

I have come home again;
Not since so very long;
But love measures meetings
As, song beyond song,
Joy turns to brooding,
And hushes its tongue.

Woman Few of Words

Lady, excellently brief
(Let me be too),

479

The sweet things you say
Are salt also,
For true.

It takes my very breath, the mixing,
As if I tried
To be both hot and cold
Together; lived,
And died.

As if within a summer sky
Some lightning hid;
Not to be found except
As on love's day
You did.

Compliment

Comparing her with gold,
Deriving her from queens,
I look for such a smile
As measures those extremes;

And seeing it, reply
With such a thankful grin
As testifies we know,
Both of us, the mean;

For which no word exists;
It is ideal and dark:
The lodestone, down there,
That keeps our love at work.

If You But Dreamed It

God's love does not compute desert
In birds and worms, in bones and dirt.

He kisses all things where they lie;
And if they run, or if they fly,
The very air they antic through
Is theirs till death, which he gives too.

Can you love me as He loves these
Great stones and bones and starting trees?
You never made me—yes, I know;
But you can slay me, quick or slow,
By not beginning, my sweet friend,
To own me without thought of end,

As He does, He does. Listen now
To that small warbler on the bough.
He lets him sit, He lets him sing,
As if he were the chiefest thing.
And so he is; and so am I
If you but dreamed it, standing by.

Little Trip

Let's go. Let's be somewhere awhile
We haven't ever been before;
And strangers cut the random grass
Or leave it ragged. That can pass;
For now the road climbs more and more,
And we are silent mile by mile
Between whose woods? We'll never know
Unless we stop to read his name.
Up and over, down and on
Around this mountain, blue then brown.
Here is a river, wild or tame
According as the rocks below
Be few or many. Next a house,
And neat or not we like it well,
For someone else does all the chores
Or doesn't do them. Churches, stores—

There, I heard the crossing bell.
So home by dark to moth and mouse.

I Am Not Ever

The desert moor, the empty glen:
I am not ever, travelling by your side, so much at home
As then.

The swept road, the swift car,
Flying, flying on the wings of those forsaken worlds,
As far

As God's body, death's end:
I am not ever, dear, so deep in love with you; nor you
With wind.

Second Thought

I have not waited to praise this woman.
Some day it will be forty years since I began.
But a tale now, and a song then—could I have believed
Stuttering like that became a man?

Well, then, the full word. I say it loud at last. . . .
What do you mean, you heard nothing?
Why, it was one wave, gathering back yonder,
That came all the way unbroken; then burst.

But I see now. It did not break. It keeps going,
Through me and on. Over, too, and back under:
One with the deep world, the dark and round.
Well, then, no praise. No insult of sound.

To the Author of Hesperides and Noble Numbers

Herrick, hello.
You cannot be asleep; and yet if so,
Kinsman, your book is not: the lyric
Spring, unquenchable, of him I know,
Robert, as my Herrick.

And I am his,
And therefore yours, like those nine mistresses
Who never spoke one word, yet wore
The crimson ribands and the stomachers
You still I think adore.

I do but read,
Herrick, I do but listen; yet indeed
All that you asked was eyes and ears.
Well, mine are thine, and I shall intercede
With others to give theirs.

Herrick, be sure
Your maids, your meadows, and your verse endure,
And your delicious lewdness, drawn
By the same sun, that loves impure with pure,
From him I dote upon.

If Mistresses

If we had mistresses, my old
Deep-sleeping friend—if you and I,
That once outwatched the flowery cold
And saw each brilliant planet die
Love's death at summer daybreak—now,
In winter, if we did somehow

Have pretty mistresses, my friend,
And I should name them, would you hear?

483

You can but feel, yet in the end
You knew those others: hot and clear
By heart you had them, so that I learned
Only from you how fierce we burned,

Yourself and me—oh, that young night,
And oh, now this decrepit day.
For I shall keep the secret tight
Of these green girls with whom I stray,
Unknown to you, unguessed by them,
Devouring blossom, bud, and stem

Till each is in me like a cool
Life-giving herb; for I confess
There is no rage in my misrule;
My lust is leaf, is marrowless.
And that is all; so sleep again
Under our snow, ancient of men.

THE SPEECH DEATH MAKES ॐ

Time Was When Death

Time was when death
Seemed mountain, or myth;
Alien to world;
Green oceans away.

Time was when the end
Seemed a pouring of sand;
And the last fine grain—
That glittered the most.

Time was; time is;
And this morning death says:
Stand there; I am here;
I am all that will be.

His language is plain:
Very like to my own.
But the one dark word
Is the sound of my name.

Time still is to be
When I am not I.
The speech death makes
Is not special for me.

Little My Soul

Little my soul,
How long will you live?
And where, if not here?
And why, if I die?

Little my life,
Who had you before?
And who will be next?
And again? What then?

Little my breath,
Did you never stop?
Were you never so cold
That known was unknown?

Little my soul,
You and I are the same;
Are warm, and are one.
Peace be till we cease.

Stronger than Minds of Men

Stronger than minds of men—
Almost than His, than His—

Strange, but the learner learns
Only what is, what is.

Learns to lie down one day;
Suffers himself to be bound;
So then the turning, turning,
Cold and slow, around.

Yet after years a pressure,
As of contraction's heat,
Sometimes to the pure center.
There is no name for that.

Nor any name for the turning,
Spread-eagled, upon a sphere
He will be learning, learning
Until light disappear.

Oldest Cemetery

I go downhill some days to a little room
Where the first people put their souls to sleep,
And where four walls of fallen fieldstone keep
Close rumor of their names, with verses cut
(I lie and read) against forgetful doom.
Remembered, they would rise in fields of rest
As far away as east is from the west;
Or farther, past all compass; for they shut
This wilderness of time, of nature out;
They thought to wake in such a world of light
As no man works for, warned of coming night;
Pure joy and peace it was. And so they put
Each weary soul to bed, with owls and crows
To watch, and weeds to deepen its repose.

Some days I think the end has come and gone.
Sound fell, and they got up, and where they lay

486

Was nothing now but litter as away
On wings they went and had their dream at last:
The universe was over. Time goes on
As always, and the same birds in the sky
Declare it, but without hope's reason why:
Tick, tick, until the finish. Or, no blast
Of horns was heard, no host of angels passed;
It all was childish error, and these stones
But tilt above time's waste. And whose the bones?
The verses tell. I ponder them, steadfast,
Expectant. No, the end is coming still
For such as these, on this forgotten hill.

Men Do Not Leave Things So

The small minds of birds,
Perfect in the wind or on the bough;
The sleek thoughts of those that go on four feet,
Eyes wide, without a mark left by their looking—
The same world is there,
Dozing in honey air—

Men do not leave things so.
Their dreaming hardens into chimneys, towers,
Walls, chambers for the living, for the dead—
Hopefully, forever; though these objects
Rot. Yet are replaced.
Idea is not erased.

Could it be spider fine,
Or finer: even no thin silk to blow;
Could man's brain not monument itself,
Not litter that sweet sleep—O tell him, **You**
That made man more than beast,
How like most is to least.

The Sacrifice

As soon kill God as kill one of His creatures.
He wrote this dying, and the doves around
Flew off in fear because the paper fluttered.
They did not know he starved on stony ground;
They did not know he saved them out of love
For every breath beneath him or above.

And though his own was lost, he loved it too,
And wondered at the end if he did well.
But there was not a sign of Yes or No;
Not a stone rose, nor softest feather fell
To say which sacrifice had been preferred
By Him who made them equal, man and bird.

If equal truly. So this man believed,
And so he proved he did, in the extreme;
But only after dark knew God's desire,
That may have been blood brother to his dream
Of such a love twixt intellect and beast
As spares those most who comprehend it least.

The Laughing Philosopher

The laughing philosopher sits on his tomb
With an old friend, a lover of cypresses,
And drinks all afternoon to lovely death;
"Who may not come tonight," he sips and says,
"But come she will; she is the only lady,
Living or no, that keeps her promises."

"Lady? Alive?" And now the friend is laughing.
He is himself a cypress, bald and green.
"If lady, why not lipless?" And he grins.
But the philosopher, as to his queen,
Lifts high another cup. "I think she lives.
I grant you, though, she never yet was seen."

"Then why say she? You are too obstinate.
Death could be animal; be wind, or worm;
Be anything; be nothing." "Nothing? No.
Death is my lady, and her lips are warm
For speech and then for kissing." "O, lovesick
Philosopher!" "Aha! And what the harm?"

And So It Was

And so it was
That Achilles, wounded of mind, called to his beautiful mother.
His honor had been hurt, and she must heal it.
She did; but opened a deeper wound, the death of Patroclus;
Whence rivers of blood in which all Troy was drowned.

And so it was
That Odysseus, grizzled darling of Pallas Athene,
Triumphed over the waves; then on dry land,
His enemies. But the grey waves, still reaching, rocked him
Nightly, and robbed the old fox of his rest.

And so it was
That Hamlet, friend of angels, was elected by the fiend
To weed the bed of Denmark, and plucked up,
Before he knew it, flowers; till all was waste
And woe, and the prince of roses died himself by prick of thorn.

And so it was
That once in poor La Mancha thought grew rich,
Put forth, and filled the world; which, being full
Already, groaned aloud, fearful of surplus; and the vine,
Weary of its own leaves at last, withdrew.

And so it was
And is, and will be ever: no good man but finds the going
Strange; and yet he goes; and we that watch him
Wish we too had gone where wolf and worm,
Surprising a brave soul, work out their wonders.

In Athens, Though

In little Greece, great mountains:
Walls of an old world that only eagles and the ghosts
Of heroes (Agamemnon in his shroud)
Remember, and that only
Women such as walk there now can wear
Like sadness on their shoulders, in their eyes.
Their smile assumes sobriety
In strangers too; the wind
Is one to them and these; the hard,
High, marvellous brown mountains are a wingèd
Weight they share with who comes up,
Comes down the stony passes, and is nightly
Glad for olives, ancient on the plain.

In Athens, though, a honey-sweet
Old wrinkled woman, captive of the suburbs,
Beamed when her son said "Delphi";
Beamed, holding my hand in hers, and said it after him
As a girl says a lesson; said it softly,
"Delphi, Delphi," twice, for then, for now:
Her birthplace, and her second childhood's
Innermost clandestine pleasure
Hugged here in this faraway new house
Where lights mean other houses, not the stars.
"Delphi." And I saw her halfway up
Parnassus, gathering thyme, the flowery food
Of old ancestor bees long since
In Hades, mourning the hot sun.
I saw her, not in shadow, bearing
Both of those huge tawny summits,
Desolate, for burden, smiling
Ruefully, remembering,
Remembering,
Not here but there,
Not now but then and then,
The cries of heroes (Laius in his car).

Once the Wind

They left him hanging for the deed
His black-eyed brother did.
And still beneath that basswood tree
No wildflower goes to bed.

No daisy but is darker there
For staring all night long
At something once the wind turned round,
Careless of right, of wrong.

They came next day and cut him down,
And the false brother groaned.
But still the black-eyed Susans gaze
At what the wind turned round.

And would, if any man could read,
Tell what was done amiss.
But no man now remembers it,
So long ago it is.

Nap

I lay me down, but down is deep
Past dark, past death, past deep's idea;
Is the soft seas themselves, that drain
Away as my own mind does, my own
Bones that will not be, not be
Again; not be my bones; not my
Own bones, that settle separately,
Softly, down and down—oh, sweet
Non-being, not my own, wherein
I sink like light in water, dimming
Slowly, oh, so slowly, deep
By deep, beyond the dark of death's idea.

Anything But Bitter

Rage in the mildest mind,
A mute world assisting—
Contradictories grown dumb;
The mystery made lasting—
Rage so deep, so pure,
Is not unwise or wasting.

It may be that the glint
Is anything but bitter
Of ardor in those eyes,
Staring out at matter:
The urgency to love
Deity's dead letter.

The Time I Wasted

The time I wasted built the world.
Lazily looking, there it was.
Piecemeal, the frame emerged;
Or most of it; some never has.
And never will; the mind's work,
Proud thing, leaves vacancies.

If I could only waste it all.
But, temporal, nobody can.
If I could only have it whole.
But mortal thought turns always in.
To know itself, the single will
Must mutilate that sizeless one.

The Waves

The waves of air and ocean
And the dark sea of nothing between stars;
Or if not nothing, something; but no matter,
There they go galloping as if in eagle
Wind, in dolphin water; yet not so—
Oh, widest world, oh, nameless,
Nervous,
Nothing if not something: curl on curl
Out, out, and out—sometimes
It causes me to tremble,
Tremble,
Sometimes it causes me down here,
Oh, way down solid here,
To shake and tremble.

Judge and Angel

The aging heart: is it more filled with kindness,
Having more room—O memory, more room—
Or does a colder person occupy it:
A dusty miller, or a rich bridegroom
Who comes too late for love, and lays him down
With icy gold for maiden and bedgown?

The youthful heart says yes: what age forgives
Is age; at greener folly it but groans;
It finds the children witless whom it else
Might wonder at; their delicate breastbones
It taps and says not tough enough, not steel;
Time aches to eat of it, poor flesh, inchmeal.

Both hearts are bitter when they think thiswise
And not of love alone: which if they do,
Then grief in them is for their own defect;
But joy is for the strength that can renew,

Oh, instantly, the charity they lost
When judge and angel, deep in them, crisscrossed.

Some Day Then

Old men's intensities are not to be believed.
Their pities and their rages, humorous, unterrible,
Return and burn again, building a whiter ash
About a hotter fire: some day, some day, unbearable.

Some day then it is clear: soul must consume itself.
After so many trials, nothing but ache, but error.
So with no world to watch, and neither with smoke nor flame,
Simply it burns and burns; and no tale of the terror.

The Time to Come

Two young hearts in five old rooms
But the first ever, being theirs:
Experience, transplanted, blooms
And with good weather wisely bears;
And will be harvested some day;
But that is worlds on worlds away.

Why do I jump the time to come?
It is but starting; will be slow;
Will stop, they think, and hang and hum
Like wind with no good where to go.
Yet in that sweetness let them be.
Time may stand still. It raced with me.

Parents' Recompense

Those that we hovered,
Holding our breath,

Suddenly see him,
Granduncle Death,
Walking close by.
So we are to die.

Not yet. We are strong.
But it is their turn
To indicate love
By excess of concern.
They do; and we smile
All the last mile.

Young Herbert

Young Herbert on his hill and I on mine
Do not forget each other. What he thinks,
I wonder. But he thinks. I know by how
He takes so long a look when we descend
And meet. And maybe smile. If we do not,
The choice was his. The younger and the stronger
Quietly decides. Immense and fair,
He rules me. When he waves I am as glad
As if a wild god noticed. When we speak,
The best I do is listen. Once he called
Me captain, and saluted my great age.
He may believe me dying: what if that,
And only that? If so, I do not tell him
Both of us are doomed. For all I know,
He isn't; generations of old men
May go downhill each morning as I do
And wait for him and gamble that he smiles.

The Child at Winter Sunset

The child at winter sunset,
Holding her breath in adoration of the peacock's tail

495

That spread its red—ah, higher and higher—
Wept suddenly. "It's going!"

The great fan folded;
Shortened; and at last no longer fought the cold, the dark.
And she on the lawn, comfortless by her father,
Shivered, shivered. "It's gone!"

"Yes, this time. But wait,
Darling. There will be other nights—some of them even better."
"Oh, no. It died." He laughed. But she did not.
It was her first glory.

Laid away now in its terrible
Lead coffin, it was the first brightness she had ever
Mourned. "Oh, no, it's dead." And he her father
Mourned too, for more to come.

Wish for the World

Wish for the world that it will never change,
Even if terrible, to total strange.
Even if good, may there be no excess
Beyond this power to think of more, of less,
That is our lone reward for living here.
May only what is missing still be clear
On any earth to come, that so can teach
Hell's difference, and heaven's—each from each,
And both from its dear self: the single place
Than which all others have exacter grace,
And yet it is the measure. Be it thus
Forever, little world that lengthens us.

In Bitterness of Heart

In bitterness of heart I write,
But gentleness of mind;
For thinking slow, I may remember
That the world is kind.

Or was; or would be; and contains,
Like dew within the rose,
Some delicate, some hidden friends.
I must remember those.

And so I do; and drop by drop
I am rewarded well;
By tincture; or as weeping gold
Tempers the harsh bell.

Carl

Like a great tree
Spread over me,
With love in every limb:
I worshipped him.

And Still the Same
(To Joseph Wood Krutch)

He differs day by day,
Or else I do.
Yet it is not my way
Thus to be ever new
And still the same:
Both wild and tame;

Both added to and one
When that is done.

It seems no more than chance
That changes him.
And molecules do dance,
I know, and atoms swim.
With this man, though,
It is not so.
Surprising to the end,
He is my friend.

Not that his wit consents.
He hides his heart.
So it is my pretense,
And both of ours the art,
Thus to despise
What never dies;
What never will be done
Till many is one.

Woe, Woe
(To Robert Lax)

Woe, woe. The long face,
Patiently, in hoarse wind,
Meditates, meditates,
Without a word that men hear.

When they do, and I have,
What a seeing, what a song.
Not a thought but thanks God
For bird and leaf and Sunday morning.

Snow, rain: exactly so.
Mountains; or if need be, none.
Men, women: who but these,
The now, the here? And what delight.

Woe, woe. The mournful eyes
Should never have misled us. Listen.
Angel clear and sparrow sweet:
Love, love is all there is.

Good, good: how get it said
In man's time? God is long.
Maybe that: he really mourns.
The night comes. So much unmentioned.

Once in Kentucky
(To Thomas Merton)

In our fat times, a monk:
I had not thought to see one;
Nor, even with my own poor lean concerns,
Ever to be one.

No. But in Kentucky,
Midway of sweet hills,
When housewives swept their porches, and March light
Lapped windowsills,

He, once my merry friend,
Came to the stone door,
And the only difference in his smiling was,
It sorrowed more.

No change in him, except
His merriment was graver.
As if he knew now where it started from;
And what the flavor.

He tasted it, the joy,
Then gave it all to me:
As much, I mean, as I could carry home
To this country,

499

To this country whose laughter
Is a fat thing, and dies,
I step across its body and consider,
Still, those eyes.

The Wonder Is
(To Robert Caldwell)

Massive the man, massive the wrath;
He girds at public liars, thieves;
Unreason so enrages him
He trembles like a tree, with leaves,
And might come down; except his strength
Is delicate, both breadth and length.

The wonder is at last the soul;
It sits in him, beside his heart,
And sings as if a stranger wound
The key to it and gave it start;
It sings of things that cannot be:
For instance, he delights in me.

In so much bigness, something perfect—
Not that I prove it—something old;
As if his giant maker said,
Let this be in him, small and gold,
To sit each day beside his wrath
And sing like love of truth and death.

Like Mice, Like Flowers
(To José Villa)

Look. The stone face—
It is not stone, but the soul's grace
That he met early (he was not young long),
Frozen.

Look. Now, years away,
See the hot subtleties that play
Like mice, like flowers, like rain, yet never
Melt it.

Look. Sweet mercy's worm,
Within him, still cannot make infirm
His judgment: silver gentle, iron
Decisive.

Anger Is, Anger Was
(*To James Thurber*)

The tumult in this shouting man
Gives way at once to dove's words.
Anger is, anger was,
But half between is holy ghost
Descending out of time gone.

The memory of this hunted man
Is barking wolves, is fool's gold.
But here a wing, and there a wing,
And all within is sleepy peace.
He walks again the good world.

Philosopher at Large
(*To Mortimer Adler*)

The ancient garden where most men
Step daintily, in specimen dust,
He bulldozes; plows deep;
Moves earth; says someone must,
If truth is ever to be found
That so long since went underground.

What truth? Why down? He shakes his head.
He does not know. But roots and rocks

Go tumbling, tearing, as his blade,
Shivering from its own shocks,
Bites farther, and upturns pure clay
He does not pause to smooth away.

And horrifies those men, by hedge
And dust plot, whom the top sufficed.
They thought the garden theirs. And still
It is; but the dead air is spiced
With damp new things dug up. Or old,
He says; like God, like buried gold.

Between Our Voices
(To Allen Tate)

He was the soonest friendly,
But then the soonest tired;
As if between our voices,
Suddenly, a third,
More intimate than either,
Said something thin and weird,

And he must listen closely,
Though not to me or him;
As if the ancient mother
Of every man had come,
And only he might fathom
Her words of sleep, of home,

Of going back to places
Before a thought was had;
As if the world's conception
Still waited, and instead
There was this womb of ocean,
And none but him inside.

502

His Thoughts Are Kisses
(To John Tagliabue)

He walks in a fine fire of atoms
So continual, like light about his head,
That he has never dreamed of cold or storm,
Or nakedness disgusted with itself, or envy
Poisoning used arrows to be shot again,
This time to reach and kill.

He walks in the first mist, the one
Before creation rested. He is affection
Not yet distilled, distinct: incapable of dying.
His thoughts are kisses, fecund as the weightless
Waters of the deep love turned that day to spray;
And still they dance in him.

My Great Friends

My great friends do not know me.
Hamlet in the halls,
Achilles by the river, and Don Quixote
Feasting with the Duke see no one there
Like me, like Mark Van Doren, who grows daily
Older while they look not, change not,
Die not save the deaths their masters made.

Those, yes, over and over.
And Bottom stands tremendous,
And Sancho rubs his head, half comprehending
Knighthood, and Malvolio's cold voice
Invites the madhouse hour. These neither die
Nor rise again. They look not, change not,
Only as folly, wonderful, lasts on.

Still my great friends ignore me,
Momently grown older

503

And dying in the west. They will be there
Forever, gods of the world, my own immortals
Who will not go along. Nor do I ask them.
Let them forever look not, change not,
Die not save as mortals may behold.

THE GOOD OF STILLNESS 🐦

Country Boredom

Whole days are city minutes if you measure
Time by persons. Less. For no one comes.
Ticktock is not a footstep, nor does wind
Wear clothes. Nor does sunset speak to sunrise;
They are not even strangers to each other,
Here in this waste of purpose, in this faceless
Forum where the atoms never argue:
Equal and indivisible; content
With the vast void between them. If you count
By voices, music fails; and if you listen
Only for wit there is no need of ears.
What then? Why stay? What is the good of stillness,
Had at so huge a cost? I will not tell you.
I do not know. Except, with stillness itself
For standard, I could be satisfied, and am.
Listen. No one comes. That wasn't the wind.
Even the clock is holding its breath; and the stars
Have stopped. Or I think they have. Be quiet. Thinking
Itself is sound. We shouldn't be here. Or if so,
We shouldn't be disagreeing. Even agreeing.

Sweet William's Breath

Sweet William's breath,
Clove pink, clear spice,

504

Has breathed upon me twice,
Boy and man:
In my gaunt grandmother's garden,
Then my own—hot, sweet,
Here it is, and candy good;
Here it is, red, white,
And small and many, like the figures
In her apron long ago.
Gaunt she was, and still, and good,
My life ago.

High August

More things thrive in the sun
Than my sweet people and me:
The snake; the venomous vine;
The weasel; the wild bee;
And over us all sometimes,
Thunder, suddenly.

The world, put forth this while,
Threatens our breathing room;
Buzzes, and strikes; but then
Winter is soon to come;
We shall be few again,
And loving, and lonesome.

Departure: September

He has driven away, and with him has gone
More even than summer, though that is as much
As I look for this morning; and see on the lawn—
Look, leaves fallen, and dry to the touch.

More than warm green, than lazy long growth,
Went down the cool hill with him only last night.

I am here, he is there: it is each, it is both
Things sicken me now with their secret delight;

As if it were good to devour an old heart;
As if it were pleasure to leave in its place
A dry, small mind whose meagerest art
Will be to remember his hands and his face:

How he did this, and how he said that,
And how he was angry for part of one day;
As if it were better to sit where he sat
Than to have him still here and deciding to stay.

Dance of Death

Fall is a crazy dancer—
Look, how he whirls in leaves;
How happy Death is to be stamping with him—
There, on the stricken body
Of grass, of mortal green.

Down with it all: he dances,
And look, she laughs in his arms;
Wicked, the bright wind is funeral music
For long days—remember?—
And hot dark, and flowers.

Death is a wild partner;
But look, she is not young.
She is the eldest daughter; she has danced
Forever, without wedding
Any warm one.

With Apples

The last leaves are down, and the iron
Trunks, solitary, say they can stand there

Seven cold months without perceptible
Change. But the green ground changes
Daily, so that Hallaway's old horses,
The brown one, the black one,
Nibble at next to nothing where the hoar frost
Of hours ago gave way before the yellow and still blowing,
Blowing—some of them purple—leaves.
These move, head down, but listen:
Someone may be coming, even now, in the bright wind,
With apples. I am coming.
Four pockets full, and extras on the hip.
Hi, there, Handsome Jerry!
Don't you know me, Slobbery Mack?

The Angle of the Sun

The angle of the sun—O, artist,
Summer and winter you dispose these bands
Of shadow with a master ease. They lie,
Dark sleepers, where you let them fall:
So beautiful, so bodiless, so less than black,
So willing to be walked on; or—
Look now—
So perfect in their stroke, so brushed,
Thick, thin, that all the world outside this window
Is one in secret cunning with your amber
Mind, O, artist cool and warm together,
Strict and sweet,
O, painter loved and loving
Of slant lines across a yard.

Say Which

This afternoon I think I'll pile
The apple wood that David split;
Or rake and sweep the dirt floor

Down cellar; or, if the wind dies,
Assemble the last mountain of this year's
Leaves, and drag it off to rot in rain
And snow while no one notices; or climb
And shut the attic louvers—it is time;
Or stuff the window cracks; or clear
The strainer by the pond; or hang
The tools where they belong; or—oh, my lucky
Stars, the list is endless; I am rich;
I can say which
Of all these good, clear, shapely,
Solitary things
I'll do;
And show to you.

Incinerator

Mornings, in a stone place,
I worship fire the cleanser.
I go there; he meets me;
And one scratch does it all.

The paper, the wet bones;
Last evening's greenstuff:
I bring them; he knows me;
And smoke is our word.

And then I am silent.
But he the undoer—
Ah, the fierce laughings
Of flame to itself.

The eggshells, the cardboard—
Matter into spirit—
No wonder he adores me,
And comes there every day.

Old Nameless

Hephaestus, Vulcan, or perhaps
Old Nameless, dancer until dead,
Lie down awhile; or if you must,
Go jig and grin on graves instead;
Go slide on ice, go walk on water;
Any cool thing can be hotter.

Trample dew; go tread the sea,
Or, rage insisting, some man's house
So far from here I'll never know
By reek of paint or roasting mouse.
And yet I would not harm my brother.
Go melt one Pole, and then the other.

Be you busy, I care not
So it be elsewhere, master mine;
For you are that, as I could prove
By taper, torch, or turpentine.
Take my left hand, right hand, both;
But swear me then this little oath,

O, master flame: that you will spare
My books and papers; these two beds;
The dishes—do not sport with those,
Nor with the frames about the heads
Of certain young ones; nor the sill
That warmed her Wednesday, lying ill.

Sodden November

Sodden November
Is weeping for summer.
Or maybe not so.
The slime of leaves, the sleep of trees
Could be cold secret luxuries:

509

Sweet shivers of content
At riches spent.

Which were not wasted.
They are the liquid
Bed he desires.
Mountains of mist, and rivers of rain:
The heart of the world can rest again,
Under this grey profound
Of water and ground.

Let Me Listen

I cannot thank you, rain, enough.
You would not hear me anyway.
You have your noises—let me listen
As the dark grass will all day.

I am not grass, I am not ground,
I do not live by water song;
Except as through this blessed glass
I feed on sound—may it be long—

Of drops that drive into the heart
And bring like blood the brightness back.
And yet not blood, and yet not mine
That cold deep world, crack under crack.

The Fields of November

The fields of November
Fit like a lion's hide:
Old, dreaming lion,
Cold, sleepy ground.

The hollows and the rises,
The boulders, the long swells,

All of them are one there,
Breathing under brown.

But faint breath, and slow beat:
The fields of November
Fit like a warm skin
The dark of the world.

December Setting

What death more wonderful
Than day's in winter?
All the cold west burns,
Burns to be near its insatiable lover,
The dark.

Cunning with hunger,
The two of them mingle
Their hectics—fiery,
Fiery the fusion, and smoky, of living
And lifeless.

Oh, the white heat of it,
Tempered to crimson:
And crimson—oh, lovers,
Oh, lovers of dying—to terrible black
Under black.

Too Old to Read

The quickest movement of the quickest bird
That comes in winter, then is gone again
(But comes again, finding our suet good;
Then off; then back; and now he wipes his bill)—

That quickest movement marks the flick of time
Mankind has been here (now he brings his mate:

Less gay, more greedy; and the two contest;
Not with each other; no, the stranger there)—

Has been in houses that the wildest dream
Of the first wing, before the world was cool,
Could never have imagined standing (six
More strangers: they descend; they have it all)—

Standing here this moment, this ticktock
Of cosy time; then gone again (Oh, God,
Oh, history. These little darting eyes:
Too old to read. Nor mind, mind to remember).

Enemy Cold

My enemy, cold,
Waits into the winter
To show me how cunning
He is, and serious.

Strange, I forget.
I think he has mellowed.
It takes him forever
To kill the good autumn.

But then he is done,
And here I am softer
Than Indian summer,
Than worm in the wainscot;

Here I am dead,
If once he can sting me.
So in by the boarding,
And thin over thresholds,

Crafty, he comes.
Then I double the doorglass;

Stuff the least crevice.
But he is not exiled.

Here he is now;
Is near; he must have me;
And may, some midnight
When I am grown listless.

December Cats

Less and less they walk the wild
Cold world of dark, of windy snow.
Curiosity comes in;
There is nothing more to know;
Examines corners; yawns and dies,
Warm under lamps and buzzing flies.

The oldest beast, with panther head,
The latest yielded: ran in tracks
Himself had punctured; hid by stones,
And pounced, and crackled mice's backs.
But now that all midwinter wests,
Even he the ranger rests.

Double Good

If I can wonder what this animal thinks,
Sitting and watching or not watching me,
Does he do likewise? That is what I wonder.
Is something in him free as I am free?

Free, I mean, to seek what is not given,
And to despise all else? For if I knew,
And he knew, and the strangeness were destroyed,
What dreadful silence then between us two.

For now we talk; absurdly, we do talk,
And neither understands more than he should.
If all, we were as one; but now in dark
We keep distinction, which is double good.

No more than with another man I know,
No more than with a second beast he sees,
Past the fine twilight of this interval,
What each one is forever, if God please.

Winter Housecleaning

THURSDAY

Tomorrow to the white pine
Patch where in November,
Solitary, I whacked off
Dead limbs, and left them.

Snow tonight, and no wind.
Well, if nothing changes,
Kerosene and old tires
Will smoke in every opening:

Will crackle as I drag there,
Thorny, a poor thousand
Pieces of the deep grove
That are at last but litter.

Once they were soft green.
Then the end of sunlight.
After that, a grey maze.
Tomorrow, woods to walk in.

SATURDAY

Not tomorrow—oh, no.
Yesterday I started:

Stumbled to the bonfire
With long ones, with short ones;

But still it is a wild place,
And I am not its tamer.
Oh, no. Time is.
(Sir, take it easy.)

SUNDAY

And yet they are a great thing:
Clean aisles to stroll in.
Possibly my strong sons—
Christmas, I'll ask them.

Lichen

Boulder in the meadow, world in the world,
And lichen upon it: field in a field.
On the smooth top there, death's grey grain
Creeping by centuries, circular, small:
Whosoever watches, still but a stain
Spreading in one place, waiting to be all.

Oh, the cold time yet, oh, the slow years
Till granite is covered, and sleep overpowers.
All the great rock there, grim as the world,
Whitened with death's wheat, motionless, mute:
Whatsoever wind, no leaf uncurled;
Whatsoever rain, no sweet green shoot.

Not that it hates this, tightening hold
On the hair of the stone, on the scalp of the world.
Ready for ice cap, ready under drought,
Ready now for nothing or for all, it lies,
Putting invisibly its feelers out
For the last great changes. Lichen is wise.

515

Wild Pansy

Delphinium, haunt of hummingbirds,
White phlox, at sunset whiter still,
Stonecrop, corpse-cold, and feverfew
That seems a daisy yet is not,

You sleep more deep than Johnny-jump-up,
Who in cold spring, impertinent,
Will stare each early riser down,
Then call that windy world his own.

And so it will be. Such an eye
Dreams nowhere else in wintry earth.
I think it opens even now.
Cat nap for him is death enough.

EPIGRAMS 𝕖𝕨

Art Is Just

Art is short and art is long.
Work done this morning waits on time.
But time waits too. The oldest song
Still burns in eternity's quicklime.

And may be diamond there or dust.
Time cannot tell. Yet it was known
From the first blazing. Art is just,
And broods in eternity's brimstone.

Comedy

The world will not be understood.
Put on a sword, put on a hood.

Listen. Can you hear me? Good.
The world will not be understood.

Tragedy

The world is something I must try,
However hard, however high.
Though I stumble, though I die,
The world is something I must try.

Freedom

To be what no one ever was,
To be what everyone has been:
Freedom is the mean of those
Extremes that fence all effort in.

Humility

Let all men be what they would be?
I will. But let them tell me too
The utmost they expect of me,
That I the more may pleasure you.

Atlantic

The ship's prow,
Great horse's head above unseen great hooves and knees,
Unflinching, through the bitterest green seas
Bites now;
And now;
And now.

Tourist

I passed Olympus in the night,
But had I passed by day
I still could tell you less of it
Than blind Homer may.

Good and Evil

There is no man alive loves evil; none
Knows how to do so even if he would.
And this is strange; yet stranger, what each one
Hugs to himself as better than the good.

Pessimist

Happy the man whose every dawn
Is last, and yet tomorrow shines.
What splendor, though it be the meanest
Morning. And tonight he dines.

Inconsistent

Let no man see my girl;
Let all see, and admire.
Why do I contradict
Myself? Do not inquire.

Congenital

Beauty and strength were born in you, my soul,
Or else are missing; nor will come by thrift.
You may not add a part unto the whole:
The effortless, original free gift.

Relative

As time goes, and lives last,
  One winter is not long.
Except to starving mice: then vast
  Eternities of wrong.

Suspense

Get out, come in. Where have you been?
I know. Things do. So you are late.
Kiss me. Lie here. I tell you, dear,
I hardly could both breathe and wait.

Sons

Riches would be well;
And happy work, and praise.
But most, may they keep liking
Each other all of their days.

Cold Beauty

Woods, flaming in winter sunset,
Had best be witnessed warm indoors.
There is no heat in all that hectic;
Nor—wait, child—from Orion's stars.

Martin House Unvisited

Sixteen rooms, and none too narrow;
All of them high, for wind and view;
But random wren or sweet tree swallow
Is so far all that fate will do.

Gravity

Snow is so light, how can it fall?
She was so sweet, how could she die?
I cannot tell you, child; but all
Things do love earth; yes, even the sky.

Warning

God will be hard to love.
Nature does not assist.
She was the jealous one
When daylight and chaos kissed.

Frankness in Friends

Frankness in friends must never be:
No words to set each other wise.
It was by love they learned to see,
Not by deliberate sunrise.

Knowledge Enough

The final freedom I desire:
To know what Homer, Shakespeare, knew;
And tough Cervantes: don and squire—
Halfway between them, that will do.

Good Appetite

Of breakfast, then of walking to the pond;
Of wind, work, rain, and sleep I never tire.
God of monotony, may you be fond
Of me and these forever, and wood fire.

Last Housecleaning

Empty, my mind, of web and dust;
Of diamond too, and sharpened gold;
Of everything, and if you must,
Of my own self, grown old and cold.

LATE POEMS
(1963)

O World

O world, my friend, my foe,
My deep dark stranger, doubtless
Unthinkable to know;
My many and my one,
Created when I was and doomed to go
Back into the same sun;

O world, my thought's despair,
My heart's companion, made by love
So intimate, so fair,
Stay with me till I die—
O air,
O stillness, O great sky.

Eternity's Low Voice

Eternity's low voice,
That no one yet has heard,
Sings peace be with you, children
Of man, beast, worm, and bird.

523

Variations upon Disaster

The stone lifted,
A little flaming salamander, startled by broad light,
Darts away among wet leaves.

The hay cut,
A spider web that danced between two blowing stalks
Has to be built again.

The tree felled,
Four blue eggs roll out of a robin's nest.
No young this year.

The basket overturned,
A mouse's brood—run, run—so many mouthfuls
For the scampering cats.

The earth quakes,
And villages fall; but rise again when all the dead
Have namesakes: the new children.

History, a hundred feet
Above high tide, comes in unnoticed; customs drown
So painlessly, nobody weeps.

True Is True

"You say you love me truly,
But then how true is true?"
"How windy is the west wind,
How watery is dew?"

"I've heard the wind shift after dark,
And grass by noon is dry."
"How windy is the east wind?
At noon how high is high?"

524

"The faith of things is not the same.
They cannot ever err."
"Then my own mind must be a sleeping
Thing. It does not stir.

"It changes only when you do,
As winds go round and round."
She laughed, and taking both his hands
They circled without sound.

Vessel

Body, don't break.
Spirit, don't spill.
Crack after crack,
However, it will.

The Cat and the Miser

Nothing could have brought him to the door,
This brown, this dripping night,
But the faint noise that did: a plucking,
Plucking at the tight
Copper crosswires of the screen.

He knew. It was the cat:
Her signal to come in.
Or thought he knew, the miser,
As with a groan, a sly grin,
Shuffling, he slid the bolt.

No eyes would have been so welcome,
Staring up and blinking.
But these, the tall thief's—
Oh, oh! the unthinking
Blow, the heavy feet.

Oh, oh! The boxes gone,
The misery. Then here she was:
Pluck, pluck—the sound,
In and out, of delicate claws.
What fiend had listened?

Out there, what sharpened face,
Vigilant, had learned the trick?
He staggered up and let her through.
Late, late! A sudden kick—
But then, caresses.

When Oh, When Ah

When water falls and wind blows
And birds fly up, flat to the blast,
And are borne high over
Mansion and meadow
To woods, their cover;
Then quiet at last;

When light lengthens, and grass greens,
And peace, old lover, kisses our world;
But wind of a sudden
Is wild in the trees,
And butterflies madden,
And birds whirl;

When oh, when ah, when what you may say,
Weather by weather, change arrives,
Look and listen
To all that is passing.
Wind is a wizard
With nine wives.

526

Prophet

He did not say anything utterly strange,
At any rate to a thoughtful person.
Why then do we honor him, and call him prophet?

Because he said what we had always understood
When we were alone, when we were thoughtful.
We honor him because he made us remember,

Why, that we ourselves were serious once,
That we were children, and loved peace.
He gave us again the quietness of our minds.

The only strange thing was, his wild look.
But of course it was terrible to be where he had been:
To have dug those utterly simple sentences out of the
    soul's grave.

Born Equal

    "Born equal? When so many—
    Look round you—are inferior?
    In God's name who believes"—
    "None but the superior."

Somebody's Breath

Could he be here? The empty house
Said no in the night. The walls and the floors
Whispered, but only to each other:
Of those long dead, and their proud ghosts.

Yet could he be here? Two miles away
His master sat with a knife in his heart.
Angry, the pursuers opened
Doors of closets and rattled the dark;

527

Climbed the stairs and thrashed at shadows,
Thinking one of them might cry out.
Nothing but silence, roughened by whispers:
Wind, or the walls, or mice at work.

He was not here. They gathered to go.
Only one lantern flickered—"Wait!"
The oldest of them, by a window,
Stared at the glass; lifted his light:

"He's here, or was." They crowded to see.
A circle of moisture: somebody's breath.
Who had been hoping they wouldn't stop?
Whom had they terrified, turning in?

Their lanterns again; loud sounds; a door
Still swinging. "There!" And they had him fast.
Blood on his hands, but none in his face:
Save for the manacles, mere ghost.

Dry Time

All things sigh
For the locust to cease;
For a darkening sun;
For the patter of peace.

Proteus

Great rocks, and greater seas:
Between those old antagonists
The formless one more often wins.

We do not watch them every day.
By night we dream of other wars.
In a whole lifetime nothing may be decided.

528

But out of the deep, and always coming on,
A monster without shape, invisible
Until it shatters, shakes the world.

Or seems to. A little inland,
Nothing is felt or heard of those old wrestlers
That never stop. The soft one will triumph.

Deathbed

There is no more time.
Goodnight, my friends.
Even eternity,
I think, ends.

The Chatter of Children

The chatter of children
Is how they learn.
Syllables, sentences:
Such labor.
Such infinite school,
With tongue for teacher.

They could be quiet,
And watch and listen.
But the time is coming;
They must be ready.
The chatter of ages
Is what they study.

Night Life

Coming home by Canaan,
I count the souls that sleep.

But not the deer, the possum,
The cat's eyes acreep.

April Burial

On this chill day
Let earth be warm,
Receiving the child,
Undoing the harm.

Death was by day.
Then let no light
Enter this grave,
This natural night.

Beneath all days
Leave these together:
Earth and the quick girl,
Quiet forever.

May Memorial

Music on that day of days
When the lady was dead that he so loved,
And rain outdoors was cold on the grass,
But the room rustled; her friends had come;

Music, a late memorial,
For the lady had died when snow lay deep,
And he was alone, and nobody knew
How often he worked, how often he wept;

Music, he told us, would contain
His lady within it: listen well.
Sad, then happy. Yet as it sounded,
All of it heartbroke us all.

Account

What have I left undone?
What have I never been?
Who am I to inquire?
Deity's blood kin?

The Sign in the Sky

Look, he said aloud,
My love across the Hollow in your father's
House—look, look! The sky is all one blackest cloud
Filled suddenly with fire, soft fire.
Look, my love, look now!

This was long ago,
And the man is dead. But on that day of days
She too was at her window, wondering; and so
She saw—and cried to him across the Hollow,
Look, dear love, look now!

Time even then was old,
And she is dead. But there has never been
Another day like that one, when a rain of gold,
Falling without falling, woke two lovers:
Now! Let it be now!

They were but neighbors then,
And both are dead. But at that burning hour,
With all the world around them rosy red, they ran
And ran, and met midway the Hollow meadows:
Now! My darling, now!

The moment never stays.
Nobody now remembers them as one
From that day on to death, that darkest day of days
When suddenly high fire consumed their doubt
And now! each answered, now!

531

The Clover Field

"Each of you an only child:
The Barton son, the Lawton daughter.
And all the countryside, I know,
Thinks you perfect for each other.
But you can never marry." "Why?"
"I will tell you when I die."

They laughed at him, their oldest friend;
And best, for he was more than neighbor.
In their houses and in his
They honored him with name of uncle.
But now, midway a world of bees,
Instead of glad sounds, only these.

Each drew the other close, to kiss:
A proof to him if one was needed.
But he had known it all too well;
The truth was what he could not suffer.
"Then I must tell you while I live.
Listen. But do not forgive."

"Listen!" Mocking him, she frowned.
"Another story, Uncle Jason?"
"My last," he looked at her and said,
"The very last." So she was silent.
Curiosity as sweet
Hummed in the blossoms by her feet.

"Your mother ought to be alive.
And his: each lovely one for witness.
But now it is my word alone.
God save us, you are both my children—
Listen!" But the buzz of wings
Went with them, those two running things,

Uphill and over, this way, that,
Until there fell so deep a quiet,

He was the last man in the world:
Not even any sound of crying.
"Children, children!" But the bees
Came back without them for heartsease.

The First Snow of the Year

The old man, listening to the careful
Steps of his old wife as up she came,
Up, up, so slowly, then her slippered
Progress down the long hall to their door—

Outside the wind, wilder suddenly,
Whirled the first snow of the year; danced
Round and round with it, coming closer
And closer, peppering the panes; now here she was—

Said "Ah, my dear, remember?" But his tray
Took all of her attention, having to hold it
Level. "Ah, my dear, don't you remember?"
"What?" "That time we walked in the white woods."

She handed him his napkin; felt the glass
To make sure the milk in it was warm;
Sat down; got up again; brought comb and brush
To tidy his top hair. "Yes, I remember."

He wondered if she saw now what he did.
Possibly not. An afternoon so windless,
The huge flakes rustled upon each other,
Filling the woods, the world, with cold, cold—

They shivered, having a long way to go,
And then their mittens touched; and touched again;
Their eyes, trying not to meet, did meet;
They stopped, and in the cold held out their arms

Till she came into his: awkwardly,
As girl to boy that never kissed before.
The woods, the darkening world, so cold, so cold,
While these two burned together. He remembered,

And wondered if she did, how like a sting,
A hidden heat it was; while there they stood
And trembled, and the snow made statues of them.
"Ah, my dear, remember?" "Yes, I do."

She rocked and thought: he wants me to say something.
But we said nothing then. The main thing is,
I'm with him still; he calls me and I come.
But slowly. Time makes sluggards of us all.

"Yes, I do remember." The wild wind
Was louder, but a sweetness in her speaking
Stung him, and he heard. While round and round
The first snow of the year danced on the lawn.

Summer Evening

I simply cannot come in.
I must sit and look at the night.
The cats could explain, so still
In the soft, warm, dark doorlight.

So Simple

Why are my songs so simple,
Now that I know the worst?
Nothing should delight me
In times so cursed.

And nothing does but singing,
And best that it be brief;

534

About the length of daydream,
Or fall of leaf.

Drowsy Season

Heavy, heavy hangs summer,
Hot, slow sleepyhead;
Hardly hears time passing;
Hardly turns in its bed,
That is changing all the while
Into sepulchre instead.

The weight of days is less and less;
Juices go back into ground.
Hardly feels the fall come,
Hardly sees, far off around,
Dry leaves, dropped pods,
Blowing here to make the mound.

Goldfinches

The hayfield is not afire,
Yet sparks fly upward.
Crisscross then, and looping,
They dive down backward.

Unanswerable

How shall I make the most of this day
So blended of cool and warm, so bright,
So mingled of breeze and yet no breeze,
So happy in lasting—ah, till night?

For the dark comes. I do remember.
Where shall I walk, then, where shall I lie

535

As the sun goes over slowly, burning
And yet not burning the deep sky?

How shall I make the utmost of it?
I should not ask this. Who am I
In a goodness so vast, in a beauty so still,
Even its master does not try?

Truth

Slowly, slowly, in it comes,
The blue that was so broad a wave.
Out there it scarcely caught the sun.
Now it is blinding: bright blades
That strike each other down and down;
Yet more rise up, and more come on.

Be careful where you stand and look.
The near annihilates the far.
Be stricken, yet survive the stroke.
The distant swells are what they were:
Too deep, too smooth for mortal mind;
Yet in these breakers breath can end.

No Communication

The wren that rages when I sit
Too close to this crabapple tree
Cannot be told, for all her wit,
I hung the gourd she guards from me.

Under This Building

Under this building
A small stream runs,

In the dark, and noiseless
Save for a frog—
Listen, that lets me
Know he is there.
Not now; he is waiting;
He takes his time.

I must not wait;
He will never begin.
It is not for me
His intervals are,
It is not to me
He says what he says,
Or to anyone warm—
Ah, there he is.

The Three Secrets

"Gentle" and "good": the parson's words
Still hovered under the trees.
The widow and her daughters lingered,
Burying even these.

Alone at last and walking home,
The mother said: "My dears,
He had his secret cruelties,
And I my hidden tears.

"I would not tell you if it meant
I love him now the less.
But rage was in him, you must know,
Deeper than kindness."

"I knew!" The elder of them stopped,
Suddenly, and cried:
"I thought I was the only one;
With me it would have died."

"It does not hurt to have it live.
The truth must ever be.
You mean you knew—" "Mother, I mean
He could be cruel to me."

"Oh, dear." And they walked on with Sue,
Who never made a sound,
But kept her eyes, so beautiful,
On the green grass and the ground.

The youngest one said not a word,
That day or any day,
Of how he called her long ago
His everlasting May,

His springtime, his only good.
He loved her more than well.
But this was not for some to see,
Nor her own tongue to tell.

Morning After

Full moon and milky light;
Deep sleep; and now the sun.
No day remembers night,
Not even that pale one.

The Young Speak Truth

The young speak truth,
But if not, no matter.
Argument ends
One day or another.

Grasshopper voices
Had better be still:

So soon to stop—
As those too will,

After more time,
After worse trial.
But the world is theirs
Meanwhile, meanwhile.

Song Sparrow

This bird does not dream I watch him
On a twig of my wayfaring tree,
The lone spot on his breast
So important to him and to me.

Little and Short

They spent the afternoon, the night,
The dayrise, the morning,
Nobody else knew how or where,
And she said again, "Do you love me?"

"What do you think?" "Why, that you don't."
He laughed and looked at the ceiling.
"Better than words"—"I want but three,
Little and short: 'I love you.' "

"Is love itself so little and short
We must lengthen it out with speaking?"
"Love itself is all of the world."
He drowsed. He did not hear her.

Then she got up, with tears in her eyes
For husband and for children,
And found the knife. It was little and short,
But it reached in to his meanness.

Ah, but the blood. Oh, but the deed.
Noon, then night forever.
Death itself, so little and short—
She must lengthen it out with screaming.

Morning Assignment

A woman, sitting and sewing in south window light,
Is silent, and so is the small granddaughter by her side,
Counting not stitches, no, but yellow and red and white
Buttons, and silver snaps, and ribbons fit for a bride.

Judgment

And the truth came tumbling down.
Not raindrops, no,
Nor noiseless snow.
It was rocks and stones, and they thundered.

And the heavens declared the glory of God.
Not anthems, no,
Nor trumpet blow.
It was crack! and the whole sky opened.

And peace was with us from that day.
Not dreaming, no,
Nor walking slow.
It was wilderness, and voiceless.

Serious Play

To leave this child alone,
Even a little while,
Is to make earth his own.
Look, he does not smile.

To Monotony

Monotony, be thou my god.
Humdrum, lie close and watch me well.
I may complain, but stop your ears,
Remembering what now I tell:
That I would have each moment's name
Be musical, and sound the same.

When I am truant, bring me home;
Then if I struggle, strike me down.
Bind me to what I most desire,
No matter how I twist and frown.
The smile you wear as I say this,
Monotony, is all I wish.

End

This bird died flying,
And fell in flowers.
Oh, what a world
Went with him. Ours.

And Then It Rained

And then it rained, oh, then it rained,
All night, all day, it rained and rained.
And the birds stayed home
And brooded their young.
And the waterfall, roaring,
Was brown with mud.

And then it stopped, oh, then it stopped.
Sun broke through, and the raining stopped.
And the birds came forth
And sang on the posts.

And the waterfall, thinning,
Was bright as glass.

The Open Soul

Vanity unconcealed,
And jealousy confessed:
Only those afflicted
Thus, I see, have rest.

The Gift of Gold

As long as he lived he saw them
And heard them: the gold pieces
She dropped in his hand that day.

He is dead now, but the glitter
Still may lighten his eyes;
Or the dark remember the sound.

She had come through the shortcut
With kisses and tears; for his father,
Angry, had exiled him.

"You will need money, too."
It was all she owned of the world.
"No!" But she wept. Then, "Well—"

And he went. It lasted forever.
The part she owned was the whole;
It saved him a thousand times.

Wherever he walked, she was there:
A kind of shining between them,
A singing deep in his ears.

She was not of the world, his mother,
Nor was her gold a thing.
It is truelove now in a grave.

Migration

This flock of sparrows flew all night
To be here now and peck my lawn.
Did they know where? But while I ask,
They fluster. They are moving on.

He That Goes There

How he that goes there touches me,
And suffering, has all my heart,
Is not for them to understand
Who think us nothing but poor earth.

There is a thinner thing than that
Divides and joins us, him and me:
Thinner than air, than parts of fire,
Than water in falling, and more free.

Nor do I know the name of this,
Nor have I sought the reason out.
But he that goes there touches me,
And I would die lest he be hurt.

The Agony

"A blow, blunt in one place,
Then spreading:
A subtle poison after all,
A pain that travels like a death
On into objects, blanching them—

543

"How live with this?" "Why,
As the world does:
A history of bruises, none
Forgotten, none enduring; all
Closed over someday." "Someday?" "Yes."

Ostracism

Not to care much what tales are told,
What laughters laughed, what judgments given;
Not to stop breathing while the world
Recovers its heart; grudges permission;

Not to mind much these silences;
These deaths, remembering; these glooms—
Ah, it is hard to learn alone
How naked pure existence seems.

Past Is Past

To wish a word unsaid,
To wish a deed undone—
Be careful, for the whole
World that was is one.

Pull the least piece away,
And bigger ones may fall;
Then granite; then great timbers,
And the end of all.

Whirlpool

Disaster brings ten thousand eyes
To stare, and some of them to weep.
The sides of sympathy set moving
Are circular, and smooth, and steep.

544

Dream of Home

It wasn't bad, the wound.
He could drag himself to the wall;
Then, slowly over that,
The sweet dark of the woods.

The battle had moved on,
But it might be coming back.
Just as well to be in
Away from the sun and the flies.

The boy on his bare elbows
Advanced a little; and stopped.
The dead horse; the worms.
Longer, then; to the left.

But the rider, too; his face
Half off; one sorry eye
Wide open. The bloody weeds,
The rags, and the cartridge clips.

Farther around; it would take
Forever, maybe. The smell.
The buzzards, high in the blue.
He must hurry. But now some rest.

Curled on his side, he heard
His mother ringing the bell.
Supper. The new-baked bread;
The company cloth, with creases.

The pitcher of milk; the meat;
And up those carpeted stairs,
Waiting only for him,
The bottomless white pillows.

Billeting

Cool the room, as if old Utter
Quiet himself lived in it, master
Of tall mahogany and much glass.

The officer in blue, dusty
And sweating, opened the high door
And stopped. The lady there, motionless,

Regarding him from the far end,
Her ivory gown swaying as the curtains
Swayed; her dark eyes not friendly.

"Madam." He bowed, touching his saber.
"Pardon, but necessity—"
"Rubbish!" Who was that behind him?

He turned, and there she was: mistress,
Not mirror. So he turned again.
The same anger blazed at him.

"Burn me, kill me. But no speeches.
Necessity!" His face, confused,
Went back and forth. Two bitter ladies.

"Madam." But two statues now,
Contemptuous. He bowed and left.
Another mansion would have to do.

Here Came the Birds

Suddenly commencing—
Boom, swish! Boom, swish!—
Artillery over the mountain:
Hell in the high woods.
We looked at one another, startled. Then

546

Here came the birds,
More startled—bullets themselves, flying
So wild, so near,
We almost could have caught them. Almost.
No, too fast, too utterly shot forth
By fear. A naked speed;
Nestless, now and
Forever.

The Mascot

If laughter is bravery, he was a lion.
Not that he looked it; he was freckled,
And three of his top teeth were broken; and his boy's voice
Was young even for its years.

Short—hardly up to our shoulders—
He swaggered when he sang, leading
The company in choruses so ribald, even old Burnside
Himself wouldn't have understood.

When we forded, what a splashing.
But on dry land he whacked at weeds
Till you would have thought the whole Army of Northern
    Virginia, beheaded,
Lay there, bloody, in green rows.

He mimicked owls and mocking birds;
Wild pigs answered when he squealed;
The last sound he made, deep in the Wilderness, was wrens
Scolding a black cat—then, whang!

A sudden, serious bullet ended
All of this for good. The impertinent
Grin, fading as we picked him up and ran for cover,
Said it was nothing. Just damn death.

A Farm Like His Father's

"Stop it! Stop it!" But the crack
Of sixteen thousand rifles thrashed
The sound he made to tatters;
If he made a sound.

He wondered. Had he cried aloud,
Or only so the place at home
Could hear: his father's place, and some day
His, if he got back alive?

They marched this morning over a mountain,
Then here it was: the sweet terrain
Identical with where his eyes
First opened. It was that he wept for—

"Stop it!"—as artillery ripped
Familiar fences, and the shapely fields
Shuddered as he did. Not the same,
But oh, so nearly. Double outrage.

"Stop it!" And the captain, cursing,
Pulled him down. "You fool! Take cover!"
Already, though, the groves were burning:
Beautiful, like his, and blasted.

Furlough Blues

"Why are you so heavy, boy,
And hang-dog all the time?
The way you wrote, it couldn't be
Too soon till you got home."

"Don't ask me, Mother, I can't say
Without it sounding mad.

548

But when I think of them down there,
Better I should have stayed."

"Them who? Them what?" "Why, all the boys.
And then there was old Jim.
I get to hearing how we sat,
Some days, and joked with him.

"We snipped his whiskers off one night
When he snored by a tree.
This brought good luck next afternoon;
The rebels they ran away."

"But they won't always." "That I know.
Still, I ought to be there."
"Here's bread, just baked"—"But I can't eat."
"You're homesick for the war."

"Oh, no, for them. There's Frank and Bill,
There's Elmer, and there's Jack."
"God bless you, go. But promise me:
Be careful now. Come back."

The Executioner

At home he was the one most hurt
By pain in horses; sat all night
With poultices for shoulders; lifted
A foot to find if hedge thorns pierced the quick.

And now this field of torture: blinded
Mares beset with noise no beast
Had dreamed of; bloated carcasses,
Torn bellies; and the screaming not to be stopped.

And yet he stopped it. He was the one
Most merciful with bullets; stood

549

And aimed between the eyes; but what
He said before the sound nobody knew.

A secret, his and theirs. Maybe
Promises to hush the guns.
Or maybe nothing at all, except
"Goodbye, old boy, old girl; poor Dapple, goodnight."

Son Against Father

"Boy, I have dreamed of this.
But the other way around.
I was the wounded one,
And you, the good, the strong—"

The son looked into the father's
Eyes, then shut his own.
"And so with me." His whisper
Might have been heard at home.

There was no war between them.
In them two armies touched:
Enemies so earnest,
Encounter was a tryst;

The laying on of glances
That made their love complete.
But oh, the separation,
And marches in the night.

"My boy, I prayed we never
Would meet until peace again."
"So I," as the waves of battle,
Eddying, washed on.

The Dead Sentry

The dead sentry, doubled with an anguish
Now gone in the direction of his gaze,
Still searching, searching for the end of it—
Couldn't I tell him it is over? wondered
The man who had shot him, coming to make sure;
Wondering too—a habit of late—who was he
Before the wild change of war? What house and where,
And who, in which room, would weep the longest, crying
His name in the night? A habit of late; a bad one;
It might be he could never do this again—
Fingering his gun—and the worst part
Was wondering if the dead knew they were dead;
If this one did. "It's over, over!" he shouted.
But still those eyes went feeling for the end.

The Spy

"An officer, I think, Sir, taken
Just before sunrise with dispatches."
"Good. Bring him in here." The captain,
Weary, didn't look up at first;
Then did; and found he was being stared at.

"Sergeant, leave us alone. At once."
For the guard of prisoners hesitated.
"And close the flap." So two young men,
Flushed with the strangeness of it, stood
Remembering summers long ago.

"How is your father? Mine is dead."
"I know. We wrote, and the letter came back
Unopened. Sorry. Mine is well,
Except that your people burned our house.
It was his pride." "I know." A silence.

551

Walnut trees, and a winding drive.
Hot days. The Mississippi
Sluggish there; they watched the steamboats.
Then next summer father and son
Came north. The boys swam in the lake.

The two old men—but not so old—
Never ceased to be classmates; each
The dearest friend of the other; and hoped
The same was true—"Damn it, Harry,
Why did you get caught?" A silence

Outside, too, as if the sergeant,
Holding his breath, listened. "Harry—"
"Do what you have to do. I know,
It's serious." "Wait." He lifted the canvas.
Nobody heard them. "Yes, quite serious."

The lean face, the long hair,
The haggard eyes watched him. Then:
"Don't be slow. Let it be over—"
"Sh-h. You can escape. I'll shoot
And miss you. Back of the tent the river

"Is muddy and not too deep; but dive,
Stay down as long as you can, and live—
For God's sake, Harry, live. Goodbye."
They didn't shake hands. It would come to that
Some lazy summer, if both lived.

The Long Burden

"Godalmighty, look!"
Men falling everywhere,
And those two went upright.
Or one did; the other,
Dead weight on his back.

The little one, the bearer,
Staggering out of bullet range,
Stumbled. The long grass
Received him and his brother.
Both lay still.

Too soon to be so weary.
"Godalmighty, up again!"
How much farther was it,
Across how many rivers,
To bury Steve at home?

෴   ෴   ෴

In Evil Times

In evil times how can so many—
All that we know—be someway good?
For the sweet will, the delicate vine,
Climbs everywhere in our dark wood
Whose giant heart no less decays
For all these leafy kindnesses.

Can the pale stems support the host?
Unthinkable. Yet lace is strong,
And gossamer has webbed the world.
Unthinkable, I say, if wrong
Poisons the root; then nothing stands.
Doomed oaks are not held up by hands.

Alone All Day

For she is there and I am here,
And try as I may I cannot see
If the light changes in her eyes
When she is not thinking of home or me.

The Lucky Pebble

Kenneth, made giant
By the stones he lifted—
If not straight up, then oh, so slowly
Tilted, oh, so gruntingly, so greatly
Over-ended: there!—

Kenneth on this day,
Apelike in the streambed, stopped
And stared. A noiseless ripple,
Slipping past his boots, revealed
Suddenly, by all the saints,

A pebble. Kenneth stooped
And took it, dripping; grinned,
Then dropped it in his pocket; said
"That's lucky" to his boy,
And went on working.

Why? But the young one wouldn't
Ask. A thumb-size thing,
Bean-black; a little world
Of night from under water.
Lucky. Why?

A band of pure milk white
Ran round it, though: a perfect
Vein. "Is that it, Pa?"
"Is what it?" "Why, the white."
"It's both. Be quiet, boy."

He shouldn't have ever asked.
But Kenneth, patting his pocket,
Bent to the big rocks
Again; and rolled them—
Oh, he was twice as strong.

"And four times safer, too,"
He said, reading the astonished
Mind. "You'll see. No more
Things thundering back and down."
So Kenneth heaved,

Sisyphus undefeated,
While the ripple
Sang. "It's proper, son,
To keep some superstition."
Kenneth whistled.

Home Truth

I was angry at myself,
Therefore I punished you.
The evilness of others,
Good God, is what I do.

Kind Oblivion

The old couple that worry all but killed
Yet lived to die
Of time, a gentler foe,
Which covered them like snow.

And still it does, although the arriving flakes
No more are numbered
As once anxieties were
By the old man and her.

Down there no pain nor fear, no counting days
Till the last son
Leaves home, and the mad daughter,
Lost, is dragged from water.

Down there no sound of going or coming, or even
Of resting, while
The deepening blanket spreads
Peace on their poor heads.

Temperance

Stop short of all.
There is nothing to gain
From more than enough
Love, money, and rain.

City Child

The bell that sounded in the street
Where I was born those years ago
Bespoke the coming of a cart
With scarlet flowers—"Oh, who will buy
Before they die?" cried Angelo.

I remember him, so sad,
And I was sorrowed by the song.
The very blossoms seemed to weep
For their own death. Nobody bought,
Or so I thought; but I was wrong.

One night I met him jogging home,
And all his merchandise was sold.
Nonetheless, when morning came
We wept again, the flowers and I,
Lest both might die and never be old.

Getting Ready

The fields mowed, and the fences clipped:
This land is a broad bed made up

For summer to creep in with fall
And wait for the night that whitens all.

Nothing Stays

Nothing stays,
Not even change,
That can grow tired
Of its own name;
The very thought
Too much for it.

Somewhere in air
A stillness is,
So far, so thin—
But let it alone.
Whoever we are,
It is not for us.

View

To look far off, to see the land in folds,
With many fields and forests not my own,
And rivers, and a few pale desert places:
Sometimes I miss this, must the truth be known.

Riddle Me This

Riddle me this, said the homely maiden:
A house all on fire, and nobody comes.
Nobody runs with ladders and hoses.
Nor is there need. It is not consumed.

Riddle me this, said the ravishing maiden:
A house all of marble, yet see what they do.

They come with their kindling, their oil, and their matches,
As if it were dry wood—oh, that it were.

Harvest Beauty

The new-mown field has a face of its own.
No lady is lovelier just then.
Even tomorrow will lessen a little
This queen made here by sickles and men.

Boy in a Tree

The ladder was below now;
He hid among the limbs;
He looked down and down;
The lawn fell away.

He saw clear over
The ridges of the house;
Birds above and under;
The garden, a grave.

Sister came, calling.
The top of her head
Moved by a miracle:
No legs at all.

"Jack, Jack!" Her echo
Was pretty in the woods.
Father came, booming:
Thunder in the pines.

They had gone in now:
Napkins and knives.
The whole world—he had it.
He held his breath.

Longer than he should, though—
Whirled—where was north?
He breathed, and it saved him.
He hugged the good wood.

This was where the quick squirrels
Watched him every day.
A foot found the ladder.
"All right!" he yelled.

Jack-o'-Lantern

They came dripping to the door.
The wet walk behind them
Glistened. It was Hallowe'en,
And a pumpkin head grinned on the gatepost.

Ten guests in raincoats, met
With smiles. "Come in, come in!"
But one woman, the prettiest,
Staring at her host, hesitated.

"Come in, come in!" Those eyes
Hated him or feared him: which?
Then she went past him, in.
The others had not noticed.

"Harry!"—in the coat room—
"You made it look like *him*."
"Who?" She wouldn't say the name.
He knew. It was his brother.

"Where is he now?" "Dead.
You killed him, marrying that—"
"Nonsense! Nonsense!"
But oh, the wry mouth,

559

The gatepost, the yellow light,
The rain running down.
She would never love anybody
But him, the dead man.

Piling Wood

Two ends, crosslaid and tilted in
As the middle is heaped that will hold them there:
Towers and a wall—O Babylon,
You were not builded in prouder air.

Donkey

Whose little beast?
Somebody owned him.
Some great angel,
I think, loaned him,
Smiling, to men;
And wants him again.

How can he leave us?
Where will he go?
He is half in love
With living below,
And habit is strong.
He has been here long.

Stoic for nothing.
Yet he will start.
Heaven must have him,
Stubborn of heart
And stiffened of hair
Even then, even there.

560

Unknown Tongue

The frozen beards of waterfalls
Still cannot hush the song behind.
Those ogre throats confound themselves,
Muttering that spring is kind.

Winter Watchman

The house there by the waterfall—
Its master, being about to go,
Had said to him, "In any danger
Do as you fancy I would do."

What now? For headlights had turned in,
And through tall trees a window blazed;
Then more, upstairs as well as down;
But one went out as Woody gazed;

And there was something worse in that.
Or was there? Woody called to Kate:
"I think I'll go when supper's done—
No, now!" There lingered but one light,

And it was in the master's room,
That maybe thieves had found at last.
So Woody went, and by the wall
Stood on tiptoe; stretched and stretched,

And saw it was no stranger there.
Or one was not: the master's wife.
The other—ah, they kissed and kissed,
Those two, like brushwood set afire.

"In danger do as I would do."
The master seemed to speak again.

561

Woody waited; then was sure;
Climbed, and broke the window in,

And with his knife did what he fancied
Any man in danger must;
Till both their voices ceased to sound,
And there was bright red on the rug.

Then down. Now home. Yet what to say
When Kate put questions, as she would?
Danger, danger. But to whom?
The beautiful mistress—she was dead,

And there was this deep stillness here;
In so much dark the danger died.
His very steps pursued themselves.
Fool, fool! How could he hide?

Elastic

How long, O Lord, can a cat become?
Is he made of rubber and thin tree gum?
Old serpent, he lies, old lizard, he hunts:
Infinity in fur for once.

Catechism

"The coming of a god resembles—
Some say it is the very same—
The coming of a god resembles
The coming of a stranger, lame
And thirsty, and you take him in;
And not to do so is a sin."

"What if he is a robber, though—
Some say it is a trick to tell—

What if he is a murderer,
Coming to do me less than well?"
"You take the chance and ask him in.
Doubting him—that is the sin."

"What if he robs me?" "Then you gain
By some of your silver, some of your gold."
"What if he kills me?" "Then we pray."
"For me?" "For him, lest he grow old
In hardness of heart. You took him in;
You died as the saints do, naked of sin."

Displacement

The stove in my study across the field
Stood once in the parlor, but long ago.
I wish I knew whose children kneeled
And thanked it, coming in from snow.

Morning Prints

New snow, and no wind.
Nothing has disturbed these little
Tracks, left by so light,
So serious a traveller between
Grey rock and not yet frozen
Stream, then back in a wide
Loop. Step over, dear—high,
That's right, and over. Such
A beeline to the brook; and then
The round trip home, in joy perhaps,
Or drunkenness from water. High,
That's right. A pity to be here
At all; but certainly to scuff
And muddle with our needless
Footmarks his that had to be. Or hers.

Winter Gossip

The wind out there, the words in here
Are cousins, could the truth be known:
Could stillness, that small stranger, slip
Between to hum the undertone.

Go Back In Now

My guest going,
I stepped out into the winter night—
No coat, no cap—
And he said: "Go back in now, you'll be cold."
I said: "But look."
And both of us beheld the unbelievable,
The blazing stars.
"So many." "Yet so few."
"So far away." "And yet they burn
As in these very trees." "That are not consumed."
"No more than black hair is by glittering
Gems." "Good night."
"Good night. But listen. They were out here
All of the time we talked." "And watched the fire."
"Ah, yes, the fire." It flickered still
Through the storm windows. "Well,
Goodnight."

First Symptom

"You told me that before." "Oh, dear.
Some day it will be fifty times.
For I am as my mother was."
"But this was twice." "The number climbs."

The Judgment of Esther

The young wife phoned up the hill
To the old one. "Is Horace there?"
He shouldn't have been; or since he was,
He shouldn't have come when Esther called.

"What is it, Nancy?" "I'm afraid.
A prowler. Will you promise something?"
"Depends." "If I should ring tonight,
Run down at once, no matter when."

He said he would and went to bed,
Esther beside him, ice-still.
There was no ring till during breakfast.
"Thank you, Horace. Nothing happened."

"That's good." "Well, being alone, you know—
It wasn't so bad until I heard—
But it was no one. Or he left.
Thank God, Bill comes this afternoon."

"What did she say?" Esther was standing
By the side window, that looked down.
It could not see the lower farm;
But she did now, behind her glasses.

"Said nothing happened." Esther nodded,
And the day passed like any other;
Except that Nancy, unbeknown,
Was hated as white lightning strikes.

Pretty and young, and full of trembles:
More dangerous because alarmed;
A bird, a deer, with eyes too bright;
All of her warm flesh aflutter.

Had Horace thought so in his sleep?
How could she know, for sure, for shame?
The lack of any answer kindled,
Behind the spectacles, such rage

That Bill came home to a burning house:
No bride there but a heap of bones.
Or so it would have been if Esther's
Heart had had the strength of suns.

But it was old, and it was cold;
All it could do was think a death.
Behind those lenses ray on ray,
Collecting, pierced the innocent roof.

Indomitable

The chickadee the cat clawed
Is here this morning on one leg.
With no tailfeathers left he lights
And, balancing, begins to beg.

Spring Ruins

When the deep snow goes
Earth is not as it was.
All winter the mice
Have tunnelled and tunnelled.
Or the moles—nobody
Was here to name them.

No other beasts
Could have lived in this world
Of no thickness whatever;
And built, just so,

In darkness, and level,
These worms of houses,

These roadways, winding
With sun now on them
And drying their sides.
Not that it matters
To those. They are gone;
And no history.

The Marriage of True Minds

No matter winds, no matter waves,
Or, suddenly, a snapped mast,
The invisible keel slides on and on
Till no more earth, air, water at last.

Patience

To wait within is hardest:
To be, while still becoming;
Doomed to all that slowness,
Never once to die.

To wait until tomorrow
Costs but a little sleep.
The wildernesses inward
Take years to cross.

Nor is the going wasted
If every stretch was loved;
The last hill then is home ground,
For all its light be strange.

Old Letters

The exultation, the despair,
Like distant waves make not a sound.
The sea of time from upper air
Is even motionless, like ground.

Like Unseen Rain

Like unseen rain
Death drifts across the land,
Bedewing whom it will—
The pale, the still—
Then having to go on; it cannot stand.

Next day, next night,
From round the world again
It moves, unknown to most—
Only the few, the lost—
And sprinkles peace on animals and men.

March

The snow is going.
Winter will pass.
Oh, but the deep
Sweet death it was.

Dr. Johnson

Monster of learning, master judge
Of poems and philosophies,
Of good and bad, of great and small
Men who prowled Fleet Street with him,
And Cheapside, and the Strand—

Within that huge, that blinking
Frightener of babies,
Nevertheless mice played: delights
In miniature—shy loves, true servants,
Friends, and taste of tea—
And nibbling fears, as now,
As now, of horrible death, oh, on hot feet
Presentiments of blank, of worms, of fire;
Of dissolution, Bozzy,
Dissolution.

Europe

We come home old from all that world,
That passion, that compacted thought.
And sleep; and wake; and lo, its wars
Are still undreamed of, still unfought.

Ho, Hum

Every day I die a little.
Ho, hum.
Every night the world is older;
Every morning wears away
Another atom.
Ho, hum.

Every day I live a little,
Nevertheless.
Every night the world is wiser;
Every morning adds a wrinkle
To the truth.
Ho, hum.

Cousins

More than strangers, less than lovers,
They keep warm the middle world
That was made as if by children,
Nor is changed with growing old.

The Little Bridge

Go get the saw, and the small
Crowbar; the hammer, and a handful
Of tenpenny nails. We must fix
This end of the little bridge.
It has rotted over the winter.

Quick, don't stand there. And while
You are gone I will find me a shapely
Stone for the first step. Nothing
In all this world is better
Than high and dry over water.

Bereavement

The grief of neighbors, like a cloud,
Hangs over all our heads as well.
We go there, but are half afraid
Of those on whom the thunder fell.

Statecraft

It could be sinister, this sudden
Spring: grass all at once, and ferns
Unfolding; sucker shoots; the wildest
Weeds; dead canes to cut; and oh,
Those bombs of blossom. Where to turn?

What first? What next? The enemy
Is on us; we are unprepared.

If enemy. If not the friend
We prayed for, winterbound. If not
Good life again. Yet all at once,
Yet everywhere! Be calm, be cunning.
Welcome the excess. Trim, dig,
Thin, snip, and shear, till all is shaven,
All is shapely; all is ours.

Plutarch

A yesterday of heroes.
A long twilight.
Another afternoon
Now. Another night.

Samantha's Confession

"A bad man, Shebie. Beat the mare to her knees,
Then me. Or tried. I wasn't fastened up.
Ran to the scary woods; was gone till morning.
The owls made me shiver, and the cold.
Then I went back there. That was when he died."

"You found him—well—how?" "I found him drunk.
That was the worst, on top of being cruel.
I found him near the hearth, the fire gone out
And mice nibbling the biscuits. I remember.
A ponderous man. He snored. He was a pig."

Sheba, looking down at the little eyes,
The little body, withered to a wisp,
Barely said aloud: "Don't tell me, Mother."

571

"Have to, Shebie. First I stepped across
And built the fire up, good." "To get him warm?"

"You listen. Next I laid the shovel on
And heated it bright red; then brought the buckshot—"
"Mother!"—"dropped a half a dozen in
And waited, watching him; he might rouse up.
But didn't. He was out for hours. Then poured them—

"Where do you think, Shebie?" "Don't you tell me."
"Have to. In his ear. He was on his right side,
Snoring. So, the left one. Did it careful;
There was no burn that showed, nor did he move
A muscle. Then the noise stopped. So I knew."

"Mother!" But Samantha's own end
Was on her, like a punishment put off;
Or could be, Sheba said, closing the shiny
Eyes, like something better: out at last.
Yet in somebody else. She pulled the shades.

I Went Among the Mean Streets

I went among the mean streets
Of such a city
As should have moved my wrath;
But it was pity.

I did not count the sad eyes,
They were so many.
I listened for the singing;
There was not any.

O thieves of joy, O thoughtless
Who blink at this,
Beware. There will be judgment,
With witnesses.

572

Ballad of Little Leaves

When all the little leaves of April
Shivered in their green,
She walked alone and wept. "Alas,
In May I must be queen.

"The frosty beard of old King Luke
Beside me in his bed,
While sweetest Arthur wanders here—
God, let me be dead!"

As if He heard, she fell and lay
A long hour in the ferns;
And dreamed that Arthur's loving hands,
Fearful and free by turns,

Now cold, now hot, unlaced her gown
To feel if she had life.
Her heart beat; and she said to him,
"Take it. I am your wife."

It was no dream. They caught them there
And hung them high in chains
Between two oaks whose little leaves
Died with them in the rains.

May Day

May Day, and morning sun:
What could be better?
Hazy in the west, though.
Let it not matter.
Let it darken, let it rain;
Winter is gone and we remain.

A song sparrow sat there,
Somewhere, and woke me.

573

That was enough. Now
No change can shake me.
Let it blacken, let it pour;
Winter is over and here we are.

Motel Guest: The Man of God

The man of God could sleep no more.
In the next room to his,
The couple that had come at midnight
Resumed their ribaldries.

And worse. The glasses they had clinked
Were silent by a bed
Wherein—whereon—the man of God
Groaned; he would pray instead.

But not a word came to his lips.
The beast and beastess there—
He listened. They were like this world:
Ravaged beyond repair.

The spread of whoredom was a mildew,
A rot in every fold
Of God's once lovely garment, given
To keep sweet; keep cold.

His own wife—quietly he said
Her name, and turned to the wall—
Her harlotry those years ago:
The sink and source of all.

The world was dead because she once,
Behind his window blinds—
The very street boys learned of it,
And lechered in their minds.

As he had done, himself a boy,
When there was woman talk;
As he was doing now—he rose,
His forehead pale as chalk,

And drove as if no road were there;
Only his roof at last;
Whereunder—oh, he struck and struck;
And wept; yet held her fast,

The beautiful, and struck again,
Till there was no more life
In this that was but cause—the whole
World's unfaithful wife.

And when there was no breath in her
He staggered to the door.
The same stars, the innocent,
Beamed as they had before;

Yet feebly; the forgiving sun,
That hid truth in its light—
The truth! He stumbled down the steps.
He knew it all last night,

Last night when she with widened eyes
Let him do what he would;
As if she too desired—Oh, God,
So cold now. So good.

My Good Friend

Each day he is the same,
Yet different; as dew,
That is as old as water,
Last night was new.

The Secret Mother

I was there early, I said I would be,
The day the foundlings had to be moved.
One to a woman, they had to be bundled
And carried down Avenue A to a building
So fine and so high—oh, it took your breath
To think of the life, to think of the death.

Nurses and nuns, in white, in black,
Then volunteers: I was one of those.
I said I would be there early, and was.
I thought they would give me a chance to choose,
Seeing I had no child of my own—
But I lied. I had her entirely alone.

Nobody knew she was made, not even
The seaman her father; we met in a street.
It was part of my plan that such be so;
I used him that night, then let him be gone.
He was handsome and good—oh, I thought I was wise;
But who will be with him when he dies?

I thought I was brave; yet I dressed her warm
And left her in Gramercy Park to be found.
I cried, but I left her. Then she was here;
I knew, for I watched. The nurses and nuns
Could never have guessed, that day of the moving,
Who wanted her most—oh, months of loving!

It was foolish to think they would hand her to me.
I reached, but a tall old sister took her;
Walked in the wind that rose, and rocked her
Stiffly; I knew by the habit that swayed.
The baby I carried I never unwrapped;
Never peeked in; it was good, and slept.

There were people that stood, and some of them smiled
At the great one that walked; but none at my daughter,

Deep in her arms—oh, hidden, my heart.
She had laughed when I laughed, she was mirror to me.
She was what I planned when I thought I was brave
And let him be gone. Oh, wind, oh, wave.

Unresponsive

I love you as a bee loves
Plums. Please look at me, she said.
All these years, and almost never
Have you even turned your head.

My life! But he couldn't say it so she heard.
This busy frown, this stiff
Walking away from the one sound
That moved him most—
I love you more than Jupiter or Mars—
It was perverse,
Or worse.

Her very eyes were stars,
And he did not look up.
Her voice was purest music,
And he stood like stone.
When would it break out of him,
The fire of his delight?
Some time it might.

Be careful, though, after so many years.
She is still with me, warm and bright,
By day, by night.
Better not step too suddenly
Out of twilight.

The Animals

So cunningly they walk the world,
So decently they lay them down,
Who but their maker sees how pride
And modesty in them are one?

These that did not conceive themselves,
Nor dream how long ago it was,
Have yet no deeper joy by night,
By day, than to continue thus.

The patience in them, and the heat,
The languor, then the sudden life:
Body and soul identical,
Their secret is forever safe.

Oh mystery, Oh perfect grace:
Duty as instant as desire;
Nature and art so indistinct
A wonder even in heaven were.

Release from Sky

The landing strip; now down, now down;
Oh, gently; ah, the hiss of wheels;
The speed terrestrial: buildings fly,
Ground runs; good old existence reels.

Last Childhood

With time the fear returns:
A second spell of clinging
Featherlike to walls:
The hating to leave home.

There will not be a third.
House might as well be grave.
Except that it still listens:
Heartbeat in the stone.

As Far Away

"As far away as the other side
Of—well, the other world to come."
"Be serious. There is no such world."
"I mean, forever and then some."

To His Book

Go straight to them, the sweet, the few,
That nourish, unaware they do,
The maker of these naked lines.
His solitude he reconsigns
To them, not him, as meriting more
Than he will of the final store.
For his most secret scowl and smile
He meant for strangers all the while.
Go tell them that, and call them friends
On whom his very pulse depends.
He does not know them save by grace
Of poetry's pure hiding place:
The charity in some to read
As it was written, and give heed.

Farewell and Thanksgiving

Whatever I have left unsaid
When I am dead,
O Muse, forgive me. You were always there,
Like light, like air,
Those great good things
Of which the least bird sings,
So why not I? Yet thank you even then,
Sweet Muse. Amen.

INDEX OF TITLES

INDEX OF FIRST LINES

An empty box, the sons of Baal said, 429
"An officer, I think, Sir, taken, 551
And did the animals in Noah's ark, 421
And so it was, 489
And the truth came tumbling down, 540
And then it rained, oh, then it rained, 541
And there is one with somewhat pointed ears, 230
Andromache, when Hector fell, 388
Ant and shrew, 85
Ants file past, 31
Anyone on the road below, 11
Apologetic, the old person in the black hat, 394
Apples, bright on the leafless bough, 25
Are you so weary? Come to the window, 14
Art is short and art is long, 516
As far as eye or tongue, as far as odor's, 283
"As far away as the other side, 579
As firelogs hiss, Orion gleams, 449
As from Arabian ashes, 119
As if a cabinet became alive, 336
As if there lay one other sky beyond, 97
As long as he lived he saw them, 542
As soon kill God as kill one of His creatures, 488
As the blue fringes of this flower desire, 105
As through the unthinking body waves of wellness, 450
As time goes, and lives last, 519
As time goes on, and tells us less, 389
At evening in the strange unlighted town, 47
At home he was the one most hurt, 549
At last inclement weather, 165
Authority is instant as a light, 275

Bad news of battles, now as long ago, 263
Be extra careful by this door, 173
Beauty and strength were born in you, my soul, 518
Beauty is not had, 442

Courage. If such a crowd, 326
Courage in sons, with wisdom's hesitation, 457
Courtesy was born among the stars, 413

Dawn came difficultly, 350
Day after day, for her, the sun, 153
Day, be long aborning, 477
Death is a tall horse, 80
Death's hands are clock hands, 274
Delphinium, haunt of hummingbirds, 516
Did he seem happy? Well, he was serious, 332
Did the gods ever, manifest in form, 419
Disaster brings ten thousand eyes, 544
Do certainties, like persons being doubted, 325
"Does he love you?" She hesitated long, 409
Down dip the branches, 377
Dressed, undressed: the difference leaps, 475

Each day he is the same, 575
"Each of you an only child, 532
Embrace it, though it be, 152
Empty, my mind, of web and dust, 521
Envy the young who have no words at all, 456
Equality is absolute or no, 418
Eternity is not to be pursued, 274
Eternity's low voice, 523
Even from themselves they are a secret, 328
Even if wars to come sleep warm and small, 266
Every day I die a little, 569
Evil abominates the good, 441

Fall is a crazy dancer, 506
Fate comes unswerving like a frightened horse, 113
Ferdinand De Soto lies, 90
Fleeing the town where every face, 92
Footprints now on bread and cake, 7
For Dinah ravished, all of Shechem's city, 425
For he so loathed the world, this nameless man, 410

596

For he so loved the world today, 160
For she is there and I am here, 553
For the grey temples, for the slippered feet, 247
For this one day much thanks, and for, 259
Frankness in friends must never be, 520
From many a mile the son, 136
From there to here, from then till now, 443
Full moon and milky light, 538

"Gentle" and "good": the parson's words, 537
Get out, come in. Where have you been, 519
Get up, I say, and see them, 463
"Giddup, giddup, you old forgotten, 354
Giving him up, she kept the art, 178
Go get the saw, and the small, 570
Go straight to them, the sweet, the few, 579
Go to your table, in the lined room, 93
God is not gone? Fear rules us as before, 417
God will be hard to love, 520
"Godalmighty, look!", 552
God's love does not compute desert, 480
Going from us at last, 131
Good monarchs have been monarchs of themselves, 320
Good old rain god, somewhere now, 439
Great rocks, and greater seas, 528
Groper up the narrow landing, 74
Growing a little older is suddenly, 112
Guilty lover of that queen, 361

Halt, commanded bombers, 250
Happy the man whose every dawn, 518
Happy the mind alone, 117
Hardly a trunk but leans, 294
Having no end to sing, he sent his heroes, 300
He cut one finger, 380
He did not say anything utterly strange, 527
He differs day by day, 497
He does not hear the struck string, 244

He has driven away, and with him has gone, 505
He is in love with patient death, 243
He is not lifted by their flight, 40
He is not yet, 41
He is so proud, recalling, 257
He is the one that meets us where the first, 232
He is the sun-white one that loves, 234
He is untouchable, or he would cry, 235
He knew a place on the mountain where he went, 15
He locked the window, 43
He made her love him, oh, he did, 370
He never heard of it. Then it was there, 76
He pushed him in and he held him down, 333
He said that we must thank the gods, 138
He suffered every fool alive, 332
He talked, and as he talked, 135
He that was deer was lion, 335
He thought some things were not to be compared, 125
He walks in a fine fire of atoms, 503
He was not helped by knowing well, 141
He was not wise to dally with the curves, 130
He was of an old mind, 140
He was the soonest friendly, 502
He was too tightly bound, 182
He will remember this; the cunning Fates, 206
Heavy, Heavy, hangs in my head, 374
Heavy, heavy hangs summer, 535
Hephaestus, Vulcan, or perhaps, 509
Here in a circle of maples I can sit, 58
Here they come, the paired brief-cases, 208
Herrick, hello, 483
He's coming. He just called. Said he was coming, 343
Higher than hate, and the abused, 68
His body wreathes the room like draughts, 233
His eyes are so, 39
His lady lacks not anything, 150
His study is the way we stand and peer, 236
His thought of it was like a button pressed, 133

I simply cannot come in, 534
I sing of ghosts and people under ground, 227
I told you I would come, he said, 205
I took my gun, 387
I wake and hear it raining, 461
I was angry at myself, 555
I was confused; I cannot promise more, 102
I was there early, I said I would be, 576
I went among the mean streets, 572
I went, I saw, but will not tell, 383
I would dislike you if you used an art, 104
Ice on a hundred highways, 348
"Identify the logs in the fireplace burning, 410
If any god comes any more, 270
If ever age, 37
If I can wonder what this animal thinks, 513
If laughter is bravery, he was a lion, 547
If luck has senses and perceives us here, 412
If nothing else let this poor paper say, 132
If the people under that portico, 27
If there were sound, the slapping, 239
If we had mistresses, my old, 483
Immensely the low sun, 457
Impossible the words, 290
In a swift chariot, with horses jingling, 426
In bitterness of heart I write, 497
In Douglas County winds do blow, 396
In evil times how can so many, 553
In jealousy of cause and pride of plan, 283
In little Greece, great mountains, 490
In our fat times, a monk, 499
In so much dark no light is little, 438
In the clear land he went to after noon, 225
In the dead middle of the longest winter, 347
In the middle of the wood it starts, 11
In the middle of their life he risked it, 289
In the mornings of my strength, 74
In the same moment, child, 82

In wanderment I came to where, 370
In wonderment I walk to music pouring, 464
Intelligence all day upon us, 322
Into the pool of silence our tears made, 342
Is there no All, 352
Is this the man who multiplied, 177
It could be sinister, this sudden, 570
It is a different avarice, 179
It is a kind of love, insisting, 252
It is a moveless moment, with no wings, 123
It is something that he handled, 75
It never is ourselves that we hear talking, 411
It should be easy, letting the small feet go, 143
It was and it was; that day, that day, 356
It was cold, it was slow anger, 343
It was no intercourse of palms, 187
It was September, and the weeds were mowed, 12
It was so mild a thing to see, 137
It was the very innocence of love, 139
It wasn't bad, the wound, 545
Item, the man by whom he was reminded, 140

Jephthah, son of a harlot, had one daughter, 428
Joy cannot be contained, 113
June now, like any June, 51
Jupiter and Mercury, 83

Keep up your humming, west wind, and your silly, 384
Kenneth, made giant, 554
Know thy good self, he said, 183
Knowledge here will overgrow, 242

Lady, excellently brief, 479
Lay them as neatly, 25
Leave me not overlong at this remove, 103
Less and less they walk the wild, 513
Let all men be what they would be, 517
Let it be always secret what we say, 105

Let me not see the one I love, 386
Let no man say that either mind, 148
Let no man see my girl, 518
Let not the mover know, 340
Let not your strictness vary, 152
Let this be true, that I have loved, 459
Let us have deities, he said, but not as indulgence, 270
Let's go. Let's be somewhere awhile, 481
Lift as he will a wordless face, 69
Like a great tree, 497
Like raining in a river; like the dove, 408
Like unseen rain, 568
Lilac alone, 26
Listen. The wind is still, 1
"Little boy, what ails me, that you walk, 456
Little my soul, 485
Little servant with the softer voice, 330
Look, he said aloud, 531
Look. The stone face, 500
Look, till all of his years, 458
Lugubrious, his legs, 284
Lying along the window sill, 34

Make way for them, who nothing see, 138
Man, breeding, hoards his form, 272
Man is the one most caught, 268
Mankind had been so rank a field, 337
Mankind the seventh morning, 280
Massive the man, massive the wrath, 500
Master of ocean stream, those men you made, 335
May Day, and morning sun, 573
Michal, that she-wife whom David had, 431
Monotony, be thou my god, 541
Monster of learning, master judge, 568
More than strangers, less than lovers, 570
More than the remaining distance, 345
More things thrive in the sun, 505
Mornings, in a stone place, 508

Most terrible the time, with nations falling, 260
Mountains, stand again, 83
Music on that day of days, 530
My darling with the single daisy, 368
My enemy, cold, 512
My fancy is less cruel than it is kind, 108
My great friends do not know me, 503
My grievance that so mounted and so mocked, 409
My guest going, 564
My love comes walking, 473
My love she is a rose that lives, 366
My one love has lighter loves, 80
My only need—you ask me, and I tell you, 111
My sin was not to measure, 290

Never be offended, 36
Never to be renewed or to increase, 109
New snow, and no wind, 563
No animal so flattens to the ground, 292
No further doubt now. He is near, 239
No hand had come there since the room was closed, 33
"No man can look upon my face and live, 427
No matter winds, no matter waves, 567
No minion of the word, 285
No throat had ever told me what I know, 97
No wandering any more where the feet stumble, 20
No way is straight, so this one wanders, 394
No wonder-deed done in the oldest time, 96
Nobody wanted this infant born, 46
Noon today, and the earth swings high, 89
Not for him, surely, 305
Not pride it was that made me say so much, 111
Not the world's width, but a deep vein somewhere, 299
Not to care much what tales are told, 544
Nothing but death could do it, 223
Nothing could be stronger, 154
Nothing could have brought him to the door, 525
Nothing could this man dismay, 445

Praise Him who makes us happy, 436
Praise is no crust of snow, 114
Praise the good angel doubt, 436
Pray never. But if no one hears, 260
Put it away in that building; rust and dust, 355

Rage in the mildest mind, 492
Rain, that wets powder, 248
Rather than ups and downs, 188
Remembered gaiety hurts mind and heart, 411
Remembering our father, said those children, 307
Report of thunder words arrives, 240
Riches would be well, 519
Riddle me this, said the homely maiden, 557
Roads are flowing everywhere, 6
Rumors of peace, rush otherwhere if policy, 261

Said the engineer to the fireman, 372
Shatter the moldy glass, 136
She fled into herself before the sun, 142
She is the youngest of the wood, 128
She is woman, she is wife, 474
She lay there in the stone folds of his life, 170
She leaves the kitten at her cream, 8
She lives with me and is my careless love, 385
She loves me or she loves me not, 367
She met him in a wild pass of the mountains, 432
She said too little, he too much, 154
She waits in a grey high house, this lady, and waits, 174
Should this end now it were the end of light, 102
Silently, every hour, a pair would rise, 33
Sir Eglamour has limped a mile, 195
Six of the other kind were one too few, 296
Sixteen rooms, and none too narrow, 519
Sleep, grandmother, sleep, 380
Sleep, sleep, slug in the sun, 362
Slow twilight bird, 23
Slowly, slowly, in it comes, 536

Snow is so light, how can it fall, 520
So close death flew that when I walked away, 324
So cunningly they walk the world, 578
So far from sirens and the fear of wings, 259
So he sat down and slowly, slowly, 194
So long had he withheld his hands, 479
So natural his grace, men called it more, 412
So smooth a field, 33
So soft her voice, so drooped her head, 473
Sodden November, 509
Soft, soft, soft, 365
Someday ten million Ithacas will have them, 344
Something about her hair among these low hills, 222
Sometimes I fear that I too soon was mastered, 106
Somewhat more slowly, lengthener of days, 129
South wind, suddenly, 374
Spread, spread, November rain, 127
Spring of the world again, 327
Starting gardens, whichway from the tracks, 298
Still there, as if the weathered house, 297
Stones of the street are notes for musical boys, 262
"Stop it! Stop it!" But the crack, 548
Stop short of all, 556
Stranger, do not think to find, 147
Strictly at noon the mist was there, 72
Strike then the rusted strings, 145
Stronger than minds of men, 485
Such power in little places, 323
Suddenly commencing, 546
Summing him, we subtracted, 189
Swallows' wings, 37
Sweet William's breath, 504
Sweetly, augustly they sway, the great dancers, 291
Swift cruelties to children are a pyramid, 144

Tell him I was beautiful, 364
That any thing should be, 159
That chime I hear, 78

606

That God should love me is more wonderful, 405
That you were there to see before I saw, 98
The aging heart: is it more filled with kindness, 493
The ancient garden where most men, 501
The angle of the sun—O, artist, 507
The animals will never know, 444
The answer came by dream, 444
The atoms of an old jealousy, rejoicing, 359
The bell that sounded in the street, 556
The big and little stars that burn by night, 420
The big bay stands in the rain with his blinders, 353
The bitterest things are sweets misunderstood, 360
The black share-cropper, grizzled in his prime, 191
The blacksmith did not hobble here, 329
The blinding shield, the gun no foeman dodges, 279
The broad-shouldered lord of rocky Ithaca, 334
The burning cheeks of lovers, the stopped breath, 357
The chatter of children, 529
The chickadee has three short songs, 351
The chickadee the cat clawed, 566
The child at winter sunset, 495
The close world of thighs that silk and cotton, 388
"The coming of a god resembles, 562
The cool fall, a little out, 358
The country is no country I have seen, 70
The dead sentry, doubled with an anguish, 551
The deepest dream is of mad governors, 416
The desert moor, the empty glen, 482
The devil in the world maintains it, 271
The difference they prophesy, 255
The dog indoors, the cat upon the stair, 408
The dream of this new man upon the earth, 168
The dust has long been settled that she rode, 333
The earth is full of spirits once again, 108
The east wind I worked in, 88
The exultation, the despair, 568
The father of the family, stoop-shouldered, 455
The fields mowed, and the fences clipped, 556

The fields of November, 510
The final freedom I desire, 520
The first triumphant man was he that drew, 38
The flakes are a little thinner where I look, 3
The forty acre oatfield, 204
The frozen beards of waterfalls, 561
The genius of these hills I see in sleep, 406
The god of galaxies has more to govern, 437
The grass is deep in the field, and her four legs, 16
The gravelly road is gone, 133
The great eyes died around this room, 169
The great machines that mouse these fields, 399
The greater world is water, 116
The grief of neighbors, like a cloud, 570
The harmony of morning, and a thrush's, 122
The hayfield is not afire, 535
The high heap that now and then, 216
The house there by the waterfall, 561
The humped back of the beaver, and the four, 126
The ladder was below now, 558
The landing strip; now down, now down, 578
The last leaves are down, and the iron, 506
The last thin acre of stalks that stood, 4
The laughing philosopher sits on his tomb, 488
"The laws that if I love them set me free, 276
The leafless road midwinters by itself, 127
The liberal arts lie eastward of this shore, 299
The little cities of New Orleans, 356
The little doctor with the black, 185
The little fellow—partly fool, 200
The little fox, demanding to be seen, 452
The little god sat bright across the board, 226
The little pine grove, trimmed of its ground branches, 295
The long life and the short life differ dimly, 321
The longest hour is swifter than I thought, 110
The lord of increase, traveling with me, 392
The lover loves the eyes that close, 474
The low, the large, the umber moon, 355

The lump of sore silence, 361
The man of God could sleep no more, 574
The meadow hedge hides meadowlarks, 398
The million little wars, 249
The millions at this solstice, 246
The mind at last fills up with men, 390
The moments he remembers? They are those, 210
The moon is in flood, 29
The morning flashed like mica, 160
The mother of life indulges all our wandering, 121
The mountain he is more than there, 349
The new-mown field has a face of its own, 558
The news of snow full driven at the face, 347
The old couple that worry all but killed, 555
The old man in the window, 371
The old man, listening to the careful, 533
"The old man of whom you spoke—your father, 425
The only thing she kept, 42
The paths again are solid green, 30
The people whom He chose to hear His word, 434
The person on the sidewalk is possessed, 142
The quickest movement of the quickest bird, 511
The rails that clicked him homeward, 312
The random eye mismates them, 209
The right one that he gave me, 215
The round old lady with the little eyes, 330
The same stones, one upon the other, stand, 446
The ship's prow, 517
The sky above us here is open again, 1
The sky is laid as low again, 88
The small minds of birds, 487
The snow is going, 568
The sorrows of this old woman taper, 221
The stalls were empty in the shed, 14
The stone lifted, 524
The stove in my study across the field, 563
The stubble is an upstart thing, 9
The sun came white upon these shingles once, 10

There was a line of frosty light, 26
There was a widow had six sons, 220
There was some kind of safety in the feathery, 196
There were six children in a house, 81
These little birds that feed all day so fiercely, 478
These things I say, no one of them can reach, 110
They are more fierce to conceal it, 303
They are new comers too, the bent-necked, 236
They are nothing but sifted, 42
They came dripping to the door, 559
They hurt us most by loving us, 341
They left him hanging for the deed, 491
They spent the afternoon, the night, 539
They told this tale of her, that dying, 331
They were good fortune's maid and man, 151
They were not old enough to be, 75
Things on my desk to be remembered, 454
This afternoon I think I'll pile, 507
This amber sunstream, with an hour to live, 123
This apple now, and this smooth block of wood, 125
This bird died flying, 541
This bird does not dream I watch him, 539
This bird is used to sitting on bright ledges, 3
This book declares my love is a condition, 109
This boy and girl, having no secret knowledge, 305
This danger that like wire, 247
This flock of sparrows flew all night, 543
This girl was not to go, 147
This is the boy that rode nine hundred, 202
This man kept courage when the map of fear, 246
This moonlight lies, 24
This valley sends another sound, 87
This wind today, 61
This woman is bewildered, 200
Those are helped who need no help, 443
Those beautiful, young, breaking eyes, 339
Those that we hovered, 494
Those waves of understanding that arrived, 337

We come home old from all that world, 569
We could not love these things in others, 328
We never could see it wound him, the tipped weakness, 192
We of this place who prowl its rectangles, 297
We shut our eyes to punish, lest a piece, 307
What beast is this, not bellowing, not stung, 414
What corner now, and do no shadows, 310
What death more wonderful, 511
What fury in the white sky, 397
What god was there, 402
What golden spider warmed himself and spun, 106
What have I left undone, 531
What held the bones together? Not belief, 161
What if it is happening now, 386
What is he doing there in the dark hour, 287
What is it, not to fear, 252
What is it then that beautifies the fields, 406
What is the hour, how loud the clock, 129
What moon presides when mosses grow, 210
What now to do on such an earth, 251
What shall be said of the lucent, the going, 256
What was this life I led, 122
What would I have then, 255
Whatever I have left unsaid, 580
When Adam fell, and Eve, and the gates closed, 419
When all the little leaves of April, 573
When Bathsheba, grown old, one day had audience, 432
When he was eighteen autumns old, 212
When I am called by Love to give account, 99
When I came back to your unlifted eyes, 103
When I did that, he faltered, 275
When I was farther away than a ship, 368
When I was twelve in that far land, 390
When icicles around the earth, 363
When one to another talks, 278
When the Atlantic upsloped itself, 171
When the deep snow goes, 566
When the last freight, dusk-musical, had gone, 163

When the new growth no more is green, 324
When the whole valley whitened and the wind split, 224
When the world ends it is too much to hope, 451
When these were idle shouting boys, 146
When they no longer lean there, 77
When they were almost there his skinny fingers, 186
When water falls and wind blows, 526
When will true love again make delicate difference, 318
Whence, whence this heat of the brain, 118
Where are we now, 375
Where did he run to, 378
Where do wars go in the night, 261
Where is that couple of slow boys, 341
Where is the bell, the horn, 467
Where is the wit that I could sometimes wield, 100
Where mild men gathered he was half at home, 156
Where she is now, with people, 366
Where the brook turns a tile brings down four inches, 292
Where the two mows divide and green hay hangs, 231
Wherever a still apron, 237
Wherever earth is home for men, 327
Whether this knight was mad no fool will know, 277
Which way this forest faces, 234
Who does not move in stream, 266
Who finds his love a whore at heart, 359
Who is more idiot noble, 279
Who is this host of folk this fair spread day, 119
Who made the evening made the fear, 31
Who made the world was not so wise, 38
Who so valiant to decide, 197
Who were the sons of heaven that looked down, 422
Whole days are city minutes if you measure, 504
Whose head is this that hangs, 287
Whose little beast, 560
Why are my songs so simple, 534
"Why are you so heavy, boy, 548
"Why do you go so fast tonight, 45
Why does it jog so slowly, the one rumor, 281